ROUTLEDGE LIBRARY EDITIONS: THE ECONOMY OF THE MIDDLE EAST

Volume 11

THE ECONOMIC DEVELOPMENT OF JORDAN

THE ECONOMIC DEVELOPMENT OF JORDAN

Edited by
BICHARA KHADER AND ADNAN BADRAN

WITH AN ADDRESS BY HIS ROYAL HIGHNESS
CROWN PRINCE HASSAN

LONDON AND NEW YORK

First published in 1987

This edition first published in 2015
by Routledge
2 Park Square, Milton Park, Abingdon, Oxon, OX14 4RN

and by Routledge
711 Third Avenue, New York, NY 10017

Routledge is an imprint of the Taylor & Francis Group, an informa business

© 1987 CERMAC

All rights reserved. No part of this book may be reprinted or reproduced or utilised in any form or by any electronic, mechanical, or other means, now known or hereafter invented, including photocopying and recording, or in any information storage or retrieval system, without permission in writing from the publishers.

Trademark notice: Product or corporate names may be trademarks or registered trademarks, and are used only for identification and explanation without intent to infringe.

British Library Cataloguing in Publication Data
A catalogue record for this book is available from the British Library

ISBN: 978-1-138-78710-0 (Set)
eISBN: 978-1-315-74408-7 (Set)
ISBN: 978-1-138-81184-3 (Volume 11)
eISBN: 978-1-315-74516-9 (Volume 11)
Pb ISBN: 978-1-138-82009-8 (Volume 11)

Publisher's Note
The publisher has gone to great lengths to ensure the quality of this reprint but points out that some imperfections in the original copies may be apparent.

Disclaimer
The publisher has made every effort to trace copyright holders and would welcome correspondence from those they have been unable to trace.

THE ECONOMIC DEVELOPMENT OF JORDAN

Edited by BICHARA KHADER
and ADNAN BADRAN

with an address by His Royal Highness
Crown Prince Hassan

CROOM HELM
London • Sydney • Wolfeboro, New Hampshire

© 1987 CERMAC
Croom Helm Ltd, Provident House, Burrell Row,
Beckenham, Kent, BR3 1AT
Croom Helm Australia, 44-50 Waterloo Road,
North Ryde, 2113, New South Wales
Croom Helm, 27 South Main Street,
Wolfeboro, New Hampshire, 03894-2069

British Library Cataloguing in Publication Data
The Economic development of Jordan.
　1. Jordan — Economic conditions
　I. Badran, Adnan　II. Khader, Bichara
　330.95695′044　　HC415.26
　ISBN 0-7099-3110-7

Library of Congress Cataloging-in-Publication Data
The Economic development of Jordan.
　　English and French.
　　Papers presented to a scientific workshop co-organized
in May 1985, in Louvain-la-Neuve (Belgium), by the
Arab Study and Research Center of Louvain University
and Yarmouk University of Jordan.
　　1. Jordan – Economic conditions – Congresses.
I. Badran, Adnan. II. Khader, Bichara. III. Hussan bin
Talal, Crown Prince of Jordan. IV. Université
catholique de Louvain (1970-　　). Centre d'étude et
de recherche sur le monde arabe contemporain. V. Jâmi'at
al-Yarmūk.
HC415.26.E26　　1986　　　338.95695　　　86-13395
ISBN 0-7099-3110-7

Printed and bound in Great Britain
by Billing & Sons Limited, Worcester.

CONTENTS

Acknowledgements
List of Abbreviations
Introductory Address by His Royal Highness Crown Prince Hassan

1. AN AGGREGATE PRODUCTION FUNCTION FOR JORDAN 1
   Khalil Hammad

2. THE ROLE OF FOREIGN AID IN THE JORDANIAN ECONOMY, 1959-1983 11
   Khalil Hammad

3. THE USE OF JORDANIAN WORKERS' REMITTANCES 32
   M.A.J. SHARE

4. THE ROLE OF COMMERCIAL BANKING IN THE JORDANIAN ECONOMY 45
   Rodney Wilson

5. JORDAN, THE GEOGRAPHIC AND ECONOMIC POTENTIAL 62
   Konrad Schliephake

6. AGRICULTURAL DEVELOPMENT AND FOOD SECURITY IN JORDAN 93
   Naji Abuirmeileh

7. LABOUR EMIGRATION POLICIES AND ECONOMIC DEVELOPMENT IN JORDAN: FROM UNEMPLOYMENT TO LABOUR SHORTAGE   118
   Ian J. Seccombe

Contents

8. INDUSTRIAL DEVELOPMENT IN JORDAN   133
   Michael B. Sullivan

9. DEVELOPMENT PLANNING IN A TURBULENT
   INTERNATIONAL ENVIRONMENT: SOME
   REFLECTIONS ON THE JORDANIAN CASE   143
   Dieter Weiss

10. TARGETS AND ACHIEVEMENTS OF JORDAN'S
    LAST FIVE-YEAR PLANS, 1976-1980 AND
    1981-1985: A SUMMARY   177
    Bichara Khader

11. JORDAN: A DISTURBING DEPENDENCE ON A
    DETERIORATING REGIONAL SITUATION ...   192
    François Rivier

12. RENTIER OR PRODUCER ECONOMY IN THE
    MIDDLE EAST? THE JORDANIAN RESPONSE   204
    Michel Chatelus

13. SOME REFLECTIONS ON THE FUTURE
    ISSUES CONCERNING ECONOMIC
    DEVELOPMENT IN JORDAN   221
    Adnan Badran, Elias Baydoun,
    Kapur S. Ahlawat and Siva Ram Vemuri

ACKNOWLEDGEMENTS

The papers published in this book were presented to a scientific workshop co-organized in May 1985, in Louvain-la-Neuve (Belgium), by the Arab Study and Research Center of Louvain University and Yarmouk University of Jordan.

More than 15 economic experts from Jordan and European countries took part in the workshop, which was also honoured by the active participation of Dr Albert Boutros, personal representative of His Royal Highness Crown Prince Hassan, and Dr Abdessalam al-Majali, President of Jordan University.

We wish here to express our gratitude to all the colleagues who helped us to carry out this project. But our warmest appreciation must be extended to His Royal Highness Crown Prince Hassan, whose videotaped address to the workshop has been unanimously praised for its clarity and precision. This special attention shows once again the importance attached by Crown Prince Hassan to a scientific approach to Jordan's present situation and future options.

We are also grateful to His Excellency, Mr Abu Nimeh, Ambassador of the Kingdom of Jordan in Belgium, for having provided his support in the preparation of the meeting.

Finally, we would like to thank Mrs Denise Mabardi for her skilful and untiring typing assistance.

ABBREVIATIONS

ACM	Arab Common Market
ACSAD	Arab Center for the Study of Arid Zones and Dry Lands
AID	Agency for International Development (US)
APC	Arab Potash Company (Jordan)
DPA	Direct productive activity
du	Dunum/s
EEC	European Economic Community
FAO	Food and Agriculture Organization (UN)
GDP	Gross domestic product
GFTU	General Federation of Trade Unions
GNP	Gross national product
GTZ	German Agency for Technical Assistance
IBRD	International Bank for Reconstruction and Development
ICARDA	International Center for Agricultural Research in the Dry Areas
ICOR	Incremental capital-output ratio
IPI	Intermediate Petrochemicals Industries (Jordan)
JD	Jordanian dinar/s
JFIC	Jordan Fertilizer Industry Company
JICA	Japan International Co-operation Agency
JPMC	Jordan Phosphate Mines Company
KD	Kuwaiti dinar/s
KFW	Kredit Instault Bank (Federal Republic of Germany)
MOE	Ministry of Education
MOL	Ministry of Labour
NPC	National Planning Council (Jordan)
NPK	Nitrogen-phosphate-potash
NRA	Natural Resources Authority (Jordan)
OAPEC	Organization of Arab Petroleum Exporting Countries
OPEC	Organization of Petroleum Exporting Countries
PLO	Palestine Liberation Organization
PVC	Polyvinyl chloride
RSS	Royal Scientific Society (Jordan)
SOC	Social overhead capital
TRA	Total resources available
UAE	United Arab Emirates
UK	United Kingdom
UN	United Nations
UNESCO	United Nations Educational, Scientific and Cultural Organization

Abbreviations

UNICEF	United Nations International Children's Emergency Fund
UNRRA	United Nations Relief and Rehabilitation Assistance
UNRWA	United Nations Relief and Works Agency for Palestine Refugees in the Near East
US	United States
USSR	Union of Soviet Socialist Republics
VAT	Value added tax
VTC	Vocational Training Corporation (Jordan)
WFP	World Food Program
WHO	World Health Organization

INTRODUCTORY ADDRESS

H.R.H. Crown Prince Hassan

It gives me great pleasure to open this workshop on the 'Economic Development of Jordan: Present Situation and Prospects for the Future', which has finally materialized after more than one postponement, for which I personally apologize. Perhaps this proves that the mechanism for Euro-Arab co-operation could benefit from an additional dose of appropriate technology and better scheduling! I am gratified that the University of Louvain has pursued the objective of holding this workshop with a measure of forbearance and a great deal of patience and goodwill. I particularly thank Professor Bichara Khader, who has served as an emissary between Yarmouk University and the University of Louvain as well as a faithful bridge between the cultures of Europe and the Arab world. I look forward to reading the published proceedings of the workshop and promise to facilitate in any way I can the implementation of proposals arising from the discussions.

Since the Second World War, Arab-European relations have been evolving towards a convergence of interests, with both Arabs and Europeans coming to terms with the newly created realities of superpower rivalry. In separate ways, Europe and the Arab world had become targets of polarization. Each turned to the task of identifying its own new role and safeguarding its independence, particularly since the process of East-West polarization itself contained within it the seeds of direct confrontation between the global powers. According to Winston Churchill, this had caused the balance of power in Europe to be replaced by a 'balance of terror'. Though Europeans may currently feel that a nuclear war is unlikely to break out in the heart of Europe, East-West confrontation remains a major and immediate European concern, as such a war might still erupt in the Middle East.

Introductory Address

Within such a context of global rivalry and with the demise of the last vestiges of European colonization, a common trust has gradually emerged between the Arabs and the Europeans, particularly with the growth of understanding on issues that had perhaps separated them in the 1950s and early 1960s. It was gradually perceived that positive relations could evolve only on the basis of positions that had to be diligently and patiently worked out and identified by the two sides. Thus, in the wake of the October war of 1973 and the Arab oil embargo, Europe and the Arabs embarked on a dialogue aimed at identifying common issues and seeking avenues for co-operation. Although the Euro-Arab dialogue has not yet produced the results originally sought by those who set it in motion, it has, albeit very slowly, moved towards bridging the gap between aspirations and the realities of an evolving relationship.

In the economic arena, while European interests are understandably linked to the problem of energy, the Arabs - involved in the process of economic development and nation-building - are concerned with long-term economic co-operation and technology transfer. On this last issue, the complexities inherent in the transfer of technology have tended to vitiate Euro-Arab co-operation. It is encouraging to observe, however, that what in the last decade or two (in the context of the technological relationship between Europe and the Arab world) seemed to be a divergent dialogue is now coalescing into one of obvious interdependence. Rather than arguing about the merits or demerits of a donor-recipient relationship, we now find ourselves in somewhat comparable straits. The present European concern that the technological divide which separates Europe from the US and Japan may, in fact, be widening is inducing a greater understanding of the underlying Arab resistance to technological dependency. Although not exactly in the same boat, we are buffeted by the same waters. Consequently, interdependence assumes a new dimension in the Euro-Arab dialogue: because a major irritant has been diluted, the dialogue can now be conducted in a more objective environment.

As we review the progress made by several Arab states in science and technology, including the establishment of national policies as well as a renewed grouping for regional scientific policy co-ordination, we can look to a future dialogue with Europe with greater optimism. This optimism is

Introductory Address

reinforced by the current debate in European circles about the relationship between technology, culture and economic development. Disparate as our several approaches may be, they nevertheless indicate that the time is not too far distant when we can, indeed when we should, develop the rudiments of a shared strategy for future co-operation.

The economic relationship between the Arab world and the European Economic Community (EEC) should not be restricted to the import and export of commodities. At present, the Arab states import a large portion of their capital and consumer goods from the EEC while exporting only one or two commodities, mainly oil, to these countries. A more extensive economic relationship ought to be worked out, on a wider base of co-operation in technology transfer and joint ventures by the private sectors in both communities. It need not be limited to individual states, but can and should be extended to other parts of Africa and Asia, within the concept of a wider co-operation between North and South, and possibly between South and South. This, I hasten to add, is not a Quixotic notion. EEC aid to the Third World increased by 14% in 1983 to reach \$1.4 bn, the highest level ever recorded by the EEC for aid flows in one year, but most of this aid went to the world's poorest countries. On the other hand, funds provided by the EEC for the Arab countries in the framework of financial and technical co-operation will be regulated by the Euro-Arab Convention for the reciprocal protection and promotion of investment. The EEC member states have already given the European Commission the go-ahead to negotiate this agreement. Talks between representatives of the Arab League and the EEC are well advanced, but a final agreement will depend on the degree of like-mindedness and political will of both parties.

Within the Arab region, Jordan has played an important economic role. Our economic achievements over the past two decades have been substantial, despite the lack of a rich base of natural resources. But it is our human resources that we regard as our major asset. Sizeable investments in the development of these resources have yielded gratifying results. The highly trained and highly skilled Jordanian workforce has been in great demand throughout the Arab oil states, to the extent that well over a quarter of a million Jordanians are currently working in these countries

Introductory Address

and have contributed to the development of the oil infrastructure. However, although the boom in the oil economies over the last decade has benefited Jordan in various ways, the energy bill has been substantial, as we continue to import most of our energy needs. We need to utilize our trained manpower and our central, almost pivotal location in the Arab Middle East. Thus we see our future role as an advanced technical and maintenance base serving the entire region, from the Gulf to the related Red Sea region (on which we border), with particular emphasis, it is hoped, on the transfer of advanced technology.

With this record of accomplishments and aspirations in the human field, Jordan hopes to build a mutually beneficial mode of co-operation with the EEC countries on the one hand and Arab oil purchasing power on the other. European know-how, skilled Jordanian manpower and Arab investments and markets can prove to be a winning trilateral combination. In particular, we believe that middle-sized European contractors and industrialists, affected by recession in recent years, can benefit from joint ventures with Jordan to serve the region's large markets and to enable us to plan development within a regional dimension. For such an enterprise to succeed, it has to be viewed as a long-term commitment, or what may be referred to as a 'contract of generations'.

Arab concern, of course, has not been confined to problems of economic development and co-operation. In its pivotal position, Jordan is well aware of the implications of the Arab-Israeli conflict. As is well known, it is the Palestine issue - speaking of politics where people matter - that lies at the core of this conflict and that has dominated the Middle East political scene for the past four decades. It has hampered the political and economic development of the countries in the region. It has created conditions that have assumed a global dimension. The continuation of the conflict has intensified a variety of forms of extremism on both the Arab and the Israeli sides.

Jordan's immediate concern is for the beleaguered indigenous Arab population under occupation whose very identity is being threatened by the continuation of Israeli measures of creeping annexation. Israel has pursued a policy of incorporating the West Bank into the context of 'Eretz Israel' by taking advantage of a situation that oscillates between 'no war' and 'no peace' or

Introductory Address

war and sterile talks about peace.

The revitalization of Arab identity and the status of the Palestinians under occupation require immediate attention and must be dealt with by the international community of nations. As long as Israel denies the Palestinians their legitimate human right to self-determination, to choose their own future, the consequences are likely to prove disastrous. Meron Benvenisti, who has served as Israeli deputy Mayor of Jerusalem, foresees the dangers inherent in a continuing state of tension between the two populations, Israeli and Arab: condemned to live under unequal systems of government, future generations will have to endure the prospect of perpetual hostility, hatred and conflict. Action is necessary to avert a situation which would only compound the present misery. Whichever option is adopted by the Israelis and the Israeli authorities, the outlook appears extremely alarming; no movement will be possible unless and until the Arab community of Palestine is accorded its right to self-determination. Our concept of such a right is derived from an aggregate of historical, cultural, social, economic and political rights, the Wilsonian concept of self-determination, common to the West in the context of Versailles. We seek a distinct Arab community, a vital and stable Arab community, in this middle ground between ourselves and Israel.

In this regard, the European community of states is called upon to strive towards an understanding whereby the identity of that middle ground - the West Bank and Gaza - is not further prejudiced by persistent occupation measures leading to <u>de facto</u> annexation. Arab municipalities in the occupied territories suffer from a chronic lack of financial assistance, despite the fact that Jordan has largely borne the cost of public services there. Financial assistance would revive their ailing institutions and services and promote their commercial enterprises. It is alarming to find that the VAT returns on Arabs in the occupied territories today, which exceed $500 mn, are in excess of the military government deficit in those territories. Apparently for Israel, at least for the time being, the occupation pays. Consequently, Israel does not allow funds from the Jordan-PLO Joint Committee in Amman to be used for Palestinian development, because it regards the money as tainted and also probably because it prefers to keep the West Bank as an ancillary economy.

Introductory Address

Disbursements of funds from various sources and private voluntary organizations have been arbitrarily halted. It is our hope, however, that Israel may find it more difficult to embargo legitimate donations from its trading partners in the EEC. Such donations could serve both the immediate interests of the people in that political middle ground and help towards a fair ultimate settlement.

The EEC has taken a positive stand on the rights of the Palestinian people. In the Venice Declaration of 13 June 1980, it addressed a core issue of the conflict by stating unequivocally that, 'The Palestinian people, who are conscious of existing as such, must be placed in a position, by an appropriate process defined within the framework of the comprehensive peace settlement, to exercise fully their right to self-determination.' The EEC has also adopted an objective attitude towards the issue of Jerusalem. The community has refused any unilateral action regarding the status of the Holy City. The particular spiritual status accorded to it by the three monotheistic religions, Judaism, Christianity and Islam, places the Holy City above all considerations of national politics and ideology. Pope John Paul II was quoted as saying, 'Jerusalem today is the object of a dispute ... God willing, it can become the crossroads of conciliation and peace.'

If we turn to Jordan's ongoing dialogue with the US and with its partners, the Palestinians and the PLO, it should be remembered that the Reagan Plan of 1 September 1982 attracted much attention at the time and held some promise. It came in the wake of the Israeli invasion of Lebanon and with the change of office from Alexander Haig to George Shultz. There was a certain momentum in the plan's conception, but the burden of steering it through was placed on the shoulders of Jordan and the Jordanian authorities. It was Jordan which was to secure a Palestinian mandate before the process of negotiations based on the plan were to begin. Israel's attitude towards the Reagan initiative, on the other hand, was clearly reflected in Prime Minister Begin's immediate rejection of it as a 'lifeless still-born'. It must be recalled that President Reagan spoke of the withdrawal of Israeli troops from Lebanon before Christmas 1983, that all-important precedent of withdrawal from occupied territories. He also spoke of the 'immediate adoption of a settlement freeze by Israel'. Optimism was not translated into action, unfortun-

Introductory Address

ately, and following the withdrawal from Lebanon, we all lived the horror of the Sabra and Shatilla Palestinian refugee camps.

As for the 'immediate adoption of a settlement freeze by Israel', the Israelis took the following attitude: '... in opposition to the political thesis of Reagan, we answer with the erection of political facts in the area'. The US, for its part, has found it difficult to pressure Israel; contrary to all expectations, the US used its power of veto to obstruct the adoption of a UN Security Council resolution against the establishment of Israeli settlements on the West Bank. In short, follow-up on the Reagan Plan showed no signs of the determination of which the US President spoke in his well-intentioned speech: 'Further settlement activity is in no way necessary for the security of Israel and only diminishes the confidence of the Arabs that a final outcome can be freely and firmly negotiated.'

Jordan has continued in its search for peace and remains committed to a just, comprehensive and durable settlement of the Palestine question. Our commitment to such a peace is underlined by our belief in an international conference in which Security Council members can participate, to ensure the realization and ratification of the provisions of Security Council Resolution 242, based on the fundamental principle of the exchange of territory for peace. We resumed our deliberations with the PLO, the sole legitimate representative of the Palestinian people since the Rabat decision of 1974, on the premise that the chain of historical, cultural, economic and political links that bind the peoples of the two Banks of the Jordan should not be broken. There is little doubt that Jordan is the natural choice as a partner, not only in the administration of economic aid in the occupied territories but also in working towards the achievement of Palestinian national rights and the determination of the Palestinians' future political status in the context of the West Bank and Gaza.

The close and deep association which has governed the relationship between the peoples of Jordan and Palestine has been repeatedly affirmed. The unity of the two Banks, promulgated in 1950, was based on the exercise of self-determination and the expression of free will. The Jordanian constitution of 1951 stipulated unreservedly that the unification of the two Banks would not, in any way, prejudice the outcome of a final settlement of

Introductory Address

the Palestine question. In the meantime, Jordan has remained determined that Palestinian rights should not be forsaken or undermined.

On 11 February 1985 Jordan and the PLO made a formal bid to meet the problem 'head on', rather than pursue a series of cul-de-sacs. The accord is straightforward, genuine and - despite its brevity - comprehensive. It is rooted in international and Arab consensus and it is more than fair to the Israelis. It spells out the substance of peace and suggests a mechanism for achieving it. All its provisions are sanctioned by international legitimacy, in which we firmly believe, as well as by time-honoured practices in international relations. Exchange of territory for peace, the right to self-determination, resolution of the status of refugees, resolution of conflict through a negotiating process, mutual respect for territorial and religious rights, the right to confederation and recourse to international approval: all are eminently respectable - and feasible - principles of human conduct. His Majesty King Hussein has said, however, that this present opportunity is the 'last chance for peace'. It provides a chance for the US and Western Europe, and gives an opportunity for their joint credibility to be restored. It is an opportunity to contain growing fanaticism in both Israel and the Arab world. The British Minister of State, Richard Luce, has recently stated that as the Arab-Israeli dispute drags on, 'extremism has grown on all sides, and will grow further if there are no perceptible moves towards a settlement'.

For the Jordan-PLO accord to succeed, much is expected from the international community. The initial response from Europe and the EEC, in their statement issued at the end of March 1985, has been encouraging, specifically since it also addressed two other issues plaguing the region: Lebanon and the Lebanese dilemma, and the Iran-Iraq war, both 'hot spots' that are related to our present unstable Middle East situation. The statement signifies that a stable and peaceful Middle East, engaging in a dynamic process of economic growth, can only enhance European prosperity and world peace. A more forceful and effective European role is called for if the peace process is to evolve. The geopolitical reality of the EEC, its proximity to the Middle East on the other side of the Mediterranean, its long historical involvement in the area and its present non-partisan role can all

Introductory Address

contribute to enhancing the prospects of understanding and compromise. Most importantly, the community has the power, through its strong relations with its ally, the US, to help us to induce the latter to adopt a more positive and even-handed approach to the peace process, by confronting the political realities of the area and addressing the requirements of peace. There are two principal requirements in this context: to open a dialogue with the Palestinians and the PLO, and to participate in an international peace conference. Such an effective and constructive role by the European community is not a flight of fancy. What it requires is a regeneration of the European will, somewhat enfeebled at the moment. We need to make a collective contribution to the settlement of a problem whose genesis was largely of European making and on European soil, and whose resolution would largely redound to Europe's advantage.

It is my belief that the selfless efforts of the academic communities of Europe and the Arab world can make a difference, at least a conceptual difference. As has been demonstrated in the past, the seeds of imaginative solutions are often sown on university soil. For this reason, I am greatly encouraged by the resolution of the European Parliament to establish a Euro-Arab University. This would bring together European and Arab scholars on a continuous basis, promote like-mindedness, seek a commonality of interests and provide an intellectual, and thus, we hope, dispassionate, impetus to Euro-Arab understanding.

Chapter One

AN AGGREGATE PRODUCTION FUNCTION FOR JORDAN[1]

Khalil Hammad

INTRODUCTION

The purpose of the present chapter is to estimate a preliminary production function for the Jordanian economy. Although many econometric models have been formulated and estimated for the country's economy, none of them has included an aggregate production function. This is due to the fact that Jordan has no statistics on capital stock. In this chapter, time series capital stock is generated for the period 1967-81 and used as an input or factor of production. It is assumed that output is a function of capital stock and labour. Output or GDP and labour services are taken from Jordanian original sources in current values and then deflated by the implicit GDP deflator.

The Cobb-Douglas production function is widely used in economic analysis and it is used in this study. The function is estimated in log-linear form by the ordinary least squares method. The statistical results will indicate what returns to scale are prevailing in Jordan. In addition, output elasticity with respect to each input, namely, capital and labour, will be examined.

GENERATING CAPITAL STOCK

A time series capital stock for Jordan was generated by the author for the period 1967-79; the series was used to construct a profit index which served as an explanatory variable in an investment demand function.[2] In this chapter, two time series capital stock will be generated for the period 1967-81. The methodology follows that of Adelman and Chenery in their study of the Greek development

An Aggregate Production Function

experiences.[3]

The first step to generate capital stock is to calculate the overall incremental capital-output ratio (ICOR) for the period under study. Capital stock figure for the first year of the study period is obtained by multiplying overall ICOR by the GDP for that year. Subsequent figures of capital stock are derived by cumulating net capital formation.[4]

In calculating the incremental capital-output ratio for the aggregate economy of Jordan for the period 1972-79, the Japan International Co-operation Agency (JICA) used the formula:[5]

$$\text{ICOR (1972-77)} = \frac{\sum_{t=1972}^{1977} I_t}{GDP_{1977} - GDP_{1972}} = 5.37$$

Where:

I_t = Net capital formation in the year t;

GDP_{1972}, GDP_{1977} = Gross domestic product in the years 1972, 1977 respectively.

Using the ICOR formula for four sub-periods of 1972-77, the JICA calculated different ICORs, which ranged from 2.02 to 5.37. High ICORs, the JICA concluded, seem to be caused by high rates of increase in capital investment in recent years. The JICA assumed, therefore, that ICOR for the aggregate economy, as well as for the study area of northern Jordan, will be 3.0 for the future until 1985.[6]

Using the JICA formula to calculate the overall ICOR for the period 1967-81 (data taken from Table 1.1) it is found that ICOR is 3.73.

$$\text{ICOR (1967-81)} = \frac{\sum_{t=1967}^{t=1981} I_t}{GDP_{1981} - GDP_{1967}} = \frac{1456.1}{389.8} = 3.73$$

An Aggregate Production Function

Table 1.1: Capital Stock Generated, Labour, Gross Domestic Product and Net Capital Formation, 1967-1981 (million constant Jordanian dinars, 1975 = 100)

Year	Net capital formation	Gross domestic product	Labour	Capital stock (K1)	Capital stock (K2)
1967	29.4	239.4	82.8	718.2	893.0
1968	36.4	285.4	115.9	747.6	922.4
1969	54.2	310.8	124.1	784.0	958.8
1970	22.8	276.4	114.3	838.2	1,013.0
1971	41.6	283.4	113.1	861.0	1,035.8
1972	50.7	307.4	122.8	902.6	1,077.4
1973	40.2	284.2	115.4	953.3	1,128.1
1974	64.7	280.4	121.5	993.5	1,168.3
1975	76.3	321.3	120.6	1,058.2	1,233.0
1976	118.3	374.2	140.6	1,134.5	1,309.3
1977	143.7	407.1	134.9	1,252.8	1,427.6
1978	139.8	447.9	160.3	1,396.5	1,571.3
1979	159.1	489.2	193.4	1,536.3	1,711.1
1980	206.5	578.4	237.5	1,695.4	1,870.2
1981	272.4	629.2	247.3	1,901.9	2,076.7

Sources: net capital stock, GDPs and labour are taken from: Central Bank of Jordan, Monthly Statistical Bulletin (Amman), vol. 19, no. 10 (Oct. 1983), tables 42, 43; Jordan, Dept of Statistics, National Accounts in Jordan 1967-1977 (Amman, 1967), pp. 14-60, and National Accounts in Jordan 1978-1982 (Amman, 1978), pp. 25-44.

It was estimated by the National Planning Council (NPC) that ICORs were 1.9:1 and 2.61:1 for the two periods 1948-61 and 1962-66 respectively.[7] A UN study (1970) estimated ICOR for the 1954-64 period and projected future ICOR as 3.00.[8]

For generating capital stock along the lines of Adelman and Chenery, however, we make two assumptions concerning ICOR: (1) we assume, with both UN and JICA studies on Jordan, that this ICOR = 3.0; (2) we assume that ICOR = 3.73, the actual one calculated in this study.

With ICOR = 3.0, capital stock for the year 1967 equals three times the GDP in 1967. Subsequent figures of capital stock for the years 1968-81 were derived by cumulating net capital formation. We call this series of capital stock K1.

With ICOR = 3.73, capital stock for the year

An Aggregate Production Function

1967 equals 3.73 times the GDP in 1967. Similarly, subsequent figures of capital stock for the years 1968-81 were derived by cumulating net capital formation. We call this series of capital stock K2.

The two series of capital stock, labour services, net capital formation and GDP are given in Table 1.1 in millions of constant JDs. These variables are plotted in Figure 1.1.

Figure 1.1: Capital Stock, Labour Services and Gross Domestic Product, 1967-81

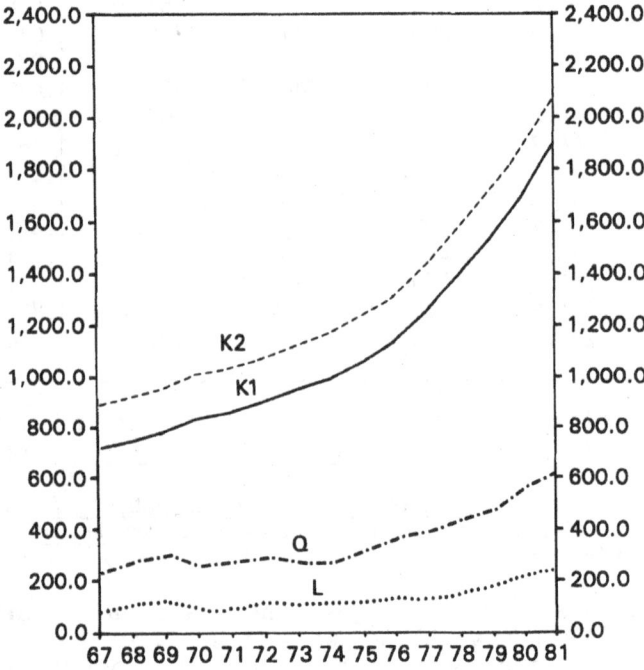

K1, K2 = Capital stock series
Q = Gross domestic product
L = Labour services

AGGREGATE PRODUCTION FUNCTION

A production function denotes the maximum output that can be obtained from a set of inputs. It is a function in the mathematical sense because it is assumed that to each set of inputs there is a unique maximum output. Hence, a production function is a mapping from the input space, X, into the output space, Q.[9]

An Aggregate Production Function

A commonly used production function in economic analysis, chosen for its mathematical properties and the possibility of being empirically estimated, is the Cobb-Douglas production function, which for the two-input case takes the form:

$$Q = A X_1^{a_1} X_2^{a_2}$$

Where Q is output;

X_1, X_2 are the two inputs;

and A, a_1, $a_2 > 0$

or more generally:

$$Q = A \prod_{i=1}^{s} X_i^{a_i} \quad ; \quad a_i > 0 \quad \forall i.$$

We shall assume that output in Jordan is a function of two inputs, capital and labour, and we also adopt a Cobb-Douglas production function specified as:

$$Q = A K^a L^b \quad \ldots\ldots\ldots\ldots\ldots\ldots \quad (1)$$

Where Q = aggregate real output.

K = capital stock.

L = labour services.

A, a, b are constants: A is a measure of technical change, a is partial elasticity of output with respect to capital, and b is partial elasticity of output with respect to labour.

In the economic literature, we have often seen a linearly homogenous production function, that is, the sum of the two exponents of the factors of production equals unity. In our model, we do not take that assumption for granted, but leave the exponents free to take any value.

In order to estimate the production function, let us take a natural log of: $Q = A K^a L^b$.

$$\ln Q = \ln A + a \ln K + b \ln L \ldots\ldots \quad (2)$$

adding an error term U;

An Aggregate Production Function

$$\ln Q = \ln A + a \ln K + b \ln L + U \quad (3)$$

Where ln = natural log

Since we have generated two time series of capital stock, we estimate equation (3), with the ordinary least squares method, using K1 and K2 respectively.

The estimated result of equation (3) for the period 1967-81 is as follows:

$$\ln Q = 0.20 + 0.41 \ K1 + 0.56 \ L \ \ldots\ldots \quad (4)$$

(t-ratio)   (0.48)   (2.86)°   (3.78)°°

$R2 = 0.9648$

D.W. = 1.04

°, °°: Coefficient is significant at 5% and 1% levels, respectively.

Where R^2 is the coefficient of determination and D.W. is the Durbin-Watson statistic.

From the above, we can see that our estimating equation can explain 96.48% of total variation in the aggregate real output. The coefficients of capital stock and labour are significant at 5% and 1% levels, respectively. The value of the Durbin-Watson statistic falls in the indeterminate region. The magnitudes of the coefficients of the variables capital and labour indicate that output elasticity with respect to capital is 0.41 and output elasticity with respect to labour is 0.56.

Estimating equation (3) using capital stock series (K2), generated on the assumption that ICOR = 3.73, the estimated result is as follows:

$$\ln Q = -0.37 + 0.49 \ln K2 + 0.54 \ln L \ldots (5)$$

(t-ratio)   (-0.65)   (2.95)°   (3.62)°°

$R^2 = 0.9657$

D.W. = 1.06

The statistical results of equation (5) are almost identical to those of equation (4). We can explain 96.57% of total variation in aggregate real output by the explanatory variables, capital and

An Aggregate Production Function

labour. The coefficients of capital stock and labour are significant at 5% and 1% levels, respectively. The sign of the constant term is negative but insignificant, and the Durbin-Watson statistic value again falls in the indeterminate region.

Returns to scale:

A production function is homogenous of degree k if $f(tx_1, tx_2) = t^k f(x_1, X_2) = t Q$

Where k is a constant and t is any positive real number.[10] If both inputs (x_1, x_2) are increased by the factor t, output is increased by the factor t. Returns to scale are increasing if $k > 1$, constant if $k = 1$, and decreasing if $k < 1$.

With respect to our specified production function, it can easily be shown that $k = a + b$. If we examine the sum of the coefficients of capital and labour in the estimated equation (4), we find that $a + b = 0.97 < 1$, implying that the Jordanian economy is operating under decreasing returns to scale. On the other hand, the sum of the two coefficients in the estimated equation (5) equals 1.03, implying that the economy is operating under increasing returns to scale.

These two diverging conclusions concerning returns to scale are the result of using two time services of capital stock in estimating the aggregate production function. However, rewriting the sum of the two coefficients of capital and labour in equations (4) and (5) as:

$a + b = 1.0 \mp 0.03$,

and approximating the sum to one decimal place, reduces the sum of the two coefficients to unity, i.e., $a + b = 1.0$. If such an approximation is warranted, then the result of both estimated equations (4) and (5) imply that constant returns to scale are prevailing in Jordan.

SUMMARY AND CONCLUSIONS

The present chapter is a preliminary attempt to specify and estimate an aggregate production function for the Jordanian economy. It is assumed that aggregate real output is a function of two factors - capital and labour - and the Cobb-Douglas

An Aggregate Production Function

function is adopted. Data deficiency on capital stock is overcome by utilizing the Adelman-Chenery approach to generate capital stock. Two series of capital stock are generated. The first series (K1) is generated on the assumption that ICOR is 3.0 for Jordan. This value of ICOR has been assumed for Jordan in two international studies. The second series of capital stock is generated on the assumption that ICOR = 3.73, the actual ICOR calculated in this study.

The ordinary least squares estimation of the log-linear Cobb-Douglas production function shows that labour and capital are significant explanatory variables. The constant term which measures technical change is found to be insignificant. With respect to returns to scale, the conclusion was not similar for the estimated equations with two series of capital stock. However, approximation to one decimal place of the sum of the two coefficients of capital and labour indicates that constant returns to scale are prevailing in Jordan.

It is hoped that this chapter will stimulate further research on the aggregate as well as on the sectoral level of the economy.

NOTES

1. The author wishes to thank Professors Peter Loeb and Vincent Lin of Rutgers University for their invaluable assistance in computer work as well as for commenting on the estimated results. Thanks are also due to M. el-Erian, a fellow of St Antony's College, Oxford, for his valuable suggestions.
2. Khalil Hammad, 'Foreign Aid and Economic Development: The Case of Jordan', unpublished PhD thesis, Southern Illinois University at Carbondale, 1981, p.110.
3. Irma Adelman and Hollis B. Chenery, 'Foreign Aid and Economic Development: The Case of Greece', Review of Economics and Statistics, vol. XLVIII, no. 1 (Feb. 1966), pp. 1-19.
4. Ibid., p. 19.
5. Japan International Co-operation Agency, Integrated Regional Development Study of Northern Jordan: Final Report (Tokyo, 1980), vol. 4, app. C-3.
6. Ibid., app. C, p.3.
7. Jordan, National Planning Council, Five Year Plan: 1976-1980 (Amman, 1976), pp. 7-10.
8. United Nations, Studies on Selected Development Problems in Various Countries in the Middle East (New York, 1970), p. 40.
9. For a detailed discussion of production functions, see, for example: R. Shone, Microeconomics: A Modern Treatment (Academic Press, New York and San Francisco, 1976); James M. Henderson and Richard E. Quandt, Microeconomic Theory: A Mathematical Approach (McGraw-Hill, New York, 1971); Alpha C. Chiang, Fundamental Methods of Mathematical Economics, 2nd edn (McGraw-Hill Kogakusha, Tokyo, 1974).
10. Henderson and Quandt, Microeconomic Theory, p.79.

BIBLIOGRAPHY

Adelman, Irma and Hollis B. Chenery. 'Foreign Aid and Economic Development: The Case of Greece', Review of Economics and Statistics, vol. XLVIII, no. 1, (Feb. 1966)

Central Bank of Jordan. Monthly Statistical Bulletin, vol. 19, no. 10 (Oct. 1983); and previous issues

Chiang, Alpha C. Fundamental Methods of Mathematical Economics, 2nd edn (McGraw-Hill Kogakusha, Tokyo, 1974)

Hammad, Khalil, 'Foreign Aid and Economic Development: The Case of Jordan', unpublished PhD thesis, Southern Illinois University at Carbondale, 1981

────── 'Capital Stock in Less Developed Countries: The Case of Jordan', Journal of Tanmiyat al-Rafidain (Iraq), vol. 5, no. 8 (June 1983)

Henderson, James M. and Richard E. Quandt. Microeconomic Theory: A Mathematical Approach (McGraw Hill, New York, 1971)

Japan International Co-operation Agency. Integrated Regional Development Study of Northern Jordan: Final Report, vol. 4 (Tokyo, 1980)

Jordan, Department of Statistics. National Accounts in Jordan: 1967-1977 (Amman, 1967)

────── National Accounts in Jordan: 1978-1982 (Amman, 1978)

Jordan, National Planning Council, Five Year Plan: 1976-1980 (Amman, 1976)

Jungshik, Son. 'An Econometric Monetary Model of Korea', unpublished PhD thesis, Southern Methodist University, 1976

Kmenta, Jan. Elements of Econometrics (Macmillan, New York, 1971)

Shone, R. Microeconomics: A Modern Treatment (Academic Press, New York and San Francisco, 1976)

United Nations. Studies on Selected Development Problems in Various Countries in the Middle East (New York, 1970)

World Bank. Jordan: Special Economic Report (May 1983)

────── World Tables: 1976 and 1980 (Johns Hopkins University Press, Baltimore, Md., 1976 and 1980)

Chapter Two

THE ROLE OF FOREIGN AID IN THE JORDANIAN ECONOMY, 1959-1983

Khalil Hammad

INTRODUCTION

The present chapter examines the role of foreign aid in the economic development of Jordan. It also gives a description of the sources of aid, its sectoral distribution and the burden of aid. The historical background for Jordan's heavy reliance on foreign aid is also given.

Jordan, formerly Transjordan, became independent in March 1946 with the ending of the British mandate established by the League of Nations in 1922. When the British government terminated its mandate in Palestine in May 1948, Transjordan forces occupied some 5,900 sq. km. of Palestine, including East Jerusalem.[1] In June 1949 the country was renamed Jordan (the Hashemite Kingdom of Jordan) and in April 1950 the West Bank was formally annexed to Jordan.[2]

In 1947 the population of Transjordan was approximately 375,000.[3] The following year about 350,000 persons left Palestine and entered Transjordan as refugees; the resident population of the West Bank was then 460,000.[4] By 1950 the population of Jordan was more than three times what the original population of Transjordan had been in 1947. Although the incorporation into Jordan of the West Bank added a mere 7% to Jordan's total area, it added some 30% to the arable land.[5] Both the influx of Palestinian refugees and the natural growth of the population of Jordan added to the numbers seeking employment. With the dearth of natural resources, Jordan had to be heavily dependent on foreign aid.

In 1955 the World Bank sent a mission to study the economy of Jordan and to make recommendations. The mission reported that Jordan had achieved a

The Role of Foreign Aid, 1959-1983

rapid expansion in economic activity since 1948, but the report added:

> Overall, the expansion of economic activity has been far from sufficient to absorb the increase in the population of the working age, and all those displaced by the Arab-Israeli war. More than half the refugee population was without any occupation (employment), even seasonally, in 1954, and most of the rest, as well as many of the indigenous population, found only casual or seasonal employment. Consequently, in 1954 the country was heavily dependent on foreign aid.[6]

The 1967 war with Israel left Israel in possession of all Jordanian territory on the West Bank of the Jordan. Israel's occupation of the West Bank has been denounced by almost all countries of the world and in many UN resolutions, particularly Security Council Resolution 242 of 22 November 1967; Jordan is thus considered to consist of both East and West Banks, although the West Bank has the status of 'occupied territory'.

The 1967 war imposed a heavy burden on Jordan. It brought a stream of refugees (estimated at 250,000-300,000)[7] from both the West Bank and the Gaza Strip and increased military expenditure both during and after the war. In April 1978 there were 677,945 refugees registered with the United Nations Relief and Works Agency for Palestine Refugees in the Near East (UNRWA) in East Jordan and a further 309,359 on the West Bank.

Thus, the influx of Palestinian refugees, the meagre natural resources and the high natural rate of population growth compounded Jordan's need for foreign aid if the country was to develop and grow.

FOREIGN AID AND THE ECONOMIC DEVELOPMENT OF JORDAN

The Balance of Payments

External trade (exports + imports) plays an important role in the economy of Jordan. The country depends to a large extent on imports to satisfy an increasing consumption demand as well as demand for capital goods.

A cursory look at Jordan's balance of payments (Table 2.1) shows a deficit in the current account for the period 1981-83. However, the deficit in the current account is mainly caused by a chronic trade

Table 2.1: Balance of Payments, 1981-83 (million Jordanian dinars)

	1981		1982		1983[a]	
	Credit	Debit	Credit	Debit	Credit	Debit
A. Goods and services	1,037.87	1,482.36	1,121.93	1,613.49	1,103.92	1,540.17
1. Merchandise	242.62	1,046.36	264.53	1,141.12	210.59	1,101.96
2. Travel	180.84	121.55	183.48	131.28	183.05	132.43
3. Investment income	66.25	37.63	72.08	39.43	62.94	46.37
4. Workers' remittances	340.79	52.00	381.87	62.40	402.90	72.80
5. Other services	207.27	224.82	219.97	239.26	244.44	186.61
Net goods & services		444.49		491.56		436.25
Trade balance		803.74		876.59		891.37
Net services	359.25		385.03		455.12	
B. Unrequested transfers	432.46	1.66	375.36	2.07	296.79	1.86
1. Private	17.13	1.66	11.64	2.07	7.23	1.86
2. Central government	415.33	–	363.72	–	289.56	–
C. Allocation of SDRs	1.21	–	–	–	–	–
D. Capital and monetary gold	52.80		171.31		146.03	
1. Non-monetary sector	69.04		113.40		156.76	
2. Monetary sector		16.24	57.91			10.73
E. Net errors and omissions		40.32		53.04		4.71

Note: a. Preliminary.
Source: Central Bank of Jordan (CBJ) Monthly Statistical Bulletin (Amman), vol. 20, no. 4 (April, 1984), table 25.

The Role of Foreign Aid, 1959-1983

deficit that dates back to the early 1950s. While the trade deficit was partly offset by an increasing surplus in the balance of services (largely remittances of Jordanians working abroad and tourism), the trade balance deficit grew steadily. Starting from the year 1959 (the first year that the Department of Statistics published annual data for Jordan), we find that the import surplus was JD 32.87 mn or 33.17% of GNP and 24.91% of total resources available (1 JD = $2.8 in 1959 and $2.57 in 1983). If we examine Table 2.2, we find that the import surplus ranged from a low of 14.8% of GNP in 1965 to a high of 34.4% of GNP in 1979. An alternative measure is the ratio of the import surplus to total resources available (TRA), defined as GNP plus the import surplus. As shown in Table 2.2, we find that the import surplus ranged from a low of 12.9% of TRA in 1965 to a high of 25% of TRA in 1979.

The large import surplus means that imports are partly paid for by the proceeds of exports. This import surplus could have been a grave problem for the Jordanian economy had it not been financed by capital inflow, mainly transfer payments where grants form the largest component.

Transfer payments of Jordan's balance of payments consist of:

1. official transfers from foreign governments and various international agencies to the government of Jordan, including a small fraction transferred by UNRWA to the Palestinian refugees;
2. private transfers from charitable institutions abroad and emigrants to their relatives in Jordan.

Table 2.3 shows the role played by foreign aid in the Jordanian economy by financing the import surplus. Net transfer payments have accommodated the trade deficit and turned the deficits in the balance of goods and services (import surplus) into surplus in 12 out of 25 years for the period under study. Furthermore, in 8 out of the other 13 years the deficit on the current account was small and manageable. The table also shows the breakdown of net transfer payments into their two components, official and private, with a dominant role for official transfers.

The Role of Foreign Aid, 1959-1983

Table 2.2: Ratio of Import Surplus to Gross National Product and Total Resources Available, 1959-83

Year	GNP	Import surplus available	Total Resources	Import % of GNP	Surplus as % of TRA
1959	99.10	32.87	131.97	33.17	24.91
1960	105.70	34.76	140.46	32.89	24.75
1961	127.10	25.46	152.56	20.03	16.69
1962	130.80	23.18	153.98	17.72	15.05
1963	137.70	36.18	173.88	26.27	20.80
1964	160.62	24.45	185.07	15.22	13.58
1965	180.54	26.83	207.37	14.86	12.94
1966	185.65	35.55	221.20	19.15	16.07
1967[a]	140.90	27.75	168.65	19.69	16.45
1968	166.90	44.36	211.26	26.58	21.00
1969	197.40	63.62	261.02	32.22	24.37
1970	187.00	46.58	233.58	24.91	19.94
1971	199.40	57.88	257.28	29.03	22.49
1972	221.00	66.98	287.98	30.30	23.26
1973	241.50	60.80	302.30	25.17	20.11
1974	279.30	83.80	361.10	30.00	23.20
1975	376.00	118.33	494.33	31.47	23.93
1976	562.40	109.21	671.61	19.42	16.26
1977	660.10	168.29	828.34	25.49	17.29
1978	781.10	192.33	973.41	24.62	19.75
1979	921.30	316.51	1,237.81	34.35	25.57
1980	1,185.30	287.13	1,472.43	24.22	19.50
1981	1,501.10	444.49	1,945.59	29.61	22.84
1982	1,695.40	491.56	2,186.96	28.99	22.47
1983	1,848.30	436.25	2,284.55	23.60	19.09

Note: a. Since 1967, data belong to the East Bank of Jordan.
Sources: Jordan, Currency Control Department, <u>Balance of Payments for the Year 1960</u> (Amman, 1961); Jordan, Department of Statistics, <u>Statistical Yearbook</u> nos. 15 (Amman, 1964) to 33 (Amman, 1982); CBJ, <u>Monthly Statistical Bulletin</u>, vol. 20, no. 4, tables 25, 43.

The Role of Foreign Aid, 1959-1983

Table 2.3: Import Surplus and Foreign Aid Compared, 1959-83 (million current Jordanian dinars)

Year	Import surplus	Net Transfer payments (total foreign aid)	Official (net)	Private (net)
1959	32.87	30.92	25.14	5.78
1960	34.76	26.89	25.49	7.27
1961	25.46	26.21	25.33	0.88
1962	23.18	25.21	23.47	1.74
1963	36.18	24.14	22.52	1.62
1964	24.45	28.52	26.57	1.95
1965	26.83	29.46	26.78	2.68
1966	35.55	34.09	31.44	2.65
1967	27.75	53.93	51.58	2.35
1968	44.36	54.48	53.07	1.41
1969	63.62	47.34	45.79	1.55
1970	46.58	40.65	39.08	1.57
1971	57.88	36.61	35.49	1.12
1972	66.98	68.29	65.96	2.33
1973	60.80	64.60	61.09	3.51
1974	83.80	86.74	84.43	2.31
1975	118.33	139.80	138.01	1.79
1976	109.21	126.55	122.75	3.80
1977	168.29	165.83	166.94	-1.11
1978	192.31	106.51	102.63	3.88
1979	316.51	314.43	318.05	-3.62
1980	287.13	398.75	390.85	7.90
1981	444.49	430.80	415.33	15.47
1982	491.56	373.29	363.72	9.57
1983	436.25	294.93	289.56	5.37

Source: As Table 2.1.

Finally, Table 2.4 measures foreign aid as a percentage of total resources available, on a per capita basis. Foreign aid reached a low of 13.6% of GNP in 1978 and a high of 37.2% of GNP in 1975. Similarly, foreign aid reached a low of 10.9% of TRA in 1978 and a high of 28.3% of TRA in 1975.

The Role of Foreign Aid, 1959-1983

Table 2.4: Total Foreign Aid as a Percentage of Gross National Product, Total Resources Available, and on a Per Capita Basis, 1959-83

Year	Total foreign aid as % of GNP	% of TRA	Total foreign aid per capita (JD)
1959	31.20	23.43	18.97
1960	25.44	19.14	16.10
1961	20.62	17.18	15.42
1962	19.27	16.37	14.42
1963	17.53	13.88	13.26
1964	17.76	15.41	15.25
1965	16.32	14.21	15.42
1966	18.36	15.41	17.30
1967	26.19	23.08	26.44
1968	27.62	22.54	25.94
1969	20.26	15.92	21.62
1970	18.27	15.11	17.67
1971	15.47	12.43	15.38
1972	25.96	20.69	27.76
1973	22.17	18.34	25.43
1974	23.19	18.95	33.11
1975	37.18	28.28	51.78
1976	22.50	18.84	45.52
1977	25.12	20.02	57.38
1978	13.63	10.94	35.74
1979	34.13	25.40	101.76
1980	33.64	27.08	123.10
1981	28.70	22.14	128.21
1982	22.02	17.07	107.57
1983	15.95	12.91	82.38

Sources: Table 2.3 and author's calculations.

On a per capita basis, every Jordanian received a low of JD 13.3 ($37) in 1963 and a high of JD 128 ($358) in 1981.

The inflow of foreign aid, with a smaller but mostly positive capital account, has more than offset Jordan's resource gap; reserves have accumulated and the country's overall balance of payments has remained strong. This reflects Jordan's ability to meet its financial obligations, maintain a stable value for its currency in the foreign exchange markets, and attain a higher rate of growth by financing a relatively large import surplus.

SOURCES AND SECTORAL DISTRIBUTION OF FOREIGN AID

Jordan's balance of payments lists three sources of foreign aid: the US, Arab countries and 'others'. The third source - 'others' - includes countries and UN agencies that do not contribute aid to Jordan on a regular basis. The purpose of this section is to investigate the sources and sectoral distribution of foreign aid for its relevance to economic development.

US Aid to Jordan
The US interest in extending aid to Jordan follows from America's interest in the Middle East in general. The Middle East is of great strategic and economic significance for the two blocs, East and West. The region's strategic importance derives mainly from its geographic location and its supply of several important materials. Its economic importance lies in its geographic location, its resources and its market.

The Middle East, by its geographic location, forms the West's military front in any potential confrontation with the Eastern bloc. The containment of Middle Eastern countries has become a Western objective, and foreign aid serves as a tool of US foreign policy. As such, countries on the periphery of the USSR receive considerable amounts of US aid. The economic importance of the Middle East lies in the fact that its underground reservoirs of oil contain possibly two-thirds of the world's petroleum reserves. Hence, the region's political stability is seen as a means of securing access to these resources.

Moving from the general to the specific, Jordan has received US aid since the early 1950s. The Agency for International Development (AID) has defined US interests and objectives in extending aid to Jordan as follows:

> Surrounded by Israel, Syria, Iraq and Saudi Arabia, Jordan is geographically and politically

Table 2.5: Total US Economic and Military Aid to Jordan, 1946-83 (million US dollars)

Programme	Total loans and grants	Repayments and interest	Total less repayments and interest	%
Economic assistance	1,468.2	51.1	1,417.1	64.5
Loans	329.1	51.1	278.0	
Grants	1,139.1	-	1,139.1	
Military assistance	1,149.0	370.5	778.5	35.5
Loans	591.3	370.5	220.8	
Grants	557.7	-	557.7	
Economic and military assistance	2,617.2	421.6	2,195.6	100.0
Loans	920.4	421.6	498.8	22.7
Grants	1,696.8	-	1,696.8	77.3
Other US loans	364.4	146.5	217.9	
Ex-IM bank loans	359.7	141.1	218.6	
All other	4.7	5.4	-0.7	

Source: Agency for International Development (AID), US Overseas Loans and Grants and Assistance from International Organizations, July 1, 1945 - September 30, 1983 (Washington, D.C., 1983), p.19.

The Role of Foreign Aid, 1959-1983

important. Jordan has long supported a comprehensive Middle East peace settlement. Jordan continues to seek a formula which will permit Jordanians and Palestinians to seize the opportunity for peace.

The primary objective of AID's program in Jordan is to assist the continued development of a moderate, Western-oriented state that is socially and politically stable. For thirty years, US economic assistance has been an important component of the US presence in Jordan, contributing to the formation of both the physical and human infrastructure which helped foster the rapid socio-economic growth of recent years.[8]

Table 2.5 examines total US aid to Jordan. This aid falls into two categories: economic and military. Total aid less repayments and interest totalled $2,195.6 mn between 1946 and 1983. The AID statistics divide total aid by period and annually. Accordingly, Jordan received $5.2 mn grants in economic aid in the period 1949-52 (called the Marshall Plan period), $275.6 mn in the period 1953-61 (called the Mutual Security Act period) and $1,185.8 mn in the period 1962-83 (called the Foreign Assistance Act period).[9] Total loans were $498.8 mn and total grants were $1,696.8 mn, or 22.7% and 77.3%, respectively, of total aid. Repayments and interest on loans were $421.6 mn for the same period.

The largest component of US aid to Jordan is economic assistance. This assistance is extended through AID and its predecessor agencies and the Food for Peace Program. US aid includes grants, which are outright gifts, and loans. The loan total covers all loans made by AID from all current and past appropriation accounts, including Security Supporting Assistance and Contingency funds. The loans total also includes 'capitalized interest': this represents interest on prior year loans that, rather than being paid when due, is added for accounting purposes to the face amount of the loan, and is thereafter treated as principal to be repaid with interest.

Total economic assistance less repayments and interest has amounted to $1,417.1 mn since 1946, or 64.5% of total US aid. Total grants reached $1,139.1 mn, or almost 80% of total economic assistance. Thus the debt burden of economic assistance was small and manageable. Repayments and

The Role of Foreign Aid, 1959-1983

interest on loans were $51.1 mn for the whole period.

US economic assistance to Jordan is provided from three sources: AID and its predecessors; Food for Peace; and other economic assistance.

AID and its predecessor agencies have extended 86.4% of total economic assistance since 1946. This includes capital assistance, technical assistance and supporting assistance. Capital assistance takes the form of shipping capital items and commodities from the US to Jordan. Technical assistance, defined as the diffusion of ideas from a technically rich country to a technically poor country,[10] involves training, advice and demonstration by the aid-giving technicians to improve or develop human skills of the natives of the recipient country. Supporting assistance involves grants to support the government budget in carrying out its routine functions.

The capital and commodity items furnished by the AID administration are primarily financed by development loans, usually for long terms and at low interest rates. Technical assistance is normally financed by development grants.

The bulk of economic aid extended by AID since 1946 has been in the form of grants to support the government budget. This means that capital and technical assistance, extended over two decades of US aid to Jordan, was very small compared to total US aid. AID statistics show that capital and technical assistance to Jordan was only about $105 mn between 1946 and 1978 (Table 2.6). The average annual amount of capital and technical assistance received by Jordan is thus $5.25 mn. The sectoral distribution of capital assistance shows that transportation, agriculture, and industry and mining received higher shares than other sectors. Technical assistance was higher in the fields of agriculture, health, education and public administration than in other sectors. Overall, agriculture received about $27 mn, transportation about $21 mn and industry and mining about $19 mn in capital and technical assistance between 1946 and 1978. Other than industry and agriculture, most of the capital and technical assistance to Jordan was for economic and social infrastructure.

In addition to the economic assistance extended by AID and its predecessor agencies,

Table 2.6: US Capital and Technical Assistance to Jordan, 1946-78 (thousand US dollars)

Sector	Capital assistance	Technical assistance	Total capital and technical assistance
Agriculture and natural resources	17,020	9,667	26,687
Industry and mining	15,184	3,583	18,767
Transportation	18,838	2,085	20,923
Health and sanitation	2,829	4,247	5,076
Education	2,362	4,854	7,216
Public safety and public administration	204	4,964	5,168
Community development and social welfare	1,563	2,844	4,407
Other general/ miscellaneous	653	14,334	14,987
Private enterprise promotion	-	1,727	1,727
Grants	44,461	48,305	92,766
Loans	12,192	-	12,192
TOTAL	56,653	48,305	104,958

Source: AID, *Capital and Technical Assistance: Completed Projects by Country and Technical Field* (Washington, D.C., 1979), pp. 71-2; 150-2.

The Role of Foreign Aid, 1959-1983

Jordan received economic assistance in the form of food. The World Food Program (WFP) (Public Law 480 - Agricultural Trade and Development Act, approved in July 1954) established as US policy 'the maximum efficient use of surplus agricultural commodities in the furtherance of the foreign policy of the United States'.[11] Title I of the act authorized the sale abroad for foreign currencies of US surplus agricultural commodities. In turn, the local currency proceeds were to be used for certain stipulated purposes, including 'loans to promote multilateral trade and economic development'.[12] Later amendments of the act allowed for sales on credit terms, repayable in US dollars. Title II covers donations under the Emergency Relief and Economic Development Programs, WFP and Voluntary Relief Agencies. Jordan has received $178.7 mn economic assistance in the form of food, $44.7 mn under Title I and $134.0 mn under Title II. Loans repayable in US dollars amounted to $58.8 mn, while loans repayable in Jordanian currency were $3.7 mn. Repayments and interest under Title I amounted to $17.8 mn during the same period. Donations under Title II amounted to $134 mn and incurred no cost to Jordan. Overall, economic assistance in the form of food amounted to 13.5% of total economic assistance and about 8.4% of US aid to Jordan since 1946. Jordan also received $1.5 mn in economic assistance under the United Nations Relief and Rehabilitation Assistance (UNRRA) Program of the US in the early 1950s.

The second category of US aid to Jordan is military assistance. Jordan received $1,149.5 mn in loans and grants in this category; loans amounted to $591.3 mn and grants amounted to $557.7 mn. Repayments and interest on military loans were $370.5 mn, compared with $51.1 mn on economic assistance. Total military assistance less repayments and interest was 35.5% of total US aid.

Arab Aid to Jordan

Jordan was one of the founding members of the Arab League, which was officially established at a meeting in Cairo on 22 March 1945.[13] After independence in 1946, Jordan continued to receive a subsidy from Britain. In 1954 a plan to develop Jordan's potash mines was introduced by the Arab League, with guarantees that members of the League would cover the expenses jointly with Jordan. In 1957 Egypt, Syria and Saudi Arabia signed a ten-year treaty with Jordan to supply it with money

The Role of Foreign Aid, 1959-1983

and arms to compensate for the deficit caused by the withdrawal of the British subsidy. Because of political circumstances, however, Egypt and Syria discontinued this aid. Between 1959 and 1963 Jordan's balance of payments showed no transfers from Arab countries. In 1964 Jordan received JD 5 mn from Kuwait to support the budget; in 1965 it received JD 7.34 mn from the Arab League (United Arab Command) in military, economic and technical development loans; and the following year it received JD 9.49 mn from Arab countries, mainly Saudi Arabia, to assist in the construction of the Ghor al-Safi/Aqaba road. Total Arab assistance to Jordan in this phase (1959-66) amounted to JD 21.37 mn.

The second phase of Arab aid to Jordan came in the aftermath of the 1967 war with Israel, which resulted in Israel's occupation of the West Bank of the Jordan. After the Khartoum Arab Summit Conference of September 1967, annual aid totalling JD 40 mn was pledged by the three oil-rich countries, Kuwait, Saudi Arabia, and Libya.[14] This emergency aid to Jordan was intended to support the government budget, increase the defensive capability of the Jordanian Army, and enhance the steadfastness of the people of the West Bank.

Because of Jordan's strained relations with the Palestinian resistance movement, however, Libya and Kuwait suspended their support to Jordan in 1970. Thereafter Jordan continued to receive aid from Saudi Arabia and other Arab oil-rich states other than Kuwait and Libya. Between 1967 and 1973 Jordan received JD 224 mn in aid from Arab countries alone, compared to JD 91.02 mn from the US and JD 37.04 mn from other sources (Table 2.7).

The third, and most important, phase of the Arab aid to Jordan came after 1973. With the quadrupling of oil prices by OPEC, Arab oil-rich countries accumulated huge reserves of surplus petrodollars. These Arab oil-rich states extended aid to developing countries in general, and to neighbouring Arab countries in particular, namely Egypt, Jordan and Syria. This is because these three countries have common borders with Israel; thus Arab aid was mainly to help their defensive capabilities and support their development efforts. The amount of aid that Jordan received in 1974 and afterwards was very large compared with that received in the previous two phases. Table 2.7 shows total government aid to Jordan, broken down into three categories: Arab, US and other sources.

The Role of Foreign Aid, 1959-1983

Table 2.7: Official Aid to Jordan by Source, 1959-83 (million Jordanian dinars)

Year	Official aid (total)	Arab aid	US aid	Other sources
1959	25.14	-	17.32	7.82
1960	25.49	-	18.20	7.29
1961	25.33	-	17.05	8.28
1962	23.47	-	15.48	7.99
1963	22.52	-	·15.51	7.01
1964	26.57	4.54	15.03	7.00
1965	26.78	7.34	11.98	7.46
1966	31.44	9.49	13.37	8.58
1967	51.58	37.57	7.62	6.39
1968	53.07	46.25	1.19	5.63
1969	45.79	41.15	1.25	3.41
1970	39.08	33.07	1.38	4.63
1971	35.94	19.11	12.82	3.56
1972	65.96	23.19	35.95	6.82
1973	61.09	23.66	30.83	6.60
1974	84.43	46.60	25.31	12.52
1975	138.01	105.65	22.44	9.92
1976	122.75	77.59	26.13	19.03
1977	166.94	132.31	15.62	19.01
1978	102.63	66.26	18.56	17.81
1979	318.05	299.66	4.59	13.80
1980	390.85	370.43	6.15	14.27
1981	415.33	394.92	-	20.41
1982	363.72	335.83	-	27.89
1983	289.56	258.31	-	31.75

Source: As Table 2.2.

After the Baghdad Arab Summit Conference, Jordan received grants from Arab states of JD 299.6 mn ($1 bn) in 1979 alone.[15] Arab aid increased steadily from JD 4.54 mn in 1964, with a slight decline in 1970 and 1971 when Kuwait and Libya suspended their support, to reach its maximum level in 1981.
Total Arab aid since 1959 amounts to JD 2332.93 mn, compared with JD 337.76 mn and JD 284.38 mn from the US and other sources, respectively. In percentage terms, Arab governments

have contributed 79.1%, the US 11.3% and other sources the remaining 9.6% of total aid.

Arab aid differs from US aid to Jordan in many respects. US aid is diversified; it consists of both economic and military assistance. Economic assistance is in the form of food, capital and technical assistance. Most US aid is tied by project. Arab aid, on the other hand, is only capital in the form of cash - the US dollar. This is because, first, Arab oil-rich states have surplus petrodollars and, second, they are in a lesser stage of development than Jordan. In fact, Jordan provides these states with skilled labour which emigrates to these states seeking higher incomes.

Thus, while it is possible to examine US aid quantitatively and qualitatively, Arab aid does not lend itself to the same sectoral distribution by source. Arab aid to Jordan has been almost entirely in the form of grants to support the budget. It has come through decisions by Arab summit conferences. Other technical and developmental loans have come from the Arab League and through bilateral agreements between Jordan and other Arab states.

We have seen earlier that budget support is used by the government to finance capital and recurring expenditures such as education, health, administration and defence. Developmental loans have been allocated to develop water resources, transport, electricity, mining, agriculture, housing, industry and mining. In short, while no precise time series or sectoral distribution of Arab aid is possible, we consider the sectoral distribution of the investments of the two development plans as representative of the allocation of Arab aid by Jordan.

Other Sources of Aid to Jordan
In addition to aid from the US and several Arab countries, Jordan receives aid from various other countries and UN agencies. UNRWA provides aid in kind to the Palestinians in Jordan. In fact, this aid is listed in the balance of payments under official transfers, while, as we have indicated, it is not governmental. Other UN agencies provide Jordan with technical and developmental loans to finance projects jointly with the government of Jordan.

Jordan also receives aid from many developed countries through bilateral agreements, but none of

The Role of Foreign Aid, 1959-1983

these countries provides aid on a continuous basis as do the US and Arab countries. Among the countries that provide aid on an occasional basis are Britain, France and Denmark. In recent years, Japan and Germany have been the most frequent aid-givers to Jordan.

Taken together, other sources of aid have contributed JD 84.38 mn, or about 9.6% of total aid since 1959 (Table 2.7). This volume of aid from other sources does not have a grant element in it to support the budget, but all of it is in the form of technical and developmental loans.

However, while all US aid has ceased since 1981 and Arab aid is declining, 'other sources' of aid have been contributing increasing amounts of loans since 1980.

THE BURDEN OF AID

Jordan has been fortunate in that most of its aid has been received in the form of grants. It should be remembered that Arab aid extended to Jordan in accordance with Arab summit conferences was in the form of outright grants to support the Jordanian budget. In addition, 77% of US aid to Jordan after 1946 was in the form of grants.

AID prepares reports on Jordan's repayments and interest for the entire period and for sub-periods. It has been shown that Jordan's repayments of principal and interest to the US have been $421.6 mn since 1946: $51.1 mn on economic loans and $370.5 mn on military loans (Table 2.5). As a fraction of total US aid, Jordan's repayments to the US have been 16% of total economic and military aid since 1946.

However, Jordan continues to borrow from various countries, both Arab and non-Arab, and from international agencies. The external debt has increased from JD 68 mn in 1973 to JD 762.9 mn at the end of 1983, or more than eleven-fold. Measured as a percentage of GNP, the external debt increased from 28% to 41% over the same period.

Consequently, the debt burden in terms of interest and amortization increased from JD 3.6 mn in 1973 to JD 171 mn at the end of 1983. Measured as a percentage of exports of goods and services, the debt burden increased from 3.7% in 1973 to 15.5% in 1983.

Thus, the external debt and its burden have been increasing in both absolute and relative terms in recent years. However, the strong position of Jordan's balance of payments (discussed earlier) indicates that the repayment problem of principal and interest on external loans is not serious as far as Jordan is concerned.

The Role of Foreign Aid, 1959-1983

NOTES

1. *The Europa Yearbook, A World Survey, 11, 1980* (Europa Publications, London, 1980), p. 666.
2. Ibid.
3. International Bank for Reconstruction and Development (IBRD), *The Economic Development of Jordan* (Johns Hopkins Press, Baltimore, Md., 1957), p. 49.
4. Ibid.
5. Yusif A. Sayigh, *The Economies of the Arab World: Development since 1945*, (Croom Helm, London, 1978), p. 190.
6. IBRD, *Economic Development of Jordan*, p.5.
7. Eliyahu Kanovsky, *The Economic Impact of the Six Day War* (Praeger, New York, 1970), p. 418.
8. Agency for International Development (AID), *Congressional Presentation: Fiscal Year 1985, Annex IV, Near East* (Washington, D.C., 1983), p. 70.
9. AID, *US Overseas Loans and Grants and Assistance from International Organizations: July 1, 1945 - September 30, 1983* (Washington, D.C., 1983), p. 19.
10. Sidney Sufrin, *Technical Assistance: Theory and Guidelines* (Syracuse University Press, Syracuse, N.Y., 1966), p. 22.
11. Charles Wolf, Jr, *Foreign Aid: Theory and Practice in Southeast Asia* (Princeton University Press, Princeton, N.Y., 1960), p. 206.
12. Ibid., p. 207.
13. Taghi Kermani, *Economic Development in Action: Theories, Problems, and Procedures as Applied in the Middle East* (World Publishing Co., Cleveland, Ohio, 1967), p. 178.
14. Sayigh, *Economies of the Arab World*, p. 191.
15. Central Bank of Jordan, *Sixteenth Annual Report* (Amman, 1979), p. 65.

BIBLIOGRAPHY

Adelman, I. and H.B. Chenery. 'Foreign Aid and Economic Development: The Case of Greece', Review of Economics and Statistics, vol. XLVIII, no. 1 (Feb. 1966), pp. 1-19

Agency for International Development. Capital and Technical Assistance: Completed Projects by Country and Technical Field (Washington, D.C., 1976)

―――― Congressional Presentation: Fiscal Year 1983 (Washington, D.C., 1983)

―――― US Overseas Loans and Grants and Assistance from International Organizations: July 1, 1945 - September 30, 1983 (Washington, D.C., 1983)

Central Bank of Jordan. Monthly Statistical Bulletin, no. 5 (Amman, 1969) - no. 10 (Amman, 1984)

The Europa Yearbook, A World Survey, 11, 1980. (Europa Publications, London, 1980)

Hammad, Khalil. 'Foreign Aid and Economic Development: The Case of Jordan', unpublished PhD thesis, Southern Illinois University at Carbondale, 1981

International Bank for Reconstruction and Development. The Economic Development of Jordan. (Johns Hopkins Press, Baltimore, Md., 1957

Jordan, Currency Control Department. Balance of Payments for the Year 1960 (Amman, 1961)

Jordan, Department of Statistics. Annual Statistical Yearbook, 1964 (Amman, 1964) - Annual Statistical Yearbook, 1975 (Amman, 1975)

―――― National Accounts in Jordan: 1952-1976 (Amman 1976)

―――― National Accounts in Jordan: 1967-1977 (Amman 1978)

―――― National Accounts in Jordan: 1967-1982 (Amman 1982)

Jordan, National Planning Council. The Three Year Plan: 1973-1975 (Amman, 1972)

―――― The Five Year Plan: 1976-1980 (Amman, 1976)

Kaplan, J.J. The Challenge of Foreign Aid: Policies, Problems, and Possibilities (Praeger, New York, 1967)

Kermani, T.T. Economic Development in Action: Theories, Problems, and Procedures as Applied in the Middle East (World Publishing Company, Cleveland, Ohio, 1967

Mason, E.S. Foreign Aid and Foreign Policy (Harper & Row, New York, 1964)

The Role of Foreign Aid, 1959-1983

Sayigh, Y.A. *The Economies of the Arab World: Development since 1945* (Croom Helm, London, 1978)
___ *The Determinants of Arab Economic Development* (Croom Helm, London, 1978)
Sufrin, S.C. *Technical Assistance: Theory and Guidelines* (Syracuse University Press, Syracuse, N.Y., 1966
Wolf, C. *Foreign Aid: Theory and Practice in Southeast Asia*. (Princeton University Press, Princeton, N.J., 1960)

Chapter Three

THE USE OF JORDANIAN WORKERS' REMITTANCES

M.A.J. Share

The purpose of the present chapter is to examine the use of the remittances from Jordanian workers abroad in the light of the limited available data. Special reference will be made to the results of a sample survey of Jordanian workers in Kuwait.[1] We start with a brief introduction to the migration process of Jordanian workers and the volume of those migrants. We then turn to the main issue of remittances.

MIGRATION OF JORDANIAN WORKERS

Labour migration in the Middle East is believed to create a pattern which is distinctive to the economies in the region because it is of a temporary rather than a permanent nature; it involves all types of worker who remain within the region, thus creating an internal flow of labour within developing countries.[2]

Over the past three decades Jordanians have been very mobile, with the oil producing states in the Middle East region providing the most popular destination. At first, the migrants' main motive was to seek employment. Later it became two-pronged: to seek employment and to achieve higher earnings than those attainable at home.

Jordanian workers show a very positive response to the high demand for their labour services in the region. This stems from the fact that Jordan's manpower enjoys a high level of education and technical skills, much needed by the oil-producing states to implement their ambitious development plans financed by substantial oil revenues.

Numerous sources agree that the detailed

picture for the various Arab nationalities in the oil states shows that Egyptians, Jordanians and Palestinians have above-average shares in professional, technical, managerial and clerical occupations.[3] The earliest reliable data on the number of Jordanians living and working abroad are contained in the first population census in 1961. Table 3.1 shows that the majority of the migrants (79% of the workers and 80% of the non-workers) choose Arab countries as their destination. During the 1970s,

Table 3.1: Jordanians Abroad by Location of Residence and Employment Status, 1961

Location	Workers	Non-workers	Total
Arab countries	15,901	24,270	50,171
Asia and Africa	105	742	847
Europe	1,683	2,177	3,860
Americas	4,912	2,597	7,509
Other countries	162	312	476
Total	22,763	30,098	62,863

Source: Jordan, Dept of Statistics, First Census of Population and Housing 1961 (Amman, 1964), vol. 1, pp. 316-23, table 5.2 and pp. 338-41, table 5.9.

the figures for Jordanian workers abroad were based on rough estimates, with such variations that they were reduced to mere guesses.[4] The author's own estimate of the number of Jordanians working abroad in 1975 ranges from 170,000 to 180,000 workers.[5] The number rose to 305,400 in 1981 (Table 3.2), of whom 85.6% were in Arab countries. This increased outflow resulted in labour shortages in specific skills and for certain sectors, to the extent that Jordan slipped out of the labour-exporting league to become both a labour-exporting and a labour-importing country during the latter years of the 1970s and the early years of this decade. Data for 1981 reveal that there were 100,000 foreign workers in Jordan, of whom 80,000 obtained work permits.[6]

Table 3.2: Jordanian Workers Abroad by Location, 1981

Location	No. of workers
Saudi Arabia	140,000
Kuwait	75,000
UAE	19,000
Qatar	7,250
Libya	6,500
Oman	6,500
Bahrain	3,250
Other Arab countries	4,000
All Arab countries	261,500
US	23,000
Britain	2,500
West Germany	10,000
Canada	5,000
Australia	3,000
Other European countries	1,400
Grand Total	306,400

Source: Jordan, Ministry of Labour, Annual Report 1981 (Amman, 1981).

JORDANIAN MIGRANTS IN KUWAIT

The Jordanian population in Kuwait in 1961 was 31,739, or 63.3% of Jordanians in all Arab countries and 50% of all Jordanians abroad.[7] Table 3.1 indicates a 56% participation rate for Jordanians abroad; applying this to Jordanians in Kuwait shows that the number of Jordanian workers in Kuwait was 17,774 in 1961.

Official Kuwaiti statistics reveal that the number of Jordanian migrants in Kuwait has been increasing since 1957. In that year Jordanians in Kuwait numbered 12,411.[8] This number increased to 31,739, 63,568, 120,815 and 172,773 for the years 1961, 1965, 1970 and 1975 respectively.[9] Of those migrants, persons actually working were 6,950, 17,774, 29,470, 33,941 and 39,110 for the same years respectively.[10]

Table 3.3: Remittances from Jordanians Working Abroad Compared with Exports, Imports and Gross Domestic Product, 1971-81 (million Jordanian dinars)

Year	Remittances	Exports	Remittances as % of exports	Imports	Remittances as % of imports	GDP at market prices	Remittances as % of GDP	Balance of payments surplus or deficit
1971	4.97	11.44	43.4	76.19	6.5	186.2	2.7	- 13.65
1972	7.41	17.01	43.7	94.88	7.8	207.2	3.6	+ 8.50
1973	14.70	18.98	77.5	107.80	13.6	218.3	6.7	+ 10.25
1974	24.13	49.75	48.5	155.68	15.5	247.3	9.8	+ 13.82
1975	53.25	48.88	108.9	232.94	22.9	278.6	19.1	+ 65.58
1976	136.41	68.71	198.5	338.74	40.3	401.7	34.0	+ 2.68
1977	154.75	82.06	188.6	453.11	34.2	477.6	32.4	+ 47.72
1978	159.38	90.92	175.3	458.94	34.7	576.7	27.6	+ 5.10
1979	180.42	120.92	149.21	588.32	30.7	712.0[a]	25.30	+ 57.40
1980	236.68	171.45	138.00	714.79	33.1	869.0[a]	27.20	+144.87
1981	340.00[a]	225.00[a]	151.11	865.00[a]	39.3	n.a.	n.a.	n.a.

Note: a. Preliminary figures.
Source: Central Bank of Jordan (CBJ), Monthly Statistical Bulletin (Amman), various issues.

MIGRANT WORKERS' REMITTANCES

From 1971 onwards, remittances from Jordanian workers abroad grew steadily and rapidly until they reached the substantial and unprecedented level of JD 340 mn in 1981 (Table 3.3).[11] In 1976 remittances represented JD 68 <u>per capita</u> and JD 798 per worker abroad. In 1981 remittances per head of the population reached JD 126 and JD 1,112.56 per worker abroad.[12] Although this volume of remittances seems remarkable, it is believed to be understated by a large margin, since the Central Bank statistics record only remittances passing through the banking system. A large proportion is thought to pass through private money-changers, be sent home with friends or brought home by the workers when they return for holidays.

The growth of the volume of remittances is attributed to various factors. First, the increase in the number of Jordanians working abroad is a major contributor to the rise in remittances. This was also accompanied by large rises in the wages and salaries of the migrant workers in the oil-producing states. These rises were made possible by the increase in oil revenues following the oil-price revolution in 1973.[13] Second, the restoration of normal conditions in Jordan after the 1970-71 disturbances resulted in renewed confidence in the country's economic stability. Workers' remittances started flowing in again, probably augmented by their savings during the unstable period prior to 1972. Third, the introduction of the three-year plan added to the confidence of investors. The plan envisaged a large contribution from the private sector, where it was hoped that 45% of its projects would be financed through private-sector participation.[14]

THE IMPACT OF REMITTANCES ON THE JORDANIAN ECONOMY

The figures in Table 3.3 reflect the ever-increasing importance of the remittances from migrant workers. Remittances amounted to 43.7% of the value of the country's total merchandise exports in 1972, while in 1981 remittances exceeded the value of exports by 51.1%. Compared with imports, remittances increased steadily from 6.5% of the value of imports in 1972 to a peak of 40.3% in 1976, then dropped to 30.7% in 1979 only to pick up again to 39.3% in 1981. This drop in relation to imports between 1976 and 1979 can be explained by the faster growth in imports during that period. In absolute terms, however, remittances were still increasing steadily. As a percentage of GDP, remittances increased from 2.7% in 1971 to 34% in 1976, then levelled off at 27.2% in 1981.

Jordan's balance of payments shows surpluses for the period 1972-80 (as measured by the balance of current transactions and capital movement in the non-monetary sector). These surpluses (Table 3.3) are mainly due to the increase in remittances from Jordanians working abroad, income from tourism and transfer payments to the central government. If remittances were excluded, the surpluses would turn into deficits for all the years except 1972 and 1975.

How does Jordan's experience compare with those of other labour-exporting countries? Table 3.4 shows migrants' remittances and their share in relation to total exports of goods for selected countries. The data furnished by the table reveal either a steady flow of remittances or an increasing trend. The amount of remittances within the Arab countries alone has shown a threefold increase since 1973, until it surpassed the $4,000 mn mark in 1978.[15] The role of remittances as a major contributor to the much-needed foreign exchange reserves of the capital-poor countries is evident. Another important role is the coverage of chronic balance of trade deficits in those countries.[16] In 1976 remittances from Jordanian workers abroad were almost double the total value of exports (Table 3.4) and one and a half times the value of exports in 1981 (Table 3.3). Relative to the value of exports, remittances show a very significant importance in Egypt, Greece, Morocco, Pakistan, Turkey and Yugoslavia (Table 3.4). Looking at remittances in relation to remitters' earnings, we observe that Portuguese and North African migrants in Europe remitted 24% of their earnings, followed by Spaniards 20%, Italians 11% and Yugoslavs 10%.[17]

A study of the Turkish experience reveals that mean remittances to the rural areas represented 15% of the mean income abroad, while remittances to the urban sector were 8%.[18] Our survey results show that Jordanian workers in Kuwait remitted on average 20.3% of their earnings.[19] The survey also reveals a positive relationship between remittances and the educational level of remitters, whereas in the Pakistani experience the remittances were found

Table 3.4: Migrant Workers Remittances and Their Share in Relation to Total Exports of Goods in Selected Labour-Exporting Countries, 1973-77 (thousand Jordanian dinars)

	1973		1974		1975		1976		1977	
	Remit-tances	as % of exports	Remit-tances	as % of exports	Remit-tances	as % of exports	Remit-tances	as % of exports	Remit-tances	As % of exports
Algeria	371	20	390	9	466	11	245	5	–	–
Egypt	85	9	189	11	367	23	445	28	1,025	–
Greece	730	59	651	37	754	39	778	35	–	–
India	183	6	276	8	490	12	750	17	1,000	–
Jordan	45	61	75	48	167	109	396	198	425	189
Morocco	249	27	356	21	533	35	548	45	–	–
Pakistan	147	16	151	15	230	22	353	31	1,110	–
Tunisia	98	24	118	13	146	17	135	17	–	–
Turkey	1,183	90	1,425	93	1,312	94	982	50	–	–
Yemen Arab Republic	108	1,200	159	1,325	221	1,556	796	5,897	1,000	–
Yugoslavia	1,390	49	1,621	43	1,695	42	1,728	35	–	–

Sources: Z. Ecevit and K.C. Zachariah, 'International Labour Migration', Finance and Development, vol. 15, no. 4 (Dec. 1978), p. 36, table 4; A.G. Chandavarkar, 'Use of Migrants' Remittances in Labour-Exporting Countries', Finance and Development, vol. 17, no. 2 (June 1980), pp. 36-7, table 1, 2; CBJ, Monthly Statistical Bulletin, various issues.

to be inversely related to the level of education of the remitters.[20] This may be explained by the fact that a large number of the Pakistani migrant workers are of the permanent type - especially the highly qualified - whereas the Jordanians are of the temporary type who have strong links with home.

USE OF REMITTANCES

The utilization of the large amounts of remittances has received little attention. Böhning, Paine and Shaw expressed their concern about the inability of the authorities in Yugoslavia, Turkey and the Arab region, respectively, to mobilize the flow of remittances towards more productive uses.[21] This concern is also shared by Birks and Sinclair, who doubt the beneficial impact of the remittances in the Arab region, particularly because of the unavailability of evidence as to the proportions of remittances channelled to investment and consumption or imports of consumer goods.[22] The Royal Scientific Society in Jordan conducted a sample survey to study the socio-economic implications of the migration of Jordanian workers, with emphasis on remittances. The results of the survey indicated that the larger part of remittances were devoted to consumer purposes. Notwithstanding a recognition of the survey's limitations and the inaccuracy of the delivered answers, it was thought safe to conclude that family maintenance was the most important outlet of remittances.[23]

Remittances of Jordanians Working in Kuwait
We conducted a sample survey of Jordanian workers in Kuwait during April-June 1978, for the purpose of estimating comparative rates of return as related to the education of Jordanian workers at home and abroad. The sample included 1,781 workers in Kuwait. The questionnaire included a section on remittances whose results are presented and examined below.[24]

Out of the sample of 1,781 Jordanian workers in Kuwait, 1,181 (66.3%) remitted part of their earnings to Jordan. The largest group of remittance recipients was 'parents' of the remitters (43.4%), followed by 'brothers and sisters' (28.2%). Remittances to the 'family' (wife and children) were only 9.6% of the total. This rather low percentage may be explained by two factors. First, many migrants are joined by their families; hence the reason for remitting to the 'family' ceases to exist. Second, people traditionally live with their parents after marriage; thus workers who leave their families behind living with their parents remit the cash to 'parents' who look after and maintain the family. Remittances to 'brothers and sisters' serve two purposes: living expenses and educational expenditure. Remittances to 'other(s)' (17.3%) include those remitted to banks, corporations and other business enterprises. When workers were asked about the purpose of their remittances, 880 (44.5%) indicated maintenance of parents, family and/or relatives. Remittances supporting education ranked second, with 20.5%.

The share of remittances earmarked for investment purposes amounted to 23.3%. Saving deposits with banks and post-office accounts led the investment league with 12.8%, acquiring 'shares and bonds' 7.0% and entering business ventures 3.4%. Overlapping exists as far as remittances are concerned. It is common for remitters to send money to their parents or relatives to be invested or used to finance a particular project on their behalf. 'Other purposes' in Table 3.6 (whose share is 7.8% of the total) includes balances such as those remitted for the purpose of building a house or buying the land on which to build the house.

A question about the regularity of the remittances revealed that 53.3% of the workers remitted at regular intervals (usually monthly), 36.4% remitted occasionally but voluntarily (i.e. without being asked to do so) and 10.3% remitted only when asked to. The reasons given by recipients for asking for remittances showed living expenses leading with 45.5%, while education yet again ranked second with 20.4%. This is remarkably similar to the percentages obtained for these two purposes. Extending help towards wedding and health expenses by the remitters was of rather smaller significance. But 'other reasons' again showed a 22.7% share of the reasons for being asked for remittances. These 'other reasons' included investments and regular obligations to banks or corporations. The importance of productive remittances is further enhanced when educational expenditures are considered as an investment outlay in human resources. The data indicate that the bulk of remitters were concentrated in the KD 1-1,000 remittance group. Remittances of KD 1,001 and over were remitted by 13.2% of the total.

Jordanian Workers' Remittances

The largest group of remitters consisted of those remitting between 5% and 15% of their earnings, followed by the 16-25%, 26-35% and 36-50% groups. In fact, 95.1% of the remitters remitted 50% or less of their earnings. Average remittances per remitter, (assuming KD 3,000 for the upper value of the open-end group), are KD 575.4 or JD 662, which comes very close to the figure found earlier for all Jordanians working abroad.

To find out whether a relationship exists between earnings and the volume of remittances, we performed the x^2 test on the sample. This shows a rather high and very significant x^2 value, indicating the existence of a relationship between earnings and remittances.

CONCLUSIONS

The survey results reveal that about 50% of the remittances of Jordanian workers in Kuwait channelled towards investment purposes, including 20.5% to education alone. In general, however, the labour-exporting countries seem to rely on incentives rather than state control for the encouragement and mobilization of the remittances. In this respect, Jordan has designed schemes which offer opportunities to workers abroad to invest, rather than consume, their savings. These include the following:

1. The enactment of the Encouragement of Investment Law No. 53/1972, which was designed to attract capital flows earmarked for investment.[25] The law provided for exemption of fixed assets from customs duties on imports, and the exemption of profits from income tax for a period of six years.
2. The introduction of the 'Post Office Fund' in 1973 and the issue of 'Development Bonds' in 1974 served two purposes: to encourage the in-flow of remittances, and to channel such cash balances into productive investment via the medium of the state.[26]
3. Liberal policies have been adopted by the Central Bank of Jordan; these allow workers abroad to hold accounts in foreign currencies with the commercial banks.[27]

Jordanian Workers' Remittances

The Jordan government appears to be aware not only of the importance of the magnitude and regularity of the remittances, but also of directing them towards useful investments as it anticipates a large contribution by the private sector in financing development expenditure.

NOTES

1. The sample survey was conducted by the author in 1978 and included almost 1,800 Jordanian workers in Kuwait. For details of the survey, see M.A.J. Share, 'A Rate of Return Analysis of the Education of Jordanian Workers', unpublished PhD thesis, University of Wales, 1980.

2. For detailed consideration of this distinction, see N. Choucri, Migration Process among Developing Countries: The Middle East (Migration and Development Study Group, Center for International Studies, Massachusetts Institute of Technology, Cambridge, Mass., May 1978).

3. See, for example: A.M. Farrag, 'Migration between Arab Countries' in International Labour Office (hereafter ILO), Manpower and Employment in Arab Countries: Some Critical Issues (ILO, Geneva, 1976); F. Halliday, 'Migration and the Labour Force in the Oil Producing States of the Middle East', Development and Change, no. 8 (1977); Peter Hopkirk, 'Jordan: A Special Report', The Times, Aug. 1977; Patrick Cockburn, 'Jordan: A Special Report', The Times, Aug. 1977; J.S. Birks and C.A. Sinclair, International Migration and Development in the Arab Region (ILO, Geneva, 1980).

4. Various estimates are reported in Middle East Economic Digest (Oct. 1976).

5. For the basis and hypothesis of the estimate, see Share, 'Rate of Return Analysis', pp. 96-9.

6. Jordan, Ministry of Labour, Annual Report 1981 (Amman).

7. Jordan, Department of Statistics, First Census of Population and Housing, 1961. vol. I (Amman, 1964), p. 316, table 5.2.

8. Kuwait, Department of Social Affairs, Population Census, 1957 (Kuwait State Press, Kuwait, March 1959), pp. 326-33, table 47.

9. Share, 'Rate of Return Analysis', p. 100, table 4.3.

10. Ibid.

11. One JD = $3.0.

12. These figures are based on the aforementioned estimate of workers abroad and on the preliminary results of the 1979 population census.

13. See M.P. Mazur, Economic Growth and Development in Jordan (Croom Helm, London, 1979), p. 122.

14. Jordan, National Planning Council, The Three-Year Development Plan (Amman, 1973), p. 34.

15. See R.P. Shaw, 'Migration and Employment in the Arab World: Construction as a Key Policy Variable', *International Labour Review*, vol. 118, no. 5, (Sept.-Oct. 1979).

16. Covering a sizeable part of Egypt's heavy balance of trade deficit is recognized as the major economic benefit to Egypt; see N. Choucri, *The New Migration in the Middle East: A Problem for Whom?* (Migration and Development Study Group, Centre for International Studies, Massachusetts Institute of Technology, Cambridge, Mass., Jan. 1977), p. 14.

17. See R. Granier and J.P. Marciano, 'The Earnings of Immigrant Workers in France', *International Labour Review*, vol. III (Jan.-June 1975), pp. 143-65.

18. S. Paine, *Exporting Workers: The Turkish Case* (Cambridge University Press, Cambridge, 1974), p. 105.

19. See below for the detailed analysis of the sample of Jordanian workers in Kuwait.

20. See S. Perwaiz, 'Home Remittances', a special report in *Pakistan Economist* (1-7 Sept. 1979), quoted in A.G. Chandavarkar, 'Use of Migrants' Remittances in Labour-exporting Countries', *Finance and Development*, vol. 17, no. 2 (June 1980).

21. See W.R. Böhning, 'Some Thoughts on Emigration from the Mediterranean Basin', *International Labour Review*, vol. III (Jan.-June 1975), pp. 251-77; Paine, *Exporting Workers*; and Shaw, 'Migration and Employment', pp. 589-605.

22. Birks and Sinclair, *International Migration*.

23. The detailed results of the Royal Scientific Society survey are presented in B.K. Saket, *Promoting the Productive Use of Remittances* (E/ECWA/Pop/conf.4/WP/18, 20 March 1981), paper presented at the Conference on International Migration in the Arab World, held in Cyprus, 11-16 May 1981, by the ECWA Division of the UN).

24. For complete details of the survey, see Share, 'Rate of Return Analysis'.

25. Jordan, 'Encouragement of Investment Law no. 53, 1972', *Official Gazette*, no. 2,386 (Amman, Oct. 1972).

26. Central Bank of Jordan, *Monthly Statistical Bulletin*, vol. 13, no. 11 (Amman, 1977).

27. Central Bank of Jordan, *Fourteenth Annual Report* (Department of Research and Studies, Amman, 1977).

Chapter Four

THE ROLE OF COMMERCIAL BANKING IN THE JORDANIAN ECONOMY

Rodney Wilson

Most economists agree that a sound financial structure is a necessary prerequisite for successful development. There is disagreement, however, over what constitutes a sound financial structure. Some see a competitive banking system as the best means of ensuring efficiency, with the Central Bank determining the rules, but allowing the banks freedom to compete for customers. The supporters of this view regard private ownership of commercial banks as crucial for successful management, as only this type of structure can provide the appropriate incentives for optimum decision-making. Conversely, others believe that the state should control how commercial bank finance is allocated, in order to ensure that finance is used for long-term development purposes, and not merely for immediate consumption aspirations. It is argued that private commercial banks are primarily interested in their own profitability, and not in wider social and developmental issues, which are more a concern of government.

In Jordan the commercial banks are privately owned and compete with each other for customers. The allocation of commercial bank finance is a matter for the banks, not the government. The state of course provides investment finance in other ways, particularly through its own expenditure. Nevertheless the banks are the major source of credit in the economy, together with the specialized financial institutions, which are also predominantly under private ownership.

The present chapter examines how well the privately owned banking system has served the Jordanian economy. Has a privately owned structure been more beneficial, from the development point of view, than a nationalized system such as that prevailing in neighbouring Arab states (including Syria) and Iran? How successful have the banks been in attracting savings which can subsequently be re-lent for productive purposes, or is hoarding still widespread? Have the commercial banks managed to attract deposits from expatriate Jordanians working in the Gulf and elsewhere? How has credit been disbursed and are the lending policies of the commercial banks consistent with the government's development objectives? Finally, has a privately owned financial system posed any problems for monetary policy, the control of inflation and economic management generally? It is hoped to provide tentative answers to at least some of these questions, which must be of interest not only to those concerned with Jordan's economy, but also to those involved in finance in other developing countries.

Table 4.1: Amman-Based Commercial Banks, Capital and Assets (million Jordanian dinars)

	Paid-up capital	Total assets
Arab Bank	22.0	3,171.6
Bank of Jordan	1.5	47.2
Cairo Amman Bank	2.5	95.5
Jordan Gulf Bank	5.0	60.6
Jordan Islamic Bank	2.9	31.6
Jordan Kuwait Bank	5.0	83.3
Jordan National Bank	3.3	104.7
Petra Bank	3.0	83.3
Syrian Jordanian Bank	2.0	12.0

Sources: *Middle Eastern Financial Directory, 1983* (Middle East Economic Digest, London, 1983, pp. 72-7; *Arab Banking and Finance Handbook, 1983* (Falcon Publishing, Bahrain, 1983), pp. 333,336.

BANKING STRUCTURE AND THE MARKET FOR FINANCIAL SERVICES

Jordan is the home of one major Arab international bank, the Arab Bank, and eight primarily local banks which serve the domestic market. Although in Table 4.1 the Arab Bank appears much larger than

The Role of Commercial Banking

the others, it is far from being the dominant force, as most of its operations are outside Jordan. The Arab Bank is a Palestinian financial institution; it was originally established in Jerusalem in 1929, making it the second oldest wholly Arab bank after Banque Misr of Egypt.[1] For operational reasons it was forced to move its headquarters to Amman after 1948, although it continued doing business in East Jerusalem and the West Bank until 1967. Since then it has expanded its operations on the East Bank, but it aims to serve the Palestinian community throughout the Arab world and overseas, not only in Jordan. For this reason it has pursued most of its expansion outside Jordan, and it has never sought to monopolize the local market.

In economic terms, the market for banking services in Jordan could be described as more competitive than that in most countries. Although there are four larger institutions among the eight main local banks, none acts as market leader, and the 'big four' account for less than half of total bank assets. The market is in fact less oligopolistic than that of most European countries, and the presence of 17 foreign banks helps increase the competitive pressures. Some of these, such as the British Bank of the Middle East, have maintained branches in Jordan since the period of the British mandate, but others arrived in the aftermath of the Lebanese civil war, when Amman seemed preferable to Beirut as a centre for regional operations.[2] Amman has not sought to become an international financial centre with offshore banking units like Bahrain, but many foreign banks find it a useful location for their remaining business in Lebanon, as well as for trade finance for Iraq, which does not permit foreign banks to operate within its borders.

Most banking business in Jordan involves domestic clients rather than international dealings, except in the case of some of the foreign banks with representative offices, as these banks often deal largely with their own nationals. The domestic need for banking services has increased rapidly in recent years, especially with the rapid growth of the Jordanian economy. In addition the economy has not only become increasingly monetized, but it seems that a large number of less affluent individuals, as well as small businesses, have acquired the banking habit. Although the tradition of paying wages in cash, especially for junior employees, remains strong, as in other parts of the

The Role of Commercial Banking

Arab world, attitudes are changing, and many appreciate the convenience of handling their finance through the banks. Savings in banks can earn interest, unlike hoarding, and a bank loan, although costly, usually comes with fewer strings than borrowing from family members. Furthermore there is general confidence in the banks, as there has never been a banking failure in Jordan.

One means of quantifying the extent to which a country has acquired the banking habit is to consider how aggregate commerical bank assets have grown rapidly over the last decade in current prices in relation to GDP. Aggregate commercial bank assets have, however, grown faster, as they now exceed GDP in terms of value. This indicates the growing use of banks to deposit funds, and as a source of borrowing. Jordan is the only Arab country where the value of bank assets exceeds GDP.[3] Bank assets are almost half the level of those of the Syrian and Iraqi banking systems, countries with much larger populations and longer histories of urban settlement. This indicates the extent to which Jordan's banks have been successful in mobilizing domestic resources. The relative impact of banking activity on Jordan's econmy corresponds more closely to that found in European countries such as Greece, Spain and Portugal rather than the countries on the southern shore of the Mediterranean.

DEPOSIT TRENDS AND THE ATTRACTION OF SAVING

Banks can, of course, only succeed in playing a major role in the economy if they are successful in attracting deposits. Table 4.2 shows the liabilities of the commercial banks in Jordan, the major proportion of which represent various types of deposit. The main source of deposits is the private sector within the country itself, comprising individuals and private businesses. The share of these in total liabilities has been fairly stable over the 1979-84 period, with no marked trends. More variable has been the share of total liabilities accounted for by non-resident depositors, most of whom are Jordanian passport holders working in the Gulf states and Saudi Arabia. Their deposits rose dramatically in the 1970s in relation to total bank liabilities, largely reflecting the boom in the oil-rich states of the Gulf during that period, and continuing emigration from both the East and

The Role of Commercial Banking

Table 4.2: Commercial Bank Liabilities (percentage)

	1979	1980	1981	1982	1983	1984
Capital	6.2	5.2	4.7	5.3	4.4	4.9
Reserves	2.0	2.0	2.2	3.2	3.1	3.3
Government deposits	7.4	8.8	9.6	7.4	7.8	5.2
Private sector deposits	56.5	54.2	53.1	56.9	55.6	55.8
Deposits of local banks	6.6	6.0	6.5	3.0	3.7	3.4
Loans from local and central bank	0.9	0.9	1.1	2.5	3.5	4.2
Deposits from foreign banks	2.0	1.4	2.5	1.9	1.7	1.7
Deposits of non-residents	8.1	12.4	10.8	11.0	11.6	13.0
Other liabilities	10.2	9.0	9.5	8.9	8.6	8.5
Total liabilities (mn JDs)	824	1,070	1,330	1,553	1,863	2,130

Source: CBJ, <u>Monthly Statistical Bulletin</u>, vol. 21, no. 2 (Feb. 1985), table 7. Percentages calculated by the author.

West Banks of the Jordan. The share stabilized in the 1980s, however, at just over one-tenth of total liabilities, as the table shows.

Deposits by government bodies, including municipalities and state-owned entities, are a relatively minor portion of total deposits, reflecting the fact that most of the Jordanian economy is in private hands. Nor has there been any marked tendency for the share of government deposits to increase. Deposits and loans from local banks are of even less significance, illustrating the underdevelopment of the inter-bank market in Amman. Most of the banking business in Jordan is of a retail nature between the banks and their private customers. There has been no attempt to establish Amman as a so-called 'wholesale' banking centre like Bahrain, where much of the bank's business is with other banks. Deposits from foreign banks are also insignificant, indicating that Amman is in no sense an international financial centre, in spite of the influx of some foreign banks from Lebanon during the civil war, as already mentioned. Banks such as American Express, Banque Nationale de

The Role of Commercial Banking

Paris, Chase Manhattan, Citibank, Credit Lyonnais and Manufacturers Hanover Trust maintain representative offices in Amman, but these serve primarily their American and French clients rather than local customers.

A further breakdown of commercial bank deposits is given in Table 4.3, from which non-deposit bank liabilities have been excluded. The data reconfirm the conclusion from Table 4.2 that private deposits from residents are of paramount importance, although non-resident private deposits are of some significance in relation to total deposits.

Table 4.3: Commercial Bank Deposits (percentage)

	1979	1980	1981	1982	1983	1984
Government	10.2	11.7	13.1	9.8	10.4	9.8
Resident private	78.5	71.8	72.2	75.5	74.1	73.0
Non-resident private	11.3	16.5	14.7	14.7	15.5	17.3
Demand deposits	35.9	35.6	32.4	30.3	27.7	25.5
Time deposits due on fixed date	34.7	36.7	38.1	42.0	48.4	51.4
Time deposits subject to notice	11.0	11.6	13.0	11.5	8.4	8.3
Savings deposits	18.4	16.0	16.5	16.1	15.4	14.7
Total deposits (mn JDs)	593	808	978	1,169	1,398	1,603

Source: CBJ, *Monthly Statistical Bulletin*, vol. 21, no.2, tables 9, 10.

Table 4.3 also provides a breakdown of different types of deposit, including demand deposits, two types of time deposit and savings deposits. Until 1980 demand deposits, on which cheques could be written, were the most popular form of deposit in Jordan, as they were the most liquid for transaction purposes. As in other developing countries, cheques have never become as popular as in some West European states or in North

America. They are more widely used by businesses than individuals, but even small businesses often prefer cash transactions with their suppliers as well as their customers. When individuals and businesses maintain substantial cash holdings, their need for liquid demand deposits is less. Consequently, the banks have increasingly found it preferable to entice depositors by offering higher interest, but less liquid time deposits. As Table 4.3 shows, by 1980 one type of time deposit, that due on a fixed date, had become more important than demand deposits. By having multiple time deposits opened at different periods with different due dates, depositors can in fact maintain a potentially liquid cash flow position with respect to their bank assets. This has become standard practice in Jordan, with the banking public wanting to combine flexibility with the maximum possible returns on their assets.

Less flexible are time deposits subject to notice: although the notice periods of 90 or 180 days are shorter than the periods for fixed time deposits, usually at least a year, the need always to give notice reduces the liquidity of the deposit. For this reason, time deposits subject to notice are the least popular type of deposit, as Table 4.3 shows, and most clients with this type of bank account will usually also maintain some funds in demand deposits. Interest rates on time deposits subject to notice are usually 0.25% lower than those on fixed time deposits, which may also account for the greater popularity of the latter. Savings schemes have been reasonably successful in Jordan, as the proportion of savings deposits in Table 4.3 shows. These are generally designed for small savers who pay in a specified sum each month on a term basis. Interest rates are at least 2% higher than those on demand deposits, but 1.5% less than those on fixed time deposits. Funds can be withdrawn on demand, but the depositor has a continuing obligation to pay into the scheme.

Figure 4.1 shows how total time deposits (fixed time deposits plus time deposits subject to notice) have increased in relation to demand deposits. The proportion had increased from 25% in 1974 to over 180% by 1984. The dotted line indicates the premium paid for time deposits on average compared to demand deposits. The premium was greatest over the 1978-82 period, as the figure shows: until 1981 interest rates on demand deposits remained at 2%, while those on time deposits

Figure 4.1: Growth of Time Deposits in Relation to Demand Deposits in Jordan's Commercial Banks

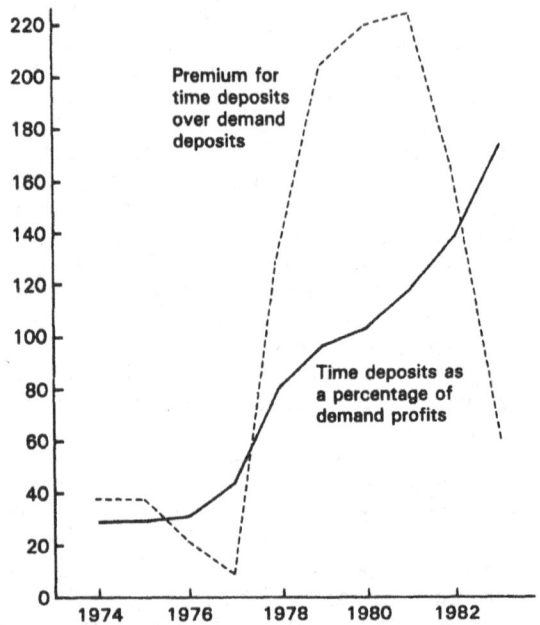

Source: Data from CBJ, <u>Monthly Statistical Bulletin</u>, vol. 15, no.7, (July 1979), tables 11, 14, and vol. 20, no. 5 (May 1984), tables 10, 12.

averaged 6.1-6.5% after 1979. This yielded premiums in excess of 200% for time deposits compared to demand deposits. In this environment the relative growth of time deposits was scarcely surprising. Even though the premium fell in 1982 and 1983, the outstanding value of time deposits continued to increase, indicating that the practice of using time deposits had become firmly established.

The significance of non-resident deposits for the Jordanian banking system has already been noted. In Table 4.4 the savings habits of residents and non-residents are contrasted. Not surprisingly, non-residents seem to have a much stronger preference for fixed time deposits than residents do. The latter may welcome the convenience of demand deposits for transaction purposes, while the former by definition are less likely to be able to make withdrawals in Jordan personally. Withdrawals can, of course, be made by post through bankers drafts or other transfer mechanisms, but as these take time to effect, even with demand deposits,

The Role of Commercial Banking

Table 4.4: Savings Habits of Residents and Non-residents Compared (percentage)

	1979	1980	1981	1982	1983	1984
Demand deposits						
Residents	37.3	37.7	38.5	33.5	31.4	27.8
Non-residents	25.3	37.2	16.7	19.7	14.8	18.0
Time deposits due on fixed term						
Residents	29.4	30.9	29.8	35.7	41.5	45.9
Non-residents	67.3	52.8	66.6	70.8	72.1	71.2
Time deposits subject to notice						
Residents	10.3	9.7	10.0	10.3	7.1	6.9
Non-residents	4.4	8.4	12.1	5.5	9.6	7.7
Savings deposits						
Residents	22.9	21.7	21.7	20.4	20.0	19.3
Non-residents	3.1	1.7	4.5	4.0	3.4	3.1
Total deposits (mn JDs)						
Residents	465	580	706	883	1,035	1,170
Non-residents	67	133	144	172	217	277

Source: CBJ, *Monthly Statistical Bulletin*, vol. 21, no. 2, tables 9, 10.

this reduces their attractiveness. Liquid assets become in practice less liquid from the depositor's point of view. Non-residents can often arrange the expiry of the fixed term of their time deposits to coincide with their visits to Jordan, and profit from higher interest in the meantime. Savings deposits also appear less attractive to non-residents, partly because, being more affluent, they can deposit enough to maintain time deposits rather than low minimum subscription savings schemes which offer lower returns. Furthermore as non-residents are not, of course, present in Jordan, time deposits imply fewer transactions than a savings scheme based on regular payments.

Jordan's banks have been extremely successful

in attracting deposits from non-residents. Workers' remittances and non-resident bank deposits have grown rapidly over the 1974-83 period. An increasing proportion of workers' remittances were being deposited with Jordanian banks, especially during the late 1970s. This was the period when record premiums were being offered on time deposits, with interest rates in excess of 6%, as already indicated. Furthermore, it was also a period when the Jordanian dinar was rising against other currencies, notably the US dollar. In 1976 the dollar was worth JD 3.32, but by December 1978 it was worth only JD 2.94. In the 1980s, however, the dollar started to appreciate again to a high of JD 3.8 by May 1984. This made dollar deposits more attractive than dinar deposits. The slower growth in deposits relative to remittances is evident after 1980. At the same time, interest rates on dollar deposits in Bahrain and elsewhere were rising to double figures, while interest rates on dinar deposits rose a mere 0.4% to 6.5%. Clearly the Jordanian banking system has lost out to some extent in the 1980s despite the strength of the dinar against other Arab currencies.

Table 4.5: Commercial Bank Assets (percentage)

	1979	1980	1981	1982	1983	1984
Reserves	12.3	10.9	8.6	7.6	7.2	6.4
Balances with local banks	6.2	6.1	7.0	3.3	5.0	4.3
Bills discounted	11.4	9.7	11.1	11.3	10.1	9.9
Loans and advances	45.0	42.9	43.0	45.8	45.2	45.5
Domestic investments	0.8	0.9	1.0	1.3	1.5	1.6
Government bonds and bills	9.0	5.6	6.0	6.6	7.9	9.8
Bills receivable	1.3	1.1	1.2	1.6	1.1	1.0
Foreign assets	9.7	19.2	17.5	16.4	16.3	15.5
Fixed assets	1.6	1.7	2.0	2.5	2.5	2.7
Other assets	2.5	1.9	2.3	3.5	3.1	3.3
Total assets (mn JDs)	824	1,070	1,330	1,553	1,863	2,136

Source: CBJ, <u>Monthly Statistical Bulletin</u>, vol. 21, no. 2, table 6.

The Role of Commercial Banking

ASSET DEPLOYMENT AND BANK LENDING

To assess the impact of commercial bank activity on the economy it is necessary to examine the banks' asset structure and patterns of lending. Table 4.5 shows the composition of Jordan's commercial bank assets over the 1979-84 period. Loans and advances account for by far the largest portion of assets, constituting almost half of total assets. Foreign asset holdings also appear to be of considerable significance, as they increased in relation to total assets during the 1979-80 period, and have remained at a high level. The banks argue that some foreign asset holding is precautionary, given their foreign liabilities because of non-resident deposits. These deposits are in dinars, however, not foreign currencies. A more likely cause of the increase in foreign asset holdings was the appreciation of the dollar, and record Eurodollar interest rates. Jordan's banks find foreign asset holding more profitable than the deployment of funds domestically, although this phenomenon has been common to many Arab and European countries with relatively liberal foreign exchange regimes for capital movements.

The increase in foreign asset holdings had a slight adverse effect on domestic loans and advances in 1980 and 1981, as the table shows, but in the longer term the effect has been countered by the reduction in the banks' liquid reserves, and a fall in relative holdings of government bonds and bills. This reduces the funding available to the government, both directly and indirectly, through the Central Bank. Commercial bank borrowing has never been a significant source of government finance in Jordan, however, in relation to aid inflows and borrowing from abroad. The only other notable development shown in Table 4.5 has been the increase in the proportion of fixed assets as Jordan's banks, like those elsewhere, have spent more and more on improvements to their own premises, some of which are without doubt unnecessary.

The pattern of commercial bank lending is illustrated in Table 4.6. A relatively small proportion of commercial bank credit is for productive activities such as agriculture or industry. Arguably this is because Jordan has specialist financial institutions such as an Industrial Development Bank and an Agricultural Credit Corporation which lend to these sectors.

Table 4.6: Distribution of Commercial Bank Credit (percentage)

	1979	1980	1981	1982	1983	1984
Municipalities and public corporations	6.0	5.6	6.2	7.3	6.3	7.2
Agriculture	3.7	3.0	2.7	2.8	2.5	2.2
Mining	0.9	0.8	0.9	1.6	2.0	2.3
Industry	12.1	12.2	11.4	11.1	11.5	12.0
Trade and commerce	28.9	29.6	31.3	32.1	26.8	25.0
Construction	32.5	32.1	27.9	24.4	26.3	27.4
Transport	2.8	2.6	3.2	3.7	4.9	4.9
Tourism, hotels and restaurants	2.1	2.1	2.2	2.3	2.5	2.0
Financial institutions	1.0	1.5	1.3	2.2	2.5	2.5
Professional and private individuals	6.4	6.9	8.4	7.8	10.5	10.2
Other	3.7	3.6	4.4	4.6	4.2	4.3
Total (mn JDs)	465	564	721	887	1,031	1,185

Source: CBJ, Monthly Statistical Bulletin, vol. 21, no. 2, table 11.

Neither of these institutions, however, advances credit to cover the total cost of the projects being backed. Borrowers are also expected to obtain some commercial bank credit, and in this sense the specialist financial institutions complement the banks' role rather than providing a substitute for their finance. The banks, however, are often reluctant to back long-term projects or schemes where collateral cannot be offered.

Most lending is for trade and commerce or construction, as Table 4.6 shows. Together these accounted historically for 60% of all credit, and despite a slight drop in 1982-83, the proportion has remained over 50%. The only other significant proportion of lending goes to professional and private individuals, who in 1983 accounted for over 10% of the total. These are mostly credit-worthy individuals who seek personal loans, perhaps to purchase a car, or finance a wedding. There is little risk to the banks as these borrowers have regular salaries paid into bank accounts, from which loan repayments can be deducted by direct debit.

The Role of Commercial Banking

Most of the lending for trade and commerce is in practice import finance, some of which is in the form of documentary credits, although most is best described as short-term inventory finance, which is not necessarily tied to the purchase of specific goods. Unsold stocks in general are regarded as collateral rather than specific items. In some cases the banks are merely financing receivables, as the stock has been sold but payments have yet to be effected. Such finance is extremely short-term, and with few risks involved. The relationship between trade finance and the value of Jordan's imports is, not surprisingly, remarkably close. When the value of imports fell in 1982-83, for example, lending for trade finance also fell. In 1976, when trade finance stabilized, imports also levelled off, but with a lag. It is difficult nevertheless to ascertain the direction of causation: whether the value of imports depends on the trade finance available, or if, with the banks so keen to finance imports, the volume of credit responds passively to the level of import demand.

Figure 4.2: Commercial Bank Construction Finance (1974 = 100)

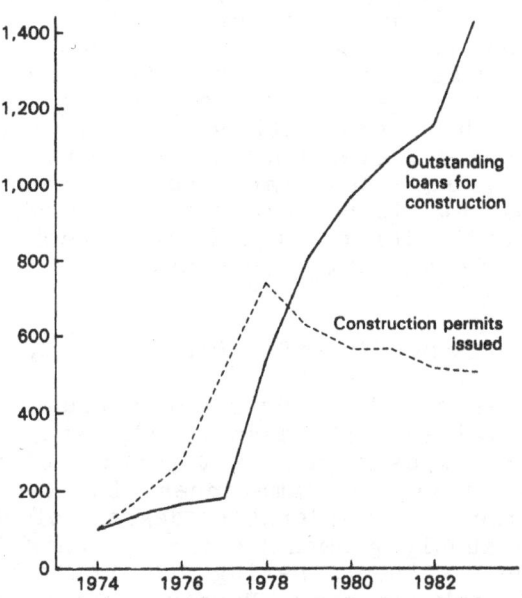

Source: Data from CBJ, <u>Monthly Statistical Bulletin</u>, vol. 15, no. 7 (July 1979), tables 12, 47, and vol. 20, no. 5 (May 1984), tables 11, 52.

The Role of Commercial Banking

The relationship between the outstanding loans approved for construction and the number of new construction permits issued appears to be less close, as Figure 4.2 shows. Although the number of permits issued for both residential and business purposes started to fall after 1978, signalling an end to the construction boom, outstanding loans for construction from the commercial banks continued to increase in value. Two possible explanations can be advanced for this discrepancy. First, there may have been a reduction in the number of new loans granted for construction, but the debt outstanding may have continued to increase as existing loans were not repaid. After the speculative property boom of the mid-1970s came to an end, many borrowers had difficulty in even servicing outstanding debts, let alone repaying the loan principal. In these circumstances loans had to be rolled over, medium-term credits becoming long-term credits, with a consequent increase in the illiquidity of bank assets.

A second explanation for the continuing growth in bank credit for construction after 1978 was that the commercial banks were providing finance for non-resident Jordanians who did not qualify for loans from the specialist, partly state-owned, Housing Bank. The prospect of bank loans for construction and home improvements was one factor which encouraged non-residents to place deposits with Jordanian banks. Therefore the commercial banks felt they were obliged to continue lending for construction, even when it was apparent to all that conditions were far from buoyant in the property market. There remain considerable risks in granting credit for construction, especially if it is property being built for rent.

CONTROL OF THE MONEY SUPPLY AND INFLATION

In Jordan as in other developing countries, with much financial activity cash-based, demand deposits account for a less significant portion of the money supply. Under such circumstances, the Central Bank can exercise a considerable degree of influence over money supply growth by merely controlling the note issue, without having to monitor closely commercial bank finances. Reserve requirements were reduced in the early 1980s, as Table 4.5 indicates, without having adverse effects on money supply growth in aggregate, and the rate of inflation.

The Role of Commercial Banking

Currency with the public in fact accounted for over two-thirds of the total money supply in 1974, narrowly defined to include currency and demand deposits only. By 1984 the proportion of narrow money in the form of currency still exceeded 61%. However, if money supply is more broadly defined to include in addition time and savings deposits in the banking system, then the proportion of currency in aggregate money appears to have fallen faster, from 53% in 1974 to a mere 32% by 1984.

To ascertain if this has any implications for the control of inflation and economic management, it is necessary to examine the relationship between both narrow money and broad money on the one hand, and wholesale prices on the other. Figure 4.3 depicts these relationships, and also shows the growth of currency over the last decade. For the reasons already discussed, time deposits have grown faster than demand deposits since the mid-1970s, and this is reflected in the more rapid rise in broad money.

Figure 4.3: Relationship Between Money Supply and Prices (1974 = 100)

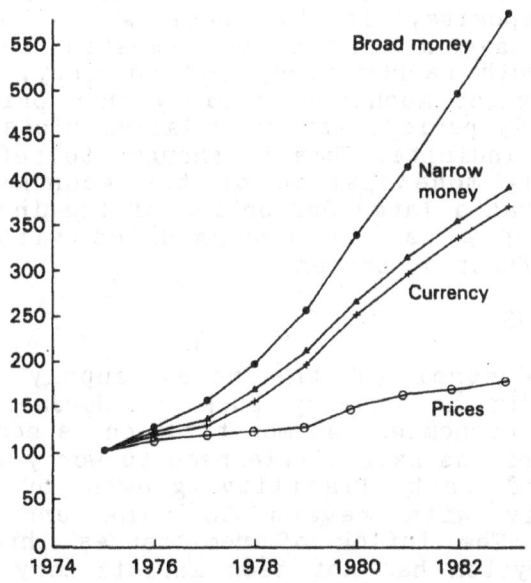

Source: Data from CBJ, Monthly Statistical Bulletin, vol. 15, no. 7 (July 1979), table 2, and vol. 20, no. 5 (May 1984), tables 2, 48.

The Role of Commercial Banking

There appears to be some relationship between both the rate of increase of narrow money and currency, considered together or separately, and price rises, as Figure 4.3 shows. When the rate of increase of narrow money and currency rose between 1978 and 1979, as indicated by the steeper slopes of both schedules, the rate of price increase also rose, although with a lag until the 1979-80 period. The slowing down in the rate of increase of both narrow money and currency after 1980 was also reflected in a less rapid rate of price increase, as the flattening of the price schedule shows. It would seem that money supply developments affect prices rather than the causation running in the other direction, with nominal money supply merely responding passively to price rises.

The relationship between the rate of increase of broad money and prices appears to be much less close, perhaps reflecting the more illiquid nature of time and savings deposits, and the larger proportion of the former held by non-residents. Time and savings deposits are also more likely to be used for the purchase of consumer durables, most of which are imported, rather than non-durables supplied domestically. As purchases of the latter will usually be made from currency holdings or demand deposits, it is these which will more probably have an effect on domestic demand and prices. Both narrow money and currency, however, also increased much more rapidly than prices over the 1975-83 period, as the relative slopes of the schedules indicate. This is thought to reflect the increasing monetization of the economy, which implies that a large proportion of the increase in money supply can be accommodated without any adverse effect on prices.

CONCLUSIONS

(1) Control of the money supply is less critical in an economy such as Jordan than in developed economies, as monetization is continuing. The authorities have little need to worry about the effect of bank liability growth on prices, especially with regard to time and savings deposits. The inflow of remittances through the banking system has not been inflationary overall.

(2) The banks have been extremely successful in attracting deposits from both residents and non-residents in recent years, particularly in the case of the latter, as the increase in non-resident

bank deposits in relation to remittances shows. Less and less money is being hoarded domestically, and the funds attracted from abroad can potentially be put to productive use within the economy.

(3) The pattern of lending, however, shows that much credit is used to finance trade and construction rather than more directly productive activities such as industry or agriculture. The banks have a natural preference for short-term lending, although in practice many of the construction loans have been rolled over into longer-term credits.

(4) If the government tightened its control over the banking system, it could probably ensure a better allocation of finance from the development point of view. There would be a high risk nevertheless in frightening away depositors, particularly non-residents, whom the government cannot force to channel their finance through Jordan's banking system. A more socially desirable allocation of credit may only result in less credit overall to allocate in the long term.

NOTES

1. For a brief history of the bank, see Rodney Wilson, Banking and Finance in the Middle East (Macmillan, London), pp. 43-9.
2. Rodney Wilson, 'Competition for Beirut's Role', Middle East Yearbook (IC Magazines Ltd., London, 1978), pp. 90-3.
3. For comparative bank asset data, see Rodney Wilson, The Arab World: An International Statistical Directory (Westview Press, Boulder, Colo., 1984), table 15.

Chapter Five

JORDAN, THE GEOGRAPHIC AND ECONOMIC POTENTIAL[1]

Konrad Schliephake

Is the Hashemite Kingdom of Jordan really the 'poor cousin' of the Arab Middle East countries, as an *International Management* reporter called it recently?[2] There is, of course, potential: not so much stemming from mineral resources, however, as from human capital and Jordan's strategic location as the link between industrialized Europe and the energy-rich Arabian peninsula. The present chapter will give a rapid survey from the viewpoint of an economic geographer.

INTRODUCTION

The raison d'être of the Emirate of Transjordan - which became the Hashemite Kingdom of Jordan after the integration of the Arab West Bank in 1948-50 - was certainly neither an economic nor a geographic one.
There had long been a self-supporting bedouin community east of the Jordan, with some continuous settlements such as Salt, Amman, Karak and Irbid in heir midst, which lived mainly as administrative centres for the Ottoman government and from trade with bedouin, peasants and possibly some Muslim pilgrims to Mecca and Medina. The First World War did not do much to change the picture. The British were fortunate to create, in 1920, a buffer state for probably three purposes: first, to counterbalance the activities of the emerging Wahhabis in what later became Saudi Arabia; second, to administer those parts of the Syrian desert which were not part of Palestine and thus not a target for Jewish immigration; and, third, to find a throne for the son of Emir Hussein, Sharif of Mecca, from the noble Hashemite family which was ousted both from

The Geographic and Economic Potential

Mecca (by Ibn Saud in 1925) and from Damascus (by the French in 1920).

The country's more recent history has not been a very happy one either. It has fought three wars with its aggressive neighbour Israel, losing with the West Bank in 1967 26% of its arable land and 48% of its population. A troubled peace has remained since, with the occupied West Bank still regarded as part of Jordanian territory - draining a substantial part of its financial resources - and with a continuous threat coming from a neighbour whose radical parties want to expand to both the Euphrates and the Nile.

Nevertheless, the country has shown a relatively good economic performance in recent years. In 1981 per capita GNP was $1,620, ranking it eleventh among the 21 Arab states and making it - nominally - the richest of the Arab non-oil producers.

Table 5.1: Jordan, Basic Figures

	1961	1974	1980	1982
Area (sq. km)	90,940	97,740	97,740	97,740
of which: settled areas (%)	24.2	22.5	22.5	22.5
of which: West Bank (%)	6.2	5.8	5.8	5.8
Population ('000)	1,706	2,660	3,190	3,490
of which: West Bank	805	770	957	1,075
% of population living in urban areas	44%	42%	57%[a]	
Agricultural surfaces[a] ('000 ha)		363	390[b]	
Per capita GNP ($)		290	1,600	1,650

Notes: a. East Bank.
b. Actually utilized: 1975 census.
Sources: Statistisches Bundesamt (1982, 1984); World Development Report 1984.

The Geographic and Economic Potential

Some basic figures may give a rough idea of the country and its population, which was estimated at 3.8 mn (including the West Bank) in 1985, of which 2.7 mn live east of the River Jordan.

In spite of the political difficulties, Jordan's economy performed relatively better than those of most other Arab countries. <u>Per capita</u> GDP at constant prices rose from 1974 to 1980 at an average 3.6% <u>per capita</u> per annum.

We shall now try to shed some light on the bases of this economic growth, for which there are several explanations.

GEOLOGICAL POTENTIAL

Most of Jordan lies within the stable Arab Plate. Palaeozoic and Mesozoic sediments, together with Neogene and Pleistocene basalt flows in the north-east, are typical for the country, with cretaceous chalks and limestones giving it relatively fertile soils.

The Wadi al-Araba-Jordan rift, with the Dead Sea at the world's deepest inland location (392 m below sea-level), and 360 km long, is a part of the East African-Red Sea-Asia Minor rift system and separates the country into two distinct parts. Whereas the mountains east of the rift slope gently to the Central Arabian Plateau towards the east, those on the West Bank form a mountainous and diversified landscape. The more recent Triassic sediments do not offer many prospects for rich mineral resources, except for phosphates. However, the Palaeozoic rocks and pre-Cambrian basements, especially in the south, have been found to contain a certain mineral wealth, as was discovered several decades ago in the Hijaz mountains in neighbouring Saudi Arabia.

Jordan lacks the large sedimentary troughs and anticlinal structures which store the world's biggest oil reserves on both sides of the Arab-Persian Gulf. Nevertheless, minerals today represent some very valuable assets for the Jordanian economy and its most important exports.

Geological and Mining Resources

Hydrocarbons.
The Arab countries possess some 52% of the world's proven oil reserves and 12 of the 21 members of the

The Geographic and Economic Potential

Arab League are today oil-producers, although quantities vary. Whereas, for several decades, the stable shelf area of the ancient Tethys Sea was considered unfavourable for the formation of commercially exploitable hydrocarbon deposits, investigations in Israel, the West Bank and Jordan have brought evidence of smaller sedimentary basins containing oil and gas (for this and the following paragraphs, see especially Bender, 1975, pp. I 26ff.)

Since ancient times asphalt floating in the Dead Sea has been found and collected, and, in 1939, an asphalt block measuring 150 cu. m was salvaged. Although no major deposits seem to be linked with this occurrence, this is the first hint of the presence of hydrocarbons. The following areas are thought to have hydrocarbon potential: the Yarmouk-al-Azraq-Wadi Sirhan basin; the al-Lisa-Ghor al-Safi area (south-eastern Dead Sea); and southern parts of the Jordan-Dead Sea depression.

Exploration activities between 1947 and 1972 by various English, Yugoslavian and US companies have not shown any commercially viable results (see also Mousa, 1974). However, in several areas of the upper-cretaceous chalk-mark sediments, and especially the Lajjun area (slightly west of al-Hasa), bituminous deposits have been investigated. In the Lajjun area they cover a surface of approx. 15 sq. km and the average yield of shale oil is calculated to be 28.1 US gal./t, or approx. 112 l/t. Reserves are thus calculated in Lajjun at about 420 mn barrels (equal to about 55 mn t), but current production costs would largely exceed the eventual benefits. Other studies, (Bender, 1975, p. IV) evaluate the 'prospective reserves' of the oil shale at between 1.3 and 10 bn metric t, with an annual production capacity of 2.3 mn t.

The al-Azraq oilfield has been explored since 1982. A first well (Qurmah 1) was struck in 1983, with a production capacity of 600 bn b/d, and a second (Qurmah 2, now Hamzah) in summer 1984, with 700 bn b/d (according to MD, 9 Nov. 1984, p. 22). The economic viability of the finds has yet to be tested, and their eventual output hardly compares with the Jordanian consumption of 55,000 bn b/d, or 2.5 mn t/year. But Jordan is expecting a great deal from the finds and, in November 1984, a Ministry for Energy and Minerals was created to administer the future wealth.

Metallic Minerals.

The outlook for metallic minerals is not very bright either. Copper deposits in the Sinai desert, associated with the Nubian sandstones, were mined during Pharaonic times and by Israel from 1958 into the 1970s. The economic success of the latter's activities was always very limited.

On the east side of Wadi al-Araba between Gharandal and the Dead Sea, similar deposits have been found in Cambrian dolomites and sandstones. Although the mineralization is very irregular, a Jordanian survey (Industry in Jordan ..., 1978) puts the reserves at approx. 60 mn t, with a copper content of about 1.36%. The proven reserves would be sufficient to produce 10,000 t/year of copper. In view of low copper prices on the world market, this potential cannot at present be economically exploited.

It is the same with manganese ore, which also occurs on the eastern side of Wadi al-Araba, around Wadi al-Dana, in dolomite-limestone shales of the Early to Middle Cambrian age. Samples from different localities showed contents of manganese (33-49%), copper (1.1-2.1%) and iron (6.1-16.3%), and ore reserves of 600,000 t have been proven.

Iron ore has been known since mediaeval times in the southern Ajlun district, where an ore body of Cenomanian-Turonian age contains approx. 561,000 t, with an iron-value of more than 60%.

Nickel and uranium have also been found in traces. Whereas the former is associated with pre-Cambrian copper mineralization in Wadi al-Araba (around Wadi al-Dana), the latter is linked with the phosphates of Rusaifa and al-Hasa. There, phosphate rocks contain an average of 100-125 ppm of U_2O_3.

Non-metallic Minerals.

In contrast to hydrocarbons and metallic minerals there is a wealth of non-metallic minerals, many of which are the origins of modern industry in Jordan. Barite has been found near Bayt Sahur and in north-east Jordan near H4 pumping station, and small-scale commercial production seems possible. Feldspar, mica and quartz are common in the igneous basic rock complexes but their quality and quantity do not seem to justify production.

Silica and glass sands abound in the Lower Cretaceous and Early Ordovician sediments. Several deposits have been identified in the south, notably around Qa'disah and Ras al-Naqab. Their quantity is practically unlimited and their quality is good. Thus, the Jordan Glass Manufacturing Company was established in 1974 to produce glass plates. Located at Ma'an, it started production in summer 1984, with a capacity of 18,000 t/year.

Clay deposits in northern Jordan (Ghor Kabid and Mahis, with reserves of nearly 50,000 t each) are the basis of a ceramics industry. Cretaceous limestone abounds and meets the requirements of raw material for the two cement factories of al-Fuhays and Rashidiyeh. The most important minerals are, however, the phosphate rocks which crop out along a 250-km 'phosphate belt' between Ras al-Naqab and Amman. The phosphorate deposits date from the Maestrichtian phase in the Late Cretaceous.

In 1894, the German geologist M. Blanckenhorn discovered the first deposits between Amman and Salt, and after the construction of the Hijaz Railway an annual production of 100-150,000 t was projected. However, the lack of capital in the Ottoman Empire and the turmoils of the First World War caused a delay, and it was not until 1934/35 that the Jordan Phosphate Mines Company (JPMC), 90% state-owned, started production in Rusaifa (Fiedler, 1984, p. 163).

Bender (1975) lists the economically interesting prospective areas as follows:

1. Ras al-Naqab/Ma'an: a phosphorate body approx. 20 m thick, south of Ma'an. The new mine of Shidiya will be producing from 1986 onwards.
2. Mahatta al-Hasa/al-Qatranah: more than 60 mn t of ore, containing more than 67% of tricalcium phosphate, have been proven and are being mined.
3. Between al-Qatranah and Amman: phosphorate layers have yet to be evaluated.
4. Rusaifa, between Amman and Zarqa: about 40 mn t of rock containing more than 62% of tricalcium phosphate.
5. In north-east Jordan, near the Jordan-Iraq border, phosphorate layers have been discovered but have yet to be evaluated.

In 1978 total proven reserves were evaluated at 130-140 mn t. With the exploration of the Shidiya deposits, halfway between Ma'an and al-Ghul (which may be exploited from 1986 onwards, with proven and indicated reserves of approx. 1 bn t), and with a better evaluation of existing mines, this figure has risen to around 1.1-1.5 bn t (<u>Joint Arab Economic Report</u> ..., 1984; <u>MD</u>, 31 Aug. 1984, p. 19).

Output from the phosphate mines in Rusaifa and al-Hasa has steadily increased from approx. 0.9 mn t around 1970 to 1.7 mn t in 1975, a figure which increased again to 3.7 mn t in 1983 and 6.3 mn t in 1984. The production target for 1985 was set at 6.7 mn t.

Jordan has fast become the world's third most important phosphate exporter, with a share of 9% (Morocco: 42%; US: 33%) of the world market. Until now the phosphate has been shipped mainly to South and East Asian countries. However, the JPMC and its affiliate, the Jordan Fertilizer Industry Company (JFIC), have constructed a phosphate fertilizer plant in Aqaba which was inaugurated in November 1982. Using 1.3 mn t of phosphate rock, its annual capacity is 740,000 t of ammonium phosphate and 105,000 t of phosphoric acid. Another project involves a scheme to set up a nitrogen-phosphate-potash (NPK) fertilizer industry (see also pp. 82-6).

Another valuable source of minerals is the Dead Sea. Some 20-26% of its water (143 sq. km) is composed of various salts, notably (according to Bender, 1975; 'Extracting Life ...', 1982, p. 9):

Sodium chloride: 13.5 bn t;
Magnesium chloride: 21 bn t;
Calcium chloride: 6.4 bn t;
Magnesium bromide: 0.9 bn t;
Rubidium salts: 12 mn t.

Most important for present activities is the potash (potassium chloride) content, which is evaluated at 2 bn t. For 20 years now, Israel has been extracting approx. 2 mn t/year of potash and 50,000 t/year of bromides; this extraction has led to a lowering of the sea-level by about 6 m since 1954.

Jordan also intended to work this valuable source and thus established the Arab Potash Company (APC) in 1955, together with several other Arab states ('Extracting Life ...', 1982). Activities started in 1975 and in 1977 the orders for the construction of a potash plant on a site between Ghor al-Safi and Lisan Island were signed. At a cost of $467 mn, the plant became operational in October 1982. The final capacity of 1.2 mn t will be reached in 1987. In 1984 output was 500,000 t, to be increased to 800,000 t in 1985.

The downstream industrialization effects of these mining activities are shown on pages 82-6.

Water Resources

Water is the lifeblood of all Arab countries, and this is all the more true for Jordan. The 200 mm/year rainfall line separates the areas suitable for rainfed farming (cereals), which is thus traditionally settled, from the Arab steppe (badiya) and the desert. Sufficient rain occurs only in the Western (300-700 mm) and Eastern Highlands (300-600 mm). Of the country's total area of 96,188 sq. km (or, including the West Bank but excluding the Dead Sea area, 95,433 sq. km), only 20% receives more than 200 mm of rain and 30% is regarded as (potentially) cultivable land (Gischler, 1979).

Not only is rainfall restricted to a small part of the territory but, as we can see from the agricultural production figures (pp. 71-5), it is very unreliable, thus creating continuous hazards for rainfed agriculture. Irrigation is therefore necessary in most regions to expand agriculture and to ensure uninterrupted production.

The surface-water potential mainly consists of the eastern tributaries of the River Jordan (the river itself and the western tributaries are tapped by Israel). Some 800-850 mn cu. m/year are available for Jordan. However, a total use of these waters would result in the river's almost drying up and in a continuous decline of the Dead Sea's water level.

The groundwater potential has yet to be thoroughly evaluated but it is thought that, in 1987, suggested demand will exceed renewable resources (MD, 2 Nov. 1984). Bender (1975) lists several potential active aquifers, the most important of which seem to be the following:

1. Lower Palaeozoic sandstones in the south and south-east, which receive little recharge.
2. Cenomanian and Turonian limestones in northern Jordan, of mainly local importance.
3. Campanian and Maestrichtian limestones from the Upper Cretaceous, which seem to be the most important and extensive aquifer systems, but which are tapped partly by the tributaries of the River Jordan and the Dead Sea rift.

The Geographic and Economic Potential

For the Amman-Zarqa conurbation, the Amman-Wadi Sir aquifer is the most important. It still seems to be under-exploited, but it is liable to pollution from household and industrial waste.

A definite groundwater balance has not yet been published. Gischler (1979, p. 102) quotes a groundwater production of 165 mn cu. m for 1975. An annual groundwater and surface-water potential of at least 1.105 bn cu. m can be compared with the consumption figures in Table 5.2).

Table 5.2: Water Consumption in Jordan, 1975 and 1990 (million cubic metres)

	1975	1990
Irrigation	375	465
Domestic use	4	286
Industry	6	30
Total	385	731

Source: Calculated after Gischler (1979), p. 102; author's own estimates for East Bank.

The figures for domestic and industrial use in Table 5.2 seem to be very low. If we compare them with current water consumption figures from European and Arab urban areas, which vary from 250 to 400 l/person/day, Jordan's population alone in 1990 (approx. 4.6 mn inhabitants) should use between 410 and 660 mn cu. m/year. Hydraulic projects like the East Ghor Canal and dam-building (King Talal Dam on the River Zarqa) are therefore essential to improve the water potential and make it available to agriculture and for human consumption.

The most spectacular project is the construction of a pipeline to bring water from the Euphrates in Iraq via two 650-km-long pipes from the Haditha Dam. Water has to be pumped to attain a height of 800 m above sea-level and costs are estimated to exceed $1 bn. The capacity will be 5 cu. m/second in the final stage (see BID, 1984, no. 8, p. 9; MD, 2 Nov. 1984, p. 22). No real judgement can be made at present as to the likely outcome of a project which is similar to the Libyan 'man-made river' and owes much to the present warmth in Iraqi-Jordanian relations.

THE AGRICULTURAL POTENTIAL

Jordan is no longer an agricultural country as measured by its socio-economic structure. Whereas in 1960, 44% of its workforce were employed in agriculture, today they account for only 20%, another 20% of the population being active in industry and 60% in services. However, figures for agriculture do not include peasants who are not gainfully employed and it is therefore assumed that one-third of the (male) labour force is actively engaged in agriculture.

Since the foundation of the state, Jordan's agriculture has not been able to feed the total population, nor will it be able to do so in the near future. The current economic development and the influx of capital allow Jordan to import whatever is needed for the nutrition of its inhabitants. But what about the future? Dependence on food imports also means a large degree of economic, and finally political, dependence. The evaluation of agricultural potential is therefore of great importance.

Climate and Soils

The climatic conditions have been described in the preceding pages. In general, the climate follows the Mediterranean regime, with cool, wet winters and dry, hot summers. Precipitation, with the rainy season extending from October to May, decreases more or less regularly towards the east.

With cereals needing an absolute minimum rainfall of 200 mm/year, some 13% of the country's surface is suitable for agriculture. Table 5.3 gives the relative and absolute shares of the total surface in the different climatic areas of Jordan (East Bank only).

In addition to the low precipitation, the variability poses a major obstacle to rainfed cereal production. Most meteorological stations show an average variability of rainfall of 30% over the last 30 years, with an increase of variability in the drier regions. The Amman Airport Meteorological Station illustrates the uselessness for agriculture of an average rainfall figure, which is 280 mm/year. There, in fact, between 1939 and 1973 (36 years) seven years showed less than 200 mm (i.e. no

Table 5.3: Climatic Zones in Jordan, Relative Share of Total Area

Province	Semi-humid zone (500-700 mm)	Semi-arid zone (350-500 mm)	Transition zone (250-350 mm)	Arid zone (less than 200 mm)	Total share
Irbid	0.6	0.9	0.5	22.6	25.6
Amman	0.2	0.3	1.6	17.8	19.9
Balqa	0.2	0.2	0.3	0.4	1.1
Karak	-	0.1	2.2	2.8	5.1
Ma'an	-	-	0.5	47.7	48.2
Total area ('000 ha)	98.9	135.9	563.4	8,456	9.255

Source: Calculated after Barham (1979), p. 42, according to figures from the Jordan Ministry of Agriculture.

cereals production possible), eight other years recorded rainfall between 200 and 270 mm (where the harvest to be expected hardly exceeds the amount of grain sown). In contrast, the four wettest years showed more than 400 mm/year.

Table 5.4: Agricultural Production in Jordan, 1961-77, Showing Minimum and Maximum Figures (kilogrammes per hectare) and Variability (percentage)

Product	Minimum production (year)	Maximum production (year)	Average yield (kg/ha) (1961-77)	Variability (%)
Wheat	276 (1973)	996 (1965)	616	41.5
Barley	139 (1973)	1147 (1969)	592	59.1
Lentils	247 (1973)	1054 (1969)	669	41.5
Chickpeas	421 (1966)	915 (1972)	638	24.4
Olives	298 (1962)	3040 (1961)	1598	50.7
Tomatoes	4615 (1976)	6918 (1964)	4762	14.1

Source: Calculated after Barham (1979), p. 54, according to figures from the Jordan Ministry of Agriculture.

The Geographic and Economic Potential

This characteristic picture is clearly reflected in the production statistics. Table 5.4 gives the minimum and maximum harvests for some typical crops between 1961 and 1977. It also shows the mean variability, which is very high for rainfed products, but lower for irrigated vegetables (tomatoes).

In contrast to the climate, the soils of the more humid regions are mostly quite favourable for agriculture (Bender, 1968; Barham, 1979). On limestone sediments red Mediterranean soils (hamra in Arabic) have developed. They are characteristic of most of the West Bank and the more humid regions (more than 350 mm) of the East Bank. Drier regions (250-350 mm) show yellow Mediterranean soils which also have a good calcium content, but have a tendency towards duricrust formation.

The yellow steppe soils and the grey desert soils are of less value to agriculture. A major problem in the more humid zone is soil erosion, which is reinforced by the relief. In fact, more than one-third of the semi-arid and arid zones (Table 5.3) shows slopes of more than 25% and cannot be used as arable land, the maximum possible slope for ploughing being 15%.

Irrigation Possibilities
Irrigation has become the most important technique for improving agricultural production under semi-arid and arid conditions. In wheat production, for instance, yields are four to six times higher with irrigation than under rainfed (350-500 mm/year) conditions.

In Jordan, pump irrigation areas have increased from 5,100 ha in 1973 to nearly 10,000 ha in 1981 (excluding the East Ghor). The Food and Agriculture Organization (FAO) indicates a figure of 85,000 ha, but this seems somewhat doubtful. Most important for irrigation activities is the East Ghor Canal, which branches off from the Yarmouk River and has a maximum carrying capacity of 300 mn cu. m/year, compared with the Yarmouk runoff of 480 mn cu. m. The canal is planned finally to reach the Dead Sea and could then irrigate a total of 50,000 ha. In 1981 some 25,700 ha were irrigated in the Ghor region, especially for the production of vegetables (70% of the area) and fruit (16%).

Other dam projects like the King Talal Dam on

the River Zarqa will also improve hydrological potential and local possibilities for additional irrigation. Besides the Jordan Valley Authority, which administers the East Ghor Project, the new Water Authority of Jordan was established at the beginning of 1984. Its task will be to undertake an integral evaluation of water resources and to suggest a strategy for their optimal employment, including the service of ever-growing Amman.

Current Agricultural Problems
The economic performance of Jordanian agriculture has been low in recent years, as has been the case for most Arab countries. The index of overall agricultural production rose slightly from an average over 1969-71 of 100 points to 112 in 1981, but this was not enough to compensate for population growth. Thus, the index of per capita production fell to 74 points in 1982. The ratio of agricultural exports to agricultural imports remained relatively stable, at a low level, as shown in Table 5.5.

Table 5.5: Ratio of Agricultural Exports to Imports, Jordan and all Arab Countries, 1970-81 (percentage)

Year	Jordan	All Arab countries
1970	24	83
1979	32	21
1980	23	17
1981	30	-

Source: Joint Arab Economic Report 1982 (1984), and author's own calculations

Whereas Jordan is a net exporter of fruit and vegetables, most of its staple foods, and also most of its meat, fish and of course cereals, have to be imported. Grain harvests have averaged 62,000 t/year over the last ten years, with a maximum of 170,000 t in 1980, whereas grain imports amounted to 620,000 t in 1981 (according to World Bank figures, 1974: only 171,000 t).

It is small wonder that the share of agriculture within GDP has decreased sharply from 14.6% in 1972 to 7%, or JD 85.3 mn, in 1982. These figures are likely to decrease still further in the near future. The winter of 1983/84 brought one of the worst droughts for nearly 40 years and wheat production tumbled from its 1982 level of 52,000 t to not more than 10,000 t (barley: 3,000 t instead of 20,000 t). Grazing areas for sheep (1 mn head), goats (500,000) and cattle (39,000) have also been reduced.

If we compare the total value of agricultural production in 1981 ($250 mn) with the balance of agricultural imports ($570 mn) and exports ($130 mn), we can calculate the share of local production within national consumption as roughly 37%.

THE HUMAN POTENTIAL

In a country with limited natural resources, the human potential must take up the slack. Due to its developmental bias, but also because of its tragic recent history, Jordan has become a pool of qualified manpower for the eastern Arab world.

Population Growth

The population growth of Jordan has been even more rapid than that in most other Arab countries. In 1961, 1.7 mn people lived in the East and West Banks. This figure rose to approx. 3.49 mn in 1982 and 3.74 mn in 1984, as shown in Table 5.6.

Table 5.6: Population, East and West Bank, 1961-82

Year	Total inhabitants ('000)	Share of East Bank (%)	Share of West Bank (%)	Population growth rate (%)
1961	1,706	52.8	47.2	3.1
1970	2,340	64.4	35.6	3.2
1975	2,741	66.1	33.9	3.5
1980	3,304	67.6	32.4	3.0
1982	3,490	69.2	30.8	2.8

Source: Statistisches Bundesamt (1980-84)

Of course, this is due not only to high natural increases (with a balance per 1,000 inhabitants of +26 between birth and death rates per annum), but also to migration from Israel and the West Bank. It is estimated that some 1.2 mn of the 4.4 mn Palestinians live in Jordan (East Bank), where they have settled in several batches since 1948. Although the natural growth rate is not spectacular, the <u>World Development Report</u> ... (1984) forecasts a further annual growth rate of 3.7% until the year 2000. It predicts a population of 7 mn at that date, to stabilize at 18 mn in the year 2110. Our analysis sheds many doubts on where to locate and how to nourish such masses in a land with scarce resources.

In terms of population density relative to the entire area, the country is, with 36 persons/sq. km, of course not overcrowded. However, if we relate population to arable land, the figure of 'physical population density' rises to 300/sq. km, which is more than in most European countries. And yet productivity is much lower. An average yield of 0.6 t/ha of wheat in Jordan (Barham, 1979, p. 54) is to be compared with more than 4 t in West Germany alone.

Most of the growth is concentrated in the area of the capital (Amman, Zarqa and Rusaifa). The combined population of the first two towns alone grew from 342,000 in 1961 to 865,000 inhabitants in 1979 (or 5.3% per annum) and the urban agglomeration must contain today some 1.5 mn inhabitants, or nearly half the Jordanian population.

Poor rural resources are one reason for this concentration; the migration of non-agricultural population from the West Bank is another. A natural annual growth rate of nearly 3% and a stagnating population figure (1961: 805,000; 1982: 1,075,000 Palestinians in the West Bank, see Statistisches Bundesamt; different figures, of 661,800 in 1967 and 797,800 in 1979 respectively, are provided by 'La viabilité ...', 1984, p. 16, but they give nearly the same growth rate of 1.56%) imply a yearly migration of 12-17,000 persons from the West Bank to Arab countries, in general to Jordan. The issue of immigration and emigration is discussed further on pages 78-9.

Education and Qualifications
The strength and potential of the population do not depend on their sheer number but rather on their educational quality. In Palestine, both by tradition and by continuous contact with the

centres of science inside and outside the Arab world, the standard of education has always been relatively high (Tuma and Darin-Drabkin, 1978). This is all the more true today. A relatively young population (see pp. 79-81) has undergone a real 'educational revolution'. Thus, from 1960 to 1980 the scholarization rate in the East Bank (primary schools) rose from 77 to 100%; 79% of the pupils (1960: 39%, see World Development Report 1983) continued their studies in secondary schools. The literacy rate among the adult population rose from 32% to 70%.

Of the 20- to 24-year-old population, 27% attend secondary schools or one of the two universities (Amman and, since 1977, Yarmouk). Some 53,600 students were enrolled at national high schools and universities, another 66,500 abroad (36.5% in Egypt, 15% in Lebanon, 9% in the US and 7% in the USSR). Table 5.7 shows the pace of educational development.

Table 5.7: Educational Figures for East Bank Students (thousands)

Type of education	1974	1978	1982
Primary schools	353	431	468
Prep. schools and secondary schools	126	231	264
High schools and national universities	12	29	55
Universities abroad	21	43	66
Students among total population (%)	27.1	34.5	35.3

Source: Statistisches Bundesamt (1980, 1984)

Of course, these figures are correlated with the fact that the population is very young, with 43.1% being between the ages of 5 and 20 in 1979. But even so, their educational standard is very much above the Arab average, as shown in Table 5.8.

Unfortunately, no figures are available to show the high professional standard of the actual manpower. But the evidence reveals a higher

Table 5.8: Jordan and Arab World, Relative Educational Standards, 1980 (percentage)

	Jordan	Arab world (weighted average)
Share of primary school pupils of this age group	108	78.4
Share of secondary school pupils of this age group	79	37.2
Share of high school and university students among 20- to 24-year-olds of the total population	27	8.7

Source: Calculated after World Development Report 1983, table 25.

standard than in most other Arab countries, as witnessed by the Jordanian workers abroad, who show a relatively high proportion of technicians, engineers, doctors, and so on.

Emigration and Immigration

By political and economic destiny, Jordan has become a country of both immigrants and emigrants. Ever since the establishment of Israel, Palestinians from the territories occupied in 1948 and 1967 have left their homes. In 1982 they were estimated to be some 5 mn people. Of these, some 0.6 mn still live in Israel and another 1.4 mn in the occupied territories (West Bank and Gaza). Probably more than 1 mn (0.8 mn were officially registered in 1982) live in Jordan (East Bank) and 560,000 in Lebanon; others live in Kuwait (260,000), Syria (215,000), Saudi Arabia (90,000) and all over the world. Much of the population growth of Jordan must be attributed to these refugees, who also brought their skills and knowledge to the country. However, in a crowded land with meagre resources, they had an early tendency to migrate to richer (Arab) countries (see also Hammouda, 1980).

The migration movement, notably towards the oil-rich countries of the Arabian peninsula, started in the early 1970s. In 1975 there were 215,000 Jordanians (and Palestinians with Jordanian passports) employed abroad. By 1980 (Birks and Sinclair, 1980) the figure had risen to 305,400, of whom 250,400 lived in Arab countries, mainly Saudi Arabia (56% of the total), Kuwait (22%), the UAE (8%) and Libya (6%); see also MEED, 14 Aug., 1981; al-Kazaz, 1983.

Recent figures (Maghreb-Machrek, no. 105 (1984), p. 69; MEED, 10 Feb. 1984, p. 23) quote between 320,000 and 350,000 Jordanians abroad. Their contribution to the national economy is important. They not only bring relief to the national labour market, but also contribute towards equilibrating the development of payments, as they transfer between $0.824 bn (1982) and $1.1 bn dollars (1983) to their country of origin. This figure is believed to have stabilized at around $1 bn/year.

The quality of Jordanian manpower abroad is highlighted by the fact that Jordan exports high-quality personnel and imports manpower for more menial jobs. In 1981 there were 103,500 foreign workers in the country, a figure which rose to 130,000 (of whom 90,000 were Egyptians) in 1984. Their transfers home amounted to $186 mn in 1983. The difference in the per capita transfers (annual rates of $1,430 by non-Jordanians to abroad and $3,500 for Jordanians from abroad) gives a rough idea of the respective quality of labour.

Quantity of Manpower
Although the quality of the manpower is quite high, the numbers involved are low when compared with the total population. It was estimated (MEED, 25 May 1984, p. 13) at the beginning of 1984 that the active population (labour force) consisted of 500,000 Jordanians and 120,000 workers from abroad (see pp. 78-9).

(Other publications (e.g. Joint Arab Economic Report ..., 1984) give a figure of 756,000 for 1980 (of which the industrial labour force is 298,000). The presence of independent peasants probably explains these statistical differences, as they are not included in the 'gainfully employed population', although they form part of the 'active population'. In general, the share of the potentially active population (51% of the total) is not much lower than the average of developing countries, but, of course, it is less than in the industrialized states (66%), resulting from the high proportion of juveniles (see pp. 75-6).

If we take the figure of 500,000 active Jordanians as accurate, this would be only 20.7% of the total (East Bank) population; 756,000 would give a ratio of 31.3%. Although the first figure is also quoted in official publications (for the East Bank, probably excluding foreign workers), it seems very low even in comparison with other Arab countries (e.g. Saudi Arabia: 23%). Three factors may be listed to explain this phenomenon: first, the fact that it is the male and active emigrants who go abroad, leaving their families behind; second, the high proportion of young people attending higher educational facilities (see pp. 76-8); and, third, the slow integration of women into the labour market because of Islamic traditions.

The emancipation of women - who already make up 46% of the high school and 41% of the local university students - will promote their accession to the labour market. As the manpower absorption capacity of the Arab oil-producing countries is receding, it is also believed that Jordanians will have to return home at the annual rate of 10,000 persons (MEED, 25 May 1984, p. 13). Whereas in the 1960s and 1970s the number of gainfully employed rose more slowly than the population figure (by 2.8% and 3.1% respectively), the former figure will increase by 4.3% per annum between 1980 and the year 2000, according to the World Bank. Some 25-35,000 additional job-seekers will need employment every year (plus re-migrants from the Arabian peninsula?). This puts a heavy strain on the labour market and shows the problems and tasks confronting economic planning for the future.

The final figures in Table 5.9 give an idea of the importance of the various economic sectors for the labour market.

Agriculture is grossly under-estimated; it accounted for some 110-120,000 workers in 1979. For the rest, the structures do not look very healthy either.

With nearly 80% of manpower in the service sectors, and only 10% in industry, Jordan is still a long way from being an industrial state. It is clear for the future, however, that the tertiary sector will remain predominant in a country which is the turn-table of transport and commerce between Europe and the Arabian peninsula (see pp. 86-7).

Table 5.9: Jordan (East Bank) - Development of Population Gainfully Employed, Share of Sectors, 1975 and 1979 (percentage)

Sector	1975	1979
Agriculture (employed only)	19.1	18.0[a]
Industry	7.6	10.7
Building trade	10.4	13.6
Commerce & tourism	6.5	9.7
Transport	5.0	8.3
Other services & administration, military services ...	34.2	47.4
Total (Absolute figures, '000)	383	450

Note: a. Including individual farmers.
Source: Statistisches Bundesamt (1980, 1984); World Development Report 1983.

Table 5.10: Gross Domestic Product, 1972-85 - Share of Sectors at Current Prices (million Jordanian dinars)

Sector	1972	1976	1980	1982	1985 (plan)
Agriculture	14.6	9.6	7.1	7.0	5.1
Industry & mining	11.5	18.5	20.3	19.5	21.7
Building trade	5.0	6.9	10.7	9.8	5.5
Commerce & tourism	19.5	20.7	18.4	18.2	13.1
Transport & communications	9.5	8.4	8.8	11.9	9.1
Others (services)	39.9	35.9	34.7	33.5	45.5
Total	182.8	387.1	907.3	1,214.5	1,695.0

Source: Statistisches Bundesamt (1984); Middle East Economic Digest (MEED), (15 Jan. 1982), p. 48.

ECONOMIC DEVELOPMENT

It has become clear that the economic development of Jordan has been hampered by relatively poor natural resources and the unfortunate (geo-)political situation. Nevertheless, the country has shown marked success in recent years. Some economic figures (Table 5.10) concerning GDP (East Bank only) give a first impression of the economy, its deformations and problems.

Agriculture's low share is not surprising and the rising share of industry is certainly a sign of healthy growth. However, it should be stressed that nearly two-thirds of GDP stems from the service sector. In fact, the high level of the Jordanian economy is only possible with the help of a massive influx of foreign capital and financial aid, as will be shown on pages 86-7.

Industrial Development and Potential

Jordan has always been a country with a liberal economic policy. Convertibility of the national currency, a free capital market, open frontiers for imports and exports and a restricted local demand for industrial goods provided no incentive for industrialization. On the other hand, the existence of qualified manpower, of strong markets and capital in the neighbouring oil-producing countries, as well as a certain protection of the national market due to relatively high transportation costs from industrialized countries, brought positive aspects for investments (Rivier, 1980). Thus the private sector supported a marked boom in the production of consumer goods, which started in the early 1970s. Unfortunately, figures on the small-scale production units which are typical of the Jordanian productive sector are defective. Official sources (see 'Role of Small- and Medium-Scale Industries ...', 1984), state that the Jordanian industrial development strategy relies on large-scale, capital-intensive, mineral-resource-based and/or export-oriented industries, aimed at the rapid infusion of advanced technology and management methods. The only survey undertaken to date on the private sector found, in 1974, 7,000 small-scale establishments with 10,964 workers (equivalent to 41% of the total industrial labour force). In 1980, 13,160 employees were registered in the private industrial sector (companies with five or more employees), a figure which had increased by 17% since 1974.

Table 5.11 shows the performance of the different sectors. After a rapid growth of production in all sectors between 1978 and 1981, mainly due to the influx of Arab capital and the rise of local and regional demand, a net stagnation has been visible since. This is all the more true if we deduct the figures for electricity production.

Table 5.11: Index of Industrial Production (East Jordan), 1978-83 (1975 = 100)

Product	1978	1981	1983
Electrical energy	153	266	404
Phosphate mining	172	300	326
Food, beverages, tobacco	142	213	169
Textiles & clothing	120	140	143
Building materials	114	230	246
Chemical industry	275	355	350
Petroleum industry	173	248	281
Total industry	159	256	276
Total industry (excluding electricity)	160	255	259

Source: calculated after Statistisches Bundesamt (1980, 1984).

The main products of the private sector today (Statistisches Bundesamt, 1984; 'Data on Installed ...', 1984) are: textiles (1.5 mn m of fabric in 1980, since then a decrease in production) and clothing, pharmaceutical products, foodstuffs and beverages, cigarettes (4.7 bn units in 1981, 4.9% of total Arab production), soaps and detergents (30,700 t in 1981), and paper and paper products (115,400 t in 1981). Some 85% of the industrial plants and 71% of the smaller production units are located in the Amman/Zarqa area (except for the Arab Pharmaceutical Manufacturing Company, established in 1960 at Salt), where manpower and infrastructural equipment are concentrated (Malkawi, 1978, p. 22 ff; Pechoux, 1984).

In contrast to the private sector, the

semi-public (with Jordanian state and Arabian foreign capital) and public sectors have shown more dynamic movement in recent years. Their activities are mostly based on the mineral resources of the country (see pp. 64-70).

Cement production doubled from 572,000 t in 1975 to 1,250,000 t in 1983, with a total capacity of 3 mn t when the Rashidiyeh plant started operating in 1984. This represents some 4% of the total Arab cement-producing capacity.

The Zarqa plant refines oil imported via the TAP-line from Saudi Arabia (Mousa, 1984). For this purpose the TAP-line, which was to be closed at the beginning of 1985, will be kept in operation. Since the start of production in 1960, capacity has risen to 100,000 b/d, or approx. 4.2 mn t/year, but only 2 mn t are presently being produced. They cover local demand, which was 1.66 mn t in 1981. The high growth rate of energy consumption is of major concern to Jordanian planners. Whereas imported energy absorbed 11% of GDP in 1980, this share is expected to rise to 20% by 1990.

The most important sector of the Jordanian industry - by reason of its financial impact - is the transformation of phosphate. In November 1982 the Aqaba plant of the JFIC was inaugurated. With a production capacity of 740,000 t of ammonium phosphate and 105,000 t of phosphoric acid, it consumes 1.3 mn t of phosphate rock. The investment costs were estimated at $435 mn. In 1983, 365,112 t of ammonium phosphate were produced, all of which was exported. With this plant, Jordan will account for 2.3% of the Arab phosphoric acid production capacity. There are more projects in Aqaba, the 'town of the future' (Fiedler, 1984, p. 200), based on this raw material. The possibility of building a plant to produce NPK fertilizer with a possible capacity of 150-250,000 t/year is at present under consideration (MEED, 6 March 1984; 'Data on Installed ...', 1984).

An aluminium fluoride plant started production in May 1984, using fluosilic acid, a byproduct from the fertilizer plant. At an investment cost of $30 mn, it will produce 20,000 t/year.

The potash plant at Ghor al-Safi has already been mentioned. Built at a cost of $450 mn, it became operational in 1982 (production: 80,000 t) and will reach its full production capacity (1.2 mn t) in 1986.

Future projects focus on the extraction of uranium from phosphate rocks and an increase of capacities within the fertilizer industries. It should, however, be realized that production capacities in the Arab world increase at an enormous rate, as shown in Table 5.12. Regional Arab demand is at present absorbing only a fraction of both existing and planned production capacity.

Table 5.12: Arab World - Production Capacities in Phosphoric Acid and Fertilizers (thousand tons)

Capacity	Phosphoric acid	P_2O_5 fertilizer	K_2O fertilizer
Present Arab capacity	3,352	-	-
Capacity under construction	2,567	4,334	2,744[b]
Capacity planned	376		
Consumption in Arab countries	700[a]	472	113

Notes: a. Rough estimate.
       b. NPK fertilizer.
Source: Calculated after 'Data on Installed ...' (1984).

The Arab countries hold approximately half of the total world phosphate reserves (<u>Joint Arab Economic Report</u> ..., 1984, p. 113) and they already account for 25% of world production. In view of a certain saturation of world demand and stagnating prices, however, caution is recommended concerning the build-up of capacities.

Services and Transport

As is clear from Table 5.10, services are the most important sector of Jordan's economy. Jordan has always been a country of trade and transit, as is evident from the ruins of Petra. The era of modern transport came with the opening of the Hijaz Railway (Dera'a - Amman - Ma'an - al-Mudawwara) in 1904-07 (Hughes, 1981; Fiedler, 1984). Today the service sector is marked by the following activities:

The Geographic and Economic Potential

1. Transport, with 618 km of railway line (mainly for phosphate transports from al-Abiadh/al-Hasa to Aqaba), 3,600 km of asphalted roads and about 95,000 vehicles.
2. Commerce and trade, which are concentrated in and around Amman.
3. Tourism, where 177 hotels, with 11,000 beds cater for 1.7 mn foreign visitors. As no distinction is made between entering tourists, foreign workers and transit travellers (e.g. to Saudi Arabia), the exact figure of the former is not known. However, the importance of tourism is highlighted by its contribution to the foreign capital balance of $404 mn in 1982.
4. Banking, in which sector Amman has been able to attract some of the activities that have moved away from Beirut since 1975.

Under the present economic and political conditions in the neighbouring Arab countries, Jordan may well become the service transit centre for the eastern Arab countries. Aqaba has become the most important single harbour for Iraqi foreign trade. In 1982 some 2,500 ships brought 7.8 mn t of goods, of which 65% went on to Iraq. Although this figure has decreased, a continuous flow of trucks bringing goods to Iraq and Saudi Arabia is a common sight on Jordanian roads. To relieve the blockade of Iraq, a further pipeline is planned from Kirkuk via Zarqa to Aqaba, with a capacity of at least 1 mn t/year, following much of the route of the old Kirkuk - Haifa pipeline (in operation from 1934 to 1948, see Mousa, 1984). The costs of at least $1 bn seem to hamper the project at present (MEED, 2 March 1984).

Capital Transfers, Arab and Foreign Aid
Jordan is by no means self-sufficient. Since the foundation of the state, the trade balance has shown a continuous deficit. In 1974 the ratio of imports to exports was 1:0.32. This figure fell to 1:0.26 in 1982 and the absolute trade deficit stood at $1.93 bn.

Nevertheless the country lives quite well, with a foreign debt of $1.95 bn at the end of 1983, less than most of the other non-oil-producing Arab countries. It lives on capital transfers, which come from several sources. The most reliable source is that of the transfers of the almost 350,000 Jordanians abroad, who remitted $0.823 bn in 1982 and between $0.7 and $1.1 bn in 1983 (differences according to sources). It is hoped that this figure will reach $1 bn and stabilize there (MEED, 20 Jan. 1984 and 25 May 1984).

In 1978, during the Baghdad Summit Conference, the Arab oil-producing countries promised budget aid to the 'front-line states' to be paid regularly until 1988; Jordan was to receive $1.25 bn/year. Unfortunately, this goal was never met and in 1984, $467 mn (1983: $581 mn) actually arrived from Saudi Arabia and Kuwait. More aid came from other Arab states (approx. an additional $0.5 mn annually), Western countries (mainly the US) and international organizations. It is calculated that Jordan received, from 1960 to 1982, approx. $2.6 bn bilateral and multilateral aid (excluding aid from the Baghdad Agreement), of which 50% came from the US.

Developmental Concepts and Planning

Because of its poor natural resources and its dependence on the (financial) goodwill of its neighbours, Jordan has never been able to elaborate a very stringent development concept (Mazur, 1979). The Jordan Development Board proposed a first five-year plan (1962-67), which was replaced in 1963 by a seven-year-plan (1964-70), with planned investments of JD 275 mn. However, the 1967 war and its aftermath made this plan obsolete, too. The newly formed National Planning Council (NPC) then proposed in 1973 a three-year plan (1973-1975), with an expected annual growth in GDP of 8% as a target and investments of JD 179 mn.

In a period of transition, several of the targets were achieved as the oil-price revolution, the absorption of Jordanian manpower abroad and the rise in phosphate prices all had a favourable impact. The following five-year-plan (1976-80) was very optimistic, aiming at an annual GDP of 11.9% (actual growth rate was 8.5%).

The sectors promoted by the state were: (a) mining and industry (+26.2% growth per annum expected); (b) water and electricity (+17.1%); and (c) transport and communications (+10.6%)

Table 5.13 gives a survey of the performance of this plan, as well as of the concept of the five-year plan (1980-85).

The Geographic and Economic Potential

Table 5.13: Jordan Development Plans (1976-80) and (1980-85), Share of Sectors (million Jordanian dinars)

Sector	Plan (1976-80) Allocated share (%)	Implemented share (%)	(1980-85) Allocated share (%)
Agriculture & co-operatives	5.2	4.2	9.3
Water & irrigation	12.7	6.0	20.8
Manufacturing & mining	29.9	25.9	30.2
Tourism & antiquities	3.2	2.7	2.6
Electricity & energy	5.6	8.1	6.5
Commerce	0.5	1.4	1.5
Transport & communications	18.3	22.6	4.6
Education, culture & information	4.9	3.7	11.1
Health	1.2	0.5	4.0
Labour development	0.6	0.1	1.0
Housing & construction	11.1	21.1	0.7
Municipal & rural affairs	5.1	3.2	7.0
Others (Awqaf, statistics, RSS)	1.5	0.4	0.5
Total	765.3	1,222.0	2,509.4

Source: MEED (15 Jan. 1982).

Whereas the share of industry (public sector only, see pp. 82-6) remains stable, agriculture's share seems definitely too low and that of other activities vary somewhat erratically. Moreover, it is not sure whether the objectives can be attained. Since 1983 the economy has been going through a period of comparative austerity (MEED, 20 Jan. 1984), during which the effects of bad harvests (see pp. 74-5), stagnating remittances of Jordanian workers abroad (in 1983 an estimated JD 0.7 bn instead of the expected JD 1.1 bn), economic stagnation in neighbouring countries (mainly Iraq, the most important market for Jordanian consumer goods) and a slack in world phosphate prices are acting together in a negative way. Real economic growth now stands at around 4-5% (12% at current prices) and it seems that the development plan (1980-85) will not be implemented at the rhythm that was originally predicted.

For the development plan (1986-90) some outlines have already been given. It aims at the optimal utilization of the country's natural resources, the completion of various infrastructural projects and a further promotion of industry which should improve the traditionally negative trade balance. Among the major new projects are investments for phosphate mining in the Ma'an area ($900 mn) and for the exploitation of the oil-shale sand (see pp. 65), which would provide 50,000 b/d at investment costs of $650 mn.

OUTLOOK - WHAT FUTURE FOR JORDAN?

Of course, it is up to the Jordanians to decide about their future. Our survey has listed positive and negative aspects relevant to Jordan's development. Among the negative aspects we should mention:

1. the continuing political threat from Israel and the uncertain future of the West Bank and of the Palestinian refugees;
2. the high population growth rate when related to the difficult natural settings;
3. the growing dependency on, first, capital influx and donations and, second, food and oil imports ($664 mn and $470 mn respectively in 1982 and 1983);
4. the coming on stream of export-oriented production units, which meet with a saturated world market.

As a counterbalance, however, there are the following positive elements:

1. highly qualified and relatively cheap manpower;
2. a liberal and stable economic regime;
3. a location on the most important transit routes to the Arabian peninsula.

Jordan will probably become neither a major industrial power like Saudi Arabia (Schliephake, 1984) nor a net exporter of agricultural products like Syria. Nevertheless its stability, its cautious policy and the optimal valorization of its natural resources, combined with its geographic setting, give it a chance to become, and remain, the most modern and most developed of the Arab non-oil-producing countries.

NOTES

1. The author's recent trip to Jordan was facilitated by grants from the German Research Society (DFG) and the University of Würzburg.
2. *International Management*, vol. 7 (1984).

BIBLIOGRAPHICAL REFERENCES

Where no other sources are cited, data come from various journals, especially the following publications:

> Middle East Economic Digest (London), various issues
> Statistisches Bundesamt (eds.), Länderberichte Jordanien (Wiesbaden, 1980, 1982, 1984)

Barham, Nasim (1979) Geographische Probleme des Regenfeldbaus in Jordanien, Hanover (Diss.)
Bender, Friedrich (1968) Geologie von Jordanien, Beiträge zur regionalen Geologie der Erde, Bd. 7, Berlin
────── (1975) Geology of the Arab Peninsula - Jordan, Geological Survey Professional Paper 560-I, US GPO, Washington, D.C.
Birks, J.S. and Sinclair, C.A. (1980 International Migration and Development in the Arab Region, ILO, Geneva
'Data on Installed and Planned Production Capacities, Consumption, Imports and Exports of Manufacturing Industries and Electricity in Arab Countries' (1984) UNIDO/IS.466 dated 14 May, Vienna 'Extracting Life from the Dead Sea' (1982) Jordan (Amman and New York) vol. 7, no. 3, pp. 6-9
Fiedler, Ulrich (1984) Der Bedeutungswandel der Hedschasbahn. Eine historisch-geographische Untersuchung, Islamkundliche Untersuchungen, Bd. 94, Berlin
Gischler, Christian (1979) Water Resources in the Arab Middle East and North Africa, Cambridge
Hammouda, Ahmad A, (1980) 'Jordanian Emigration, An Analysis of Migration Data', International Migration Review (New York), vol. 14
Hughes, Hugh (1981) Middle East Railways, Oxford
Industry in Jordan 1978 (1978) Ministry of Information, Amman, 50 pp.
Joint Arab Economic Report 1982 (1984), Arab Monetary Fund, Dubai
Al-Kazaz, Aziz (1983) 'Die internationale Arbeitskräfte-Emigration in der Region des Nahen und Mittleren Ostens' in Jahresbericht des Nah-und Mittelostvereins, Hamburg, pp. 8-13
Malkawi, Ahmad (1978) Regional Development in Jordan - Some Aspects of the Urban Bias, Amman

Mazur, Michael P. (1979) *Economic Growth and Development in Jordan*, Boulder, Colo.
Mousa, Suleiman (1984) 'The Impact of Oil on Jordan' in K.J. Gantzel and H. Mejcher (eds.), *Oil, the Middle East, North Africa and the Industrial States*, Internationale Gegenwart, Bd. 6, Paderborn, pp. 239-50
Pechoux, Paul-Yves (1984) 'Le démarrage de la grande industrie en Jordanie et en Irak', *Annales de Géographie*, vol. 93, no. 518, pp. 457-61
Rivier, François (1980) *Croissance industrielle dans une économie assisté: le cas jordanien*, Cermac, Beirut, 227 pp.
'The Role of Small-and Medium-Scale Industries in OIC Member States' (1984) UNIDO/IS. 487 dated 9 Oct., Vienna
Schliephake, Konrad (1984) 'Micro- and-Macro-regional Effects of the Oil Industry' in K.J. Gantzel and H. Mejcher (eds.), *Oil, the Middle East, North Africa and the Industrial States*, Internationale Gegenwart, Bd. 6, Paderborn, pp. 171-84
Statistisches Bundesamt (eds.) (1980, 1982, 1984) *Länderberichte Jordanien* (Wiesbaden)
Tuma, Elias and H. Darin-Drabkin (1978) *The Economic Case for Palestine*, London
'La Viabilité économique d'un état palestinien indépendant (1984) *Cahiers du CERMAC* (Louvain-la-Neuve), no. 24
World Development Report 1983, World Bank, New York

Chapter Six

AGRICULTURAL DEVELOPMENT AND FOOD SECURITY IN JORDAN

Naji Abuirmeileh

INTRODUCTION

Jordan is a country with limited land and human resources available for agricultural development and utilization. With the gap widening between food products and consumption demand, the need has grown for an adequate response from agricultural activities towards development efforts.

The present study is based on the information available to the author. It includes a compilation of the economic agricultural land, human, water and animal resources as well as an exposition of the agricultural development plans between 1963 and 1980. It also assesses the achievements of the agricultural development plan (1981-85), which laid the foundations and adopted the concept of national food security, and tried to achieve this security through carrying out agricultural developmental projects and building storage silos to secure a strategic stock of cereals and other foodstuffs.

AGRICULTURAL ECONOMIC RESOURCES

The area of the East Bank of the Hashemite Kingdom of Jordan is about 92.6 mn du. Land in the East Bank can be divided into four environmental agricultural regions in addition to the Ghor (Jordan Valley) and Semi-Ghor areas. This division is based upon homogeneity in the natural plant cover and annual average rainfall. These regions are shown in Table 6.1.

Table 6.1: Environmental Agricultural Regions of the East Bank Lands

Region	Average rainfall (mm)	Area (mn du)	%
Arid (desert)	below 200	84.6	91.4
Less arid	200-300	5.3	5.7
Semi-arid	300-500	1.7	1.8
Semi-humid & humid	500-800	1	1.1
Total		92.6	100.0

As to human agricultural resources, the East Bank population totals 2,153,273 people, 20% of whom are agriculturists. The ratio of human labour in agriculture to the total labour force is 18%, the latter amounting to nearly 450,000 people.

A reliance on rain for cultivating over 90% of the cultivable land makes water a particularly important resource for agricultural production. The average annual rainfall varies from 600 mm or more in high regions to less than 200 mm in desert areas. The aggregate amount of annual rainfall is estimated at about 6,885 mn cu. m. Annual water consumption is estimated at 550 mn cu. m, as shown in Table 6.2.

Table 6.2: Estimates of Water Consumption, 1975 and 1980 (million cubic metres)

Purpose	1975	1980
Drinking	40	60
Industry	6	30
Agriculture	375	460
Total	421	550

Surface waters are concentrated in the areas of the Jordan Valley, the Dead Sea basin and Wadi al-Arab. The productive capacity of these sources is about 850 mn cu. m, except for the Jordan Valley. The waters of these sources are primarily used for irrigation. Available water sources in the Jordan Valley are sufficient to irrigate approximately 325,000 du.

Animal wealth in Jordan includes sheep, goats, cattle, camels, poultry and fish. Sheep are considered the main source for the production of red meat as well as milk and wool. The average number of sheep in the period 1976-80 was nearly 826,000 with a minimum of 566,000 and a maximum of 924,000. In terms of agricultural wealth, goats rank next to sheep in importance. The average number of goats in the period 1976-80 was about 454,000. Cows in Jordan averaged about 37,000 head during the period, 85% of which were of local stock, the rest being Frisian. There is a tendency towards an expansion in raising milk cows. The average number of camels over the same period was some 16,000. The number of camels is decreasing annually owing to the bedouins' aversion to raising camels and their increasing desire for a settled life.

The period also witnessed a rapid and widespread development in keeping meat poultry. The productive capacity of meat poultry farms rose from 4,095,000 birds in 1976 to 5,446,000 in 1980. The productive capacity of egg-laying poultry also rose: from 958,000 birds in 1976 to 3,000,000 in 1980. The average productive capacity during this period was 1,892,000 birds. This progressive increase in the productive capacity of the farms of egg-laying and meat poultry is due to both private-sector investments and government policy, in addition to the modern technology of the poultry industry and the absorption of this technology by the farmers.

AGRICULTURAL DEVELOPMENT PLANS (1963 AND 1980)

Planners of economic and social development tend to divide the economic changes in the Jordanian economy from 1963 to 1980 into five successive stages, based on the permanent consequences of the 1948 disaster, and the nature of planning and the challenges of development after the occupation of the West Bank in 1967. The stages through which the Jordanian economy has passed are described below.

Stage I (1948-61) was characterized, despite the economic and social problems after 1948, by an annual average growth in local production of 11.5%. Developmental effort was directed towards the preparation of an economic infrastructure. Investment in various sectors was made without a pre-planned programme, as comprehensive planning for development had not yet crystallized. Although agriculture represented an economic base - with its contribution of 26% to local GNP, and its providing jobs for about 35% of the economic labour force - the frequent years of drought on the unirrigated land had a severe adverse effect upon agricultural production, particularly cereals and pasture land. Annual growth between 1954 and 1961 averaged only 2%.

Stage II (1963-67) witnessed accelerated growth in all aspects of economic activity. This stage saw comprehensive development through the five-year economic and social development plan (1963-67), which was a modification of the seven-year economic development plan (1964-70). This plan stressed productive ability, as well as continuity in carrying out large projects. The economy continued to grow rapidly until it was hindered by the 1967 war. GNP was increasing at an approximate annual rate of 9%. The value-added to the agricultural sector displayed progressive growth at 6% per annum. Most of this increase came from expanding irrigated areas after the completion of the East Ghor Canal, in addition to good harvest seasons on unirrigated lands. During this stage, the agricultural sector provided employment for about 40% of the economic labour force, and a livelihood for more than 60% of the entire population working in this sector and other complementary sectors. Agricultural income ranged between 15 and 35% of total GNP.

Stage III (1967-72), which came in the wake of the 1967 war, saw many development projects of the seven-year plan come to a standstill. The loss of the West Bank led to negative growth trends at stable prices, which amounted to 2% in agriculture. The mean average growth of GNP receded to 3.8% per annum. Jordan faced internal difficulties related to security and stability, in addition to a slump in agricultural production after some important Arab markets were closed to Jordanian agricultural products.

During Stage IV (1973-75), which included the implementation of the three-year development plan (1973-75), the Jordanian economy emerged safe from its ordeal and the challenges facing it. The march of development, planning and the setting in motion of economic activities was resumed. GNP achieved a real rise, averaging 7% per annum. Value-added in the agricultural sector decreased at stable prices at an average of 1%. The contribution of agriculture to local production was 12%. The agricultural sector, however, remained unable to meet the food needs of the people.

Stage V (1976-80), which was concerned with the five-year development plan (1976-80), aimed at continued development momentum with a comprehensive view of development strategy. Average growth in the real gross local product reached 8.5%.

In spite of the drought conditions which plagued Jordan throughout the years 1976-79, the agricultural sector achieved remarkable growth during the period of this development plan. Income from this sector increased, at current prices, from JD 26 mn in 1975 to JD 60 mn in 1980, at an annual growth rate of 18.2%. In real terms, agricultural income grew at an annual rate of 5.7%.

In comparison with the 1973-75 figures, annual production levels of field crops and meat registered a decline as a result of successive droughts. However, large increases were achieved in the production of vegetables, fruit, poultry meat and eggs. The change in production levels for some of the main agricultural commodities is shown in Table 6.3.

Table 6.3: Change in Production Levels from 1973-75 to 1976-80 (thousand tons)

	1973-75	1976-80	1973-75	1976-80	
	Minimum annual production	Maximum annual production	Average production	Average production	% change
Field crops	32	225	109	170	- 36
Vegetables	225	480	346	214	+ 62
Melons	26	48	30	50	- 40
Fruit	37	103	76	48	+ 58
Olives	7	45	24	19	+ 26
Meat	6	8	7	9	- 23
Dairy Products	35	44	39	43	- 10
Poultry	21	28	25	14	+ 79
Eggs (mn)	144	360	280	90	+210

Agricultural Development and Food Security

In the Jordan Valley, a total of 64,000 du were put under permanent irrigation, and 20,000 du were changed from a surface to a sprinkler irrigation system. In addition, 8,000 du were put under irrigation in the highland areas. This was accompanied by the introduction of new technologies in irrigation, especially with regard to drip irrigation and agriculture under plastic covers, together with the local manufacture of required materials.

In the rainfed areas, 128,000 du were planted with fruit trees, mainly olives and grapes, and 7,000 du with citrus trees; 90,000 du were afforested.

In the field of livestock production, the private sector was active in establishing poultry farms for broilers, layers and breeders. The production of eggs rose from 144 mn in 1975 to about 360 mn in 1980, while that of broiler meat increased from 21,000 t to 28,000 t. A number of pilot projects for sheep raising, involving the introduction of Atriplex shrubs into the marginal areas, have been established in recent years.

With regard to agricultural marketing, an agricultural marketing centre has been built in the al-Arda area in Jordan Valley. The centre consists of a wholesale market, a grading and packing station, and a factory for the manufacture of wooden boxes, with an annual output of 6 mn boxes. A similar marketing centre is being constructed in the Wadi Yabis area, while the necessary technical studies are being prepared for the establishment of a marketing centre in South Shuna.

During the period of the five-year plan (1976-80), certain basic organizational measures were taken in order to promote agricultural development. However, the agricultural sector still faced the constant demand for food.

THE AGRICULTURAL DEVELOPMENT PLAN (1981-85) AND FOOD SECURITY

Stage VI (1981-85) is designed to meet the local need to provide food security for the population of Jordan through the economic and social development plan (1981-85). This plan, which deals with national food security, is discussed below.

Agricultural Development and Food Security

Table 6.4: Merchandise of Foodstuffs, 1979 (tons)

Category	Production	Export	Import	Merchandise	Per capital share (kg)
Cereals	16,521	18,468	522,151	520,204	240
Vegetables	353,290	180,745	243,498	31,687	179
Fruit	68,934	180,745	143,498	11,687	15
Oils and fats	734	1,834	14,487	13,387	15
Sugar	-	555	97,301	96,746	45
Red meat	11,886	785	19,300	30,401	14
Poultry meat	31,700	-	1,180	30,570	15.2
Fish	36	24	3,700	1,721	1.7
Eggs (no.)	287,335,000	90,000,000	338,000	27,867,600	132
Dairy products	72,893	3,898	16,868	85,863	40

The concept of food security goes back to the early 1960s when the international community was faced with famines ravaging entire continents, not to mention malnutrition affecting millions of human beings. Responding to the conscience of their peoples, world governments took action and began to work together to solve the problem through a World Food Seminar. This was followed by seminars and regional and national conferences which discussed methods of solving the food crisis and achieving a state of food security. Food security has become one of the most attractive slogans put forward by the national development plans in Third World countries.

Food security can be defined as the situation which enables any government to provide and secure the food requirements of its citizens at all times and in all areas, particularly in the difficult circumstances resulting from a shortage in production owing to unexpected causes such as drought, natural disaster or a politico-economic boycott and the inability to import from the country of origin.

Agricultural Development and Food Security

Food security has taken on three dimensions. The first is the international dimension represented by the care of the international community, FAO and the World Food Program (WFP) for world food security, which showed the need for the so-called early warning for food security and the existence of a strategic international stock of food. The second dimension is the regional one, where each group from a certain region or area tries to study and define the problem of food within its countries, especially those countries forming one geographical region with mutual interests (such as the governments of the Arab countries). The third dimension is the national one, at which some countries have started to work towards securing food stocks (particularly of grain) and achieving national food security. This third dimension is the one that is dealt with in Jordan's development plan (1981-85).

The agricultural development plan (1981-85) is committed to a development strategy which achieves a balance between the agricultural sector and other sectors, and ensures the minimum requirements of food security. This strategy includes the following elements:

1. Trying to develop agriculture within the framework of integrated rural development; and the creation of sources of additional income for agricultural workers and small-holders.
2. Increasing participation in the development of the agricultural sector through the establishment of co-operatives or organizing workers via popular organizations.
3. Intensification of efforts in the field of irrigated and unirrigated agricultural land and raising its productivity by means of introducing modern techniques and overcoming the problems of fragmentation of holdings.
4. Attempts to integrate animal and plant production; and paying more attention to animal wealth.
5. Turning production towards commodities where Jordan enjoys relative advantages, and at the same time keeping to the minimum of national and Arab food security.

6. Creating a strategic stock of basic foodstuffs, and the completion of the infrastructure.

Former agricultural development plans did not aim directly at achieving food security. However, the concept of national food security is a recurrent theme in the development plan (1981-85): organizational measures in the plan include a special item to provide for an Arab food security plan through co-operation with the concerned organizations and institutions. These organizational measures are:

1. Establishing a directorate, reporting directly to the Minster of Agriculture, to manage the development of the Zarqa catchment area.
2. Intensifying efforts in the field of applied agricultural research, publication of the findings of such research, support of extension services, preparation of bulletins for guidance in agricultural development, and the formation of a committee for agricultural research with representatives from the agencies concerned.
3. Setting up three joint boards for grain, livestock, and fruit and vegetables. These boards will emanate from the Higher Agricultural Council and are to be responsible for formulating and following up the implementation of policies relating to the production, marketing, and consumption of these commodities.
4. Forming a permanent commission for agricultural credit to be entrusted with the task of reviewing and co-ordinating agricultural credit policies, developing lending criteria, assessing financial needs and securing the requisite funds.
5. Encouraging the establishment of mixed companies and co-operative societies specializing in plant and animal production to provide agricultural inputs, fruit tree seedlings and vegetable transplants, and marketing services. Supporting semi-governmental organizations such as the Co-operative Organization and the Jordan Valley Farmers' Association to enable them to provide agricultural inputs, in competition with the private sector.

6. Expanding the method of contract farming with individual farmers or groups of farmers, to produce agricultural products which are in demand; and developing this system to include the provision of agricultural inputs, support services, means of transportation and other facilities that will encourage farmers to enter contract farming.
7. Adopting marketing policies which will ensure the maintenance of existing markets and the identification of new markets for agricultural exports.
8. Formulating integrated programmes to deal with violations of state lands, and to decide upon a method of exploitation of marginal lands within environmental and climatic limitations.
9. Enacting the necessary legislation and taking the decisions required to deal with the problem of land fragmentation by consolidating ownership into holdings of a suitable size.
10. Carrying out a comprehensive survey of agricultural land in order to demarcate the different ecological zones, and to determine the crops most suited to these zones.
11. Expanding the planting of fruit trees in the Highlands through the provision of subsidies to farmers, so as to encourage them to increase and continue production.
12. Reviewing legislation that defines the responsibilities of government agencies dealing with agriculture in order to attain the highest possible level of efficiency in performance, co-ordination and integration.
13. Taking the necessary steps towards a unified Arab plan for agricultural integration and Arab food security, in co-operation with the Arab organizations and institutions concerned.
14. Amending the Agricultural Credit Corporation Law to enable the corporation to participate in the equity capital of companies established to initiate and manage agricultural projects and agricultural inputs.
15. Augmenting the resources of the Agricultural Credit Corporation to meet the necessary

financial requirements of agricultural development.

The agricultural development plan includes both numerical and general objectives. The numerical objectives are the following:

1. To increase agricultural income from JD 60 mn in 1980 to JD 86 mn in 1985 at 1980 prices, i.e. an increase of 43% at an annual rate of 7.5% by increasing average annual production of the main agricultural commodities as shown in Table 6.5.

Table 6.5: Average Production (thousand tons)

	1976-80	1981-85	% change
Field crops	109	142	30
Vegetables, melon & watermelon	376	600	60
Olives	24	32	33
Grapes	26	40	54
Citrus	30	50	67
Other fruit	20	25	25
Dairy products	39	45	15
Meat	7	15	114
Poultry	25	36	44
Eggs (mn)	280	450	61

2. To carry out afforestation of 300,000 du of state forestry land, giving priority to lands within the main catchment areas and to lands most subjected to soil erosion.
3. To plant 245,000 du with fruit trees, giving priority to sloping lands, and lands within the main catchment areas having a slope of more than 9%.
4. To limit the production of the main field crops (wheat, barley, lentils) to areas most suitable for them, and to improve yields to achieve a 30% increase in average production during the period of the plan.
5. To provide loans of JD 48 mn through the Agricultural Credit Corporation to finance the following categories of projects:

Agricultural Development and Food Security

(a) Land reclamation and development in rainfed areas, especially in the Zarqa catchment area and the Highlands.
(b) Establishment of irrigation projects, installation of modern irrigation systems, and drilling and equipping of artesian wells.
(c) Establishment of livestock development projects, including cattle and sheep farms.
(d) Mechanization of agriculture and development of food processing projects.
(e) Construction of farm buildings, and establishment of nurseries for fruit tree seedlings and vegetable transplants as well as extending seasonal loans to the Farmers' Association to enable it to supply its members with the necessary inputs.

The general objectives are the following:

1. To minimize the deficit in the agricultural balance of trade.
2. To conserve agricultural resources, i.e. soil, water and natural vegetation, and to develop their use in accordance with the ecological conditions of each agricultural area; and to prepare the corresponding land use maps.
3. To expand the production of broiler meat and eggs to meet local demand and increase exports; and to establish cattle and sheep farms.
4. To organize, develop and protect the rangeland in order to increase its bearing capacity and increase the production of meat.
5. To raise productivity in the agricultural sector and enhance the introduction of farm mechanization.
6. To increase the storage capacity for agricultural products to regulate consumption and marketing operations.
7. To strengthen collective and co-operative programmes in the sector, especially in the fields of production and marketing.
8. To integrate planning for agricultural development through comprehensive development planning at the regional level.

9. To initiate participation by the Agricultural Credit Corporation in the equity capital of companies formed to establish and manage agricultural enterprises, including those dealing with agricultural inputs.
10. To support joint Arab action in the field of integrated agricultural production aimed at achieving Arab food security.

The plan has come up against various obstacles, however. These are listed below:

1. Dependence of 90% of agricultural land on rainfall, leading to yearly fluctuations in production.
2. Lack of a scientific and economic basis for the current patterns of agricultural land use, management and conservation.
3. Land fragmentation and dispersion of holdings, especially in rainfed areas. This hinders the introduction of modern agricultural practices and discourages investment in rainfed areas.
4. Improper utilization of agricultural resources, namely soil, water and natural vegetation, and the non-enforcement of laws regulating their use.
5. Low efficiency in the use of the scarce water resources available for irrigation.
6. Low production levels in respect of quality and quantity, relative to those that could be attained by the proper utilization of available agricultural resources.
7. Absence of a suitable marketing policy to encourage and direct agricultural production, and a lack of effective means of disseminating market information to farmers.
8. Weakness of government agencies in the indentification, planning and implementation of projects in the agricultural sectors.
9. Low standard of agricultural support services, such as research, extension and plant protection, leading to the aggravation of agricultural problems and the improper use of agricultural resources and inputs.
10. Lack of co-ordination among agencies serving the agricultural sector, as well as conflicts and duplication in their functions.

Agricultural Development and Food Security

11. Increased shortage of trained technical staff and manpower in the agricultural sector.
12. Absence of an integrated and co-ordinated Arab agricultural policy, together with the continuation of trade barriers between Arab countries, leading to a general failure, in these countries, to utilize their agricultural resources for achieving maximum production levels, considering their different agro-ecological conditions.

Despite limited natural resources such as land and water in Jordan, the agricultural upswing there has absorbed modern techniques, particularly in irrigated agriculture, vegetable production, livestock meat and eggs. If productive capacity for a number of agricultural commodities has reached its maximum limits, there is still room for increasing production via vertical and horizontal expansion.

Food security has been among the priorities of agricultural development plans. To achieve a minimum of national food security, the government has adopted an agricultural developmental policy involving the execution of: (a) agricultural projects; and (b) a national strategic stock of basic foodstuffs such as wheat, rice and sugar, and increased storage capacity to help ensure this stock by building stores and silos.

Projects Provided for in the Agricultural Development Plan
The plan envisages a wide range of projects, which are discussed below.

Annual Afforestation. This project aims to plant 162,000 du with forests during the plan period: 18,000 du in 1981 and 36,000 du/year from 1982 to 1985. The cost of the project is estimated at JD 6.8 mn.

The National Afforestation Programme. This project aims to involve the private- and public-sector institutions in planting 50,000 du with forests, through allocating plots to these institutions for afforestation. The institutions will be required to plant the allocated areas with forest trees and maintain them, in return for using them as entertainment spots. Participating institutions will have the right to use these areas as long as they maintain them, but will not be granted ownership rights. The implementation of this project will be governed by a special by-law. The Ministry of Agriculture will provide the required forest tree seedlings free of charge.

Development of Forest Tree Nurseries. This project aims to increase the number of forest tree nurseries and raise the productive capacity of the existing ones, with the objective of producing 6 mn forest tree seedlings annually. Of these seedlings, 4.8 mn will be used in afforestation projects and the rest by individuals and public- and private-sector institutions. The cost of this project is estimated at JD 1.3 mn.

Development of the Zarqa River Catchment Area. The project aims to conserve soil and water in the Zarqa River catchment area and cultivate the land in accordance with its agricultural capabilities, in order to prevent soil erosion, minimize sedimentation in the King Talal Dam, and increase agricultural production. The project, which is to be implemented within seven years according to the study prepared by the German Agency for Technical Assistance (GTZ), was to lead to conserving and developing 830,000 du in the lower Zarqa catchment area through the following measures:

1. Afforestation of 225,000 du, of which 90,000 du are government property and 135,000 du are privately owned.
2. Subsidies to farmers to enable them to construct stone wall terraces and contours, and plant fruit trees over 170,000 du of sloping land.
3. Development of about 140,000 du of rangelands situated in the lower part of the catchment area and having an average annual rainfall of less than 250 mm. This will be achieved by converting the area currently under grain crops into improved grazing areas, by introducing shrub cultivation and by applying a controlled grazing system to the remaining area.

The following project components will be implemented during the plan period:
(a) planting 60,000 du with forest trees;

(b) patching 31,000 du of the already existing forests;
(c) managing 140,000 du of rangeland;
(d) planting fruit trees in 120,000 du;
(e) constructing 1,000 km of agricultural roads.

The total cost of this project is estimated at JD 30 mn.

Soil Conservation and Fruit Tree Planting. This project aims to plant fruit trees over 125,000 du of rainfed area (with an average annual rainfall of more than 250 mm and a slope of 9-25%) which is currently either not being used or under uneconomical crop cultivation. This will be done by extending credit facilities, technical and supporting services to farmers to enable them to protect their land from soil erosion, maintain soil humidity and plant it with suitable fruit trees.

The Ministry of Agriculture will supervise the implementation of the project and provide assistance to farmers with the co-operation of the WFP.

The project will include construction of agricultural roads, soil conservation measures, digging of water cisterns, farm building, construction of stone wall terraces, wired fences and planting fruit trees.

The cost of the project is estimated at JD 12.6 mn, of which JD 6.5 mn will be contributed by the WFP; the remainder will be financed from the general budget.

Production of Fruit Tree Seedlings. The project is designed to expand the production of fruit tree seedlings to meet the needs of the five-year-plan projects, which aim to plant 245,000 du with fruit trees. This will be accomplished through establishing new nurseries and expanding seedling production in the existing nurseries of the Ministry of Agriculture. The project cost is estimated at JD 5,370,000.

Development of Grain Production. This project aims to increase yields of field crops to offset the anticipated shortage resulting from the reduction of the area allocated for field crops in favour of other crops. The project is to be implemented by the Ministry of Agriculture in co-operation with the Arab Center for the Study of Arid Zones and Dry

Lands (ACSAD), and the International Center for Agricultural Research in the Dry Areas (ICARDA), through the introduction of modern production techniques and methods of planting field crops, and by carrying out experiments to develop suitable varieties to be propagated through the seed production stations of the Ministry of Agriculture and on private farms as a step towards large-scale production of these varieties.

The project will be supported by 24 centres for farm machinery services, which will provide mechanized services and modern production techniques to farmers.

The cost of the project is estimated at JD 500,000, of which JD 350,000 will come from ACSAD, JD 54,000 from ICARDA and the remainder from the general budget.

Production of Vegetable Transplants. The project aims to provide disease-free transplants, of suitable varieties, through producing these in separate nurseries under strict technical supervision. This is particularly important for tomato transplants, which need to be protected, at an early stage of growth, against virus diseases.

Three production units will be established, two of which will be set up in the Jordan Valley in 1981-82 and 1984-85, each with an annual production capacity of 30 mn transplants. A third unit will be established in the South Ghor in 1982, with an annual production capacity of 15 mn transplants. The cost of the project is estimated at JD 2.1 mn, of which JD 1.4 mn will be in the form of assistance from the European Economic Community (EEC) and the remainder from the general budget.

Production of Potato Seeds. The project aims to produce potato seeds locally, so as to enable potato planting in autumn. (This is currently ruled out by the impossibility of procuring potato seeds from abroad.) The project, which will be carried out through co-operation between the Jordanian and Dutch governments, will be located at the Wadi Dhuleil and Shaubak research stations. The project involves carrying out experiments to determine the varieties most suited to climatic conditions in Jordan, and the provision of selected potato seeds in sufficient quantities. The cost of the project is estimated at JD 725,000.

Collective Agricultural Pest Control in the Jordan

Valley. This project aims to establish seven mechanized units for agricultural pest and plant disease control, five in the North Ghor and two in the South Ghor.

The Ministry of Agriculture will extend this service to farmers at cost price. The cost of the necessary facilities and equipment is estimated at JD 1.7 mn.

Development of Meat Production. This project aims to produce about 2,000 t/year of red meat, through fattening about 300,000 lambs annually, starting from 1983, in centres distributed throughout various regions of Jordan. Half of the requirements of lambs will be purchased locally and the remainder will be imported.

The project will be implemented by a public shareholding company, with 51% of the shares subscribed by the public sector and 49% by the private sector. The cost of the project is estimated at JD 8.6 mn.

Establishment of a Grand Parent Stock Poultry Farm. The project, which aims to supply Jordan and the neighbouring Arab countries with their requirements of parent stock, eggs for hatching and chicks, is expected to produce 496,000 parent stock, 17.6 mn eggs for hatching and 6 mn chicks annually. It will be established on an area of 16,000 du in the al-Azraq area. The project is to be implemented by the Arab Livestock Company, with the Jordanian Government contributing the land, providing the required services at cost price and subscribing JD 0.5 mn of the capital. The company will itself bear the remaining cost and expenses. The cost of the project is estimated at JD 6.5 mn.

Production of Veterinary Serum and Vaccines. The project aims to produce veterinary serum and vaccines to meet the entire local requirements and partly cover the needs of the neighbouring Arab countries. It is designed to produce around 64 mn doses of different kinds of vaccine annually. The cost of the project is estimated at JD 350,000.

Improving Methods of Production and Marketing of Poultry Products. The project aims to regulate the production of broilers and eggs to meet domestic consumption and export requirements. This is to be accomplished through regulating production, procurement and marketing of broilers and eggs. This involves the establishment, in the main consumption centres (Amman, Dhuleil, Irbid, Karak), of slaughterhouses for slaughtering, packing and quick-freezing of broiler meat, together with the processing of slaughterhouse by-products. It will also involve the establishment of centres for the assembly, sorting and packing of eggs in the main towns, and the provision of means of transporting broilers to slaughterhouses, as well as of freezing tunnels and any other installations or works required to implement the project.

The project will be implemented through the establishment of a public shareholding company with subscriptions from both the private and public sectors. The cost of the project is estimated at JD 4 mn.

Establishment of a National Centre for Agricultural Research. The project aims to establish a National Centre to be staffed with specialists capable of undertaking agricultural research. The centre will also be responsible for disseminating the results of its research and co-operating with the agencies concerned in the publication and application for research results.

The project includes the establishment of a main office and three specialized research stations: one for irrigated agriculture, one for rainfed agriculture, and the third for rangelands and livestock.

Agricultural Research Unit for the Ghor. The project aims to establish a specialized unit for agricultural research and extension in the Ghor. The centre will undertake specialized research oriented towards increased agricultural production. It will also publish the results of its research and provide guidance to farmers to assist them in increasing and improving production. The cost of the project is estimated at JD 2.9 mn.

Agricultural Marketing Centres. This project aims to establish three agricultural marketing centres:

1. Wadi Yabis agricultural marketing centre. Construction started in 1980. The centre is to have two lines for the grading of tomatoes with a total capacity of 16 t/hour, and two other lines for grading other vegetables with a capacity of 16 t/hour.

2. <u>South Shuna agricultural marketing centre</u>. The tender documents for building this centre were floated in 1980. The centre will have a grading and packing unit consisting of one line for the grading of tomatoes with a capacity of 10 t/hour, and two lines for grading other vegetables, each with a capacity of 5 t/hour.
3. <u>Ghor al-Safi agricultural marketing centre</u>. The project aims to construct the necessary facilities over an area of 20,000 sq. m. These will consist of a unit for grading and packing, auction halls and offices for management. The grading unit consists of two lines for tomato grading with a total capacity of 15 t/hour, and one line with a capacity of 5 t/hour for grading other vegetables.

The cost of constructing these centres is estimated at JD 3.1 mn, to be financed from the general budget and loans from the German Kredit Instault Bank (KFW) and the British government.

<u>Two Tomato Paste Factories in the Jordan Valley and the South Ghor</u>. This project aims to produce tomato paste from the tomato production of the Jordan Valley and the South Ghor. The project will involve establishing two factories, one in the agricultural marketing centre in al-Arda with a capacity of 30 t/hour and the other in the South Ghor with a capacity of 10 t/hour. The cost of the project is estimated at JD 1.3 mn.

<u>Refrigerated Warehouses</u>. The Ministry of Supply will build a refrigerated warehouse with a capacity of 6,000 t to preserve vegetables, fruit and eggs for an extended period. The cost of the project is estimated at JD 2.3 mn.

<u>Feed Concentrate Plant</u>. The Ministry of Supply will establish a feed concentrate plant to provide the necessary concentrates to the animal feed industry. The plant will have an annual capacity of 30,000 t. This project will be implemented through a partnership arrangement between the public sector, the Jordan Co-operative Organization and the private sector, in the form of a mixed company. The cost of the project is estimated at JD 2 mn.

<u>Feed Plant</u>. The Ministry of Supply, with the

co-operation of the Jordan Co-operative Organization, will establish a feed plant to provide good quality animal feed in sufficient quantity. The cost of the project is estimated at JD 3.5 mn.

Poultry Slaughterhouse. The Ministry of Supply will establish a modern poultry slaughterhouse with a capacity of 30 t/day. It will be provided with automatic equipment for most of the operations, including packing, chilling and quick-freezing, to store surplus production for domestic use in some seasons or for export. The cost of the project is estimated at JD 2 mn.

Water and Irrigation Sector. This sector provides for implementation of the following projects at a total cost of JD 282 mn:

1. constructing the Wadi al-Arab Dam;
2. raising the height of the King Talal Dam;
3. raising the height of the Kafrein Dam;
4. constructing small dams in the desert area;
5. execution of the second phase of the Jordan Valley irrigation project;
6. irrigation of the South Ghor;
7. irrigation of Wadi al-Araba;
8. sub-surface drainage;
9. underground water resources in the Jordan Valley.

Private Sector Investments. In addition to its participation in the implementation and financing of the plan projects outlined above, the private sector will invest in various other agricultural projects. Investments will be financed from personal savings and from loans that farmers can obtain from the Agricultural Credit Corporation, the Co-operative Organization and other sources. Private sector investment is estimated at JD 133.7 mn.

The National Strategic Stock of Grain

A short-term minimum of national food security can be achieved through providing a strategic grain stock. A national strategic grain stock may be defined as a definite quantity of grain that is used as a national reserve inside Jordan, and administered by the Ministry of Supply, to ensure the needs of Jordan against several risks, such as a sharp decline in local or world production resulting from natural disasters or a political boycott by grain-exporting countries.

The Ministry of Supply is establishing and expanding silos. The storage capacity for wheat and flour used to be 5,000 t, sufficient to meet the needs of Jordan for ten days; it has now risen to 315,000 t, sufficient to meet these needs for a period of one year.

The Ministry of Supply's present plan includes a scheme to expand grain silos and increase grain storage capacity, according to the policy of providing a reserve stock of wheat of about 500,000 t, in addition to 250,000 t of maize for fodder manufacture. It has been decided to increase the storage capacity of the Aqaba silos by 100,000 t and of those of Amman by 80,000 t. New silos have been built in Irbid Governorate with a capacity of 50,000 t. The cost of this project is estimated at JD 15.5 mn. On the level of Arab food security, studies on the 'strategic food stock' of the Arab food security programme have come to the conclusion that a stock sufficient for human consumption of wheat and maize in all Arab countries, over a three months' period, is sufficient to face all risks. The study has also concluded that a national location of this project, and its administration by an Arab corporation separate from national policies, is the better alternative for the location of the proposed stock.

Thus, to achieve a minimum national food security, horizontal agricultural development schemes have to be carried out for a long-term policy. Moreover, the provision of a strategic national stock and the execution of horizontal agricultural projects will bring about a minimum short-term food security.

Jordan's emphasis on agricultural development dates back to the 1960s. But its imported food needs have been growing, placing it at the minimum limits of self-sufficiency, and consequently of its food security. The 1981-85 plan has made the slogan of food security a strategy for agricultural development, responding thereby to the joint Arab effort to achieve Arab food security within the framework of Arab agricultural integration. Jordan has committed itself to international and Arab resolutions concerning participation in the food security programme. At the national level, Jordan

Agricultural Development and Food Security

has tried to insure a minimum of both short- and long-term food security. Developmental agricultural schemes, aiming at horizontal expansion of agriculture, will deal with the long-term food security problem, while agricultural projects concerned with vertical expansion and strategic grain stocks will help to achieve the required short-term levels of food security.

RECOMMENDATIONS

By analysing the present agricultural situation, and following up agricultural development and its future trends, together with the aspirations of the current agricultural development scheme, it is possible to put forward the following recommendations:

1. Give strategic significance to the agricultural sector and endow it with high priority among other economic production sectors, through increasing the rate of investments allocated to it within the economic and social development plan in the future.
2. Define food security projects in the agricultural plan by adopting definite standards and giving them special priority in execution in relation to other projects.
3. Stress the ability of development strategy related to food security in the current agricultural development scheme, particularly in providing a strategic stock of foodstuffs and meeting its requirements in infrastucture.
4. Consider the achievement of national food security within the present development plan as a merely tentative objective; national food security must be seen as a part of Arab food security. The real food security of Jordan lies in Arab food security at large.
5. Continue co-operation with international organizations, the WFP and FAO, to accumulate a strategic stock to help towards food security and to execute productive agricultural products within the framework and with the help of the WFP.

Agricultural Development and Food Security

6. Adopt a national agricultural policy, co-ordinated with the Arab strategy of agricultural development, and stress the national dimension of the economy in order to achieve Arab agricultural and economic integration.
7. Continue support for Arab food security projects. Propose that the Council of the Arab Agricultural Development Organization consider the project of development of non-irrigated agriculture in Jordan as one of the projected Arab food security schemes, owing to the importance of this project in the field of grain production and in raising the standard of living of the farmers in the poor non-irrigated areas.
8. Set up a national committee for national food security as a specialized standing committee of the Agricultural Council. This committee should be entrusted, among other things, with co-ordination with international and Arab organizations in the field of food security, and with participation in the preparation of the specific plans and programmes that deal with national food security in Jordan.

BIBLIOGRAPHY

Arab Agricultural Development Organization. <u>The Future of Food Economy in the Arab Countries (1975-2000)</u> (Khartoum, 1979), part iv: Statistical Data

Arabeyyat, Suliman, 'Food Security in the Agricultural Development Plans in Jordan', working paper submitted to the Seminar on Planning for Food Security in Jordan (Amman, 1981)

Jordan, Department of General Statistics. <u>Agricultural Census</u> (Amman, 1980)
____ <u>Statistical Agricultural Sample</u> (Amman, 1980)

Jordan, National Planning Council. <u>Five Year Development Plan 1976-1980</u> (Amman, 1976)
____ <u>Five Year Plan for Economic and Social Development 1981-1985</u> (Amman, 1981)

al-Khalidi, Ghanem. <u>Food Crisis and Food Security in the Arab World</u>, part I (Arab Economic Unity Council, Amman, 1980)

al-Qassim, Subhi. <u>Analytic Outlook into the Food Problems in Arab Countries</u> (Shoman Foundation, Amman, 1981)

Sunna'a, Sami <u>et al</u>. 'Strategical Aims of Agricultural Development', working paper submitted to the Agricultural Sector Symposium (Amman, 1980)

Swaiti, Rasmy <u>et al</u>. 'Trends of Production and Consumption of Agricultural Products', working paper submitted to the Agricultural Sector Symposium (Amman, 1980)

Chapter Seven

LABOUR EMIGRATION POLICIES AND ECONOMIC DEVELOPMENT IN JORDAN: FROM UNEMPLOYMENT TO LABOUR SHORTAGE

Ian J. Seccombe

The question of whether, and to what extent, a country benefits from labour emigration is critically dependent on how that migration is organized and by whom. However, labour emigration policy has been largely neglected in the migration literature (Seccombe et al., 1984). This neglect stems from the assumption that, since the international labour market is effectively controlled by the labour-importing states, the question of policy should be approached from the perspective of the immigration countries. However, while the scale of labour emigration may be demand-determined, it is apparent that potential labour-supply countries are faced with an immediate policy decision; that decision is not whether to participate in the international labour market, but the extent of government intervention in that participation. Although some writers assert that labour emigration policies are determined in the main by ad hoc and short-term considerations (Höpfner and Huber, 1978), they are nevertheless influenced by, and in the long term may be an influence on, the broader development strategy adopted by the government.
     Emigration for employment has been an important, and increasingly a dominant, feature of the Jordanian economy since the early 1950s. Successive Jordanian administrations have adopted a consistently laissez-faire approach towards labour emigration, despite recent evidence that the effects of labour outflow on social and economic development have, at best, been equivocal. The present chapter will briefly outline the evolution of Jordanian participation in the international labour market and assess the formulation of, and constraints on, the Jordanian government's response towards emigration.

THE GROWTH IN TEMPORARY LABOUR EMIGRATION

Although Transjordanian labour had been involved in seasonal migration to Palestine during the British mandate period (1921-46), the flood of refugees into the independent and enlarged Kingdom of Jordan after the 1948 Palestine war generated a new scale and pattern of migration (Seccombe, 1983). High rates of unemployment (conservatively estimated at 17% nationally in 1955 by the International Bank for Reconstruction and Development (IBRD)) and under-employment, coupled with low levels of capital investment, encouraged a steady labour outflow. Much of that emigration was from the West Bank sub-districts, where overtly political motives joined the economic imperative for emigration. From the late 1950s increasing numbers of Jordanians were finding employment in the expanding oil economies of the Arab Gulf. Kuwait and Saudi Arabia accounted for more than 72% of the almost 63,000 Jordanians who were enumerated as being resident abroad in the November 1961 census of Jordan. Of those abroad some 35,000 were economically active. A comparison of their occupational characteristics with those of the domestic labour force demonstrates the significant skill selectivity of labour outflows: less than 45% of migrant workers were engaged in unskilled occupations.

Labour outflows continued to rise steadily throughout the 1960s, with annual net departures averaging 26,000 in the three years prior to 1967. The demographic upheavals and political uncertainty of the 1967-71 period, beginning with the Israeli occupation of the West Bank and culminating in the conflict with the Palestinian fedayeen, served to increase out-migration. In 1972 unemployment in Jordan still stood at over 14% nationally (World Bank, 1976), while the number of Jordanians working abroad had increased to over 80,000 with 41,000 in Kuwait alone.

It is apparent then that Jordan's role as a major regional labour supplier was already well established before the transformation in the scale of labour demand provoked by the rapid increase in financial assets of the major oil-producing states after 1973-74. In addition, receipts of workers' remittances were, in the mid-1960s, already in excess of income from domestic exports (over the period 1960-66 workers' remittances and domestic exports were JD 52.8 mn and JD 41.8 mn respectively).

With this tradition of emigration for employment and a relatively skilled labour force, Jordan was well placed to meet the growing regional demand for manpower which followed the 1973-74 oil price increases. While there is little doubt that the rate of emigration for employment accelerated rapidly during the mid-1970s, there is almost no information with which to establish the scale and direction of labour outflows (Birks and Sinclair, 1978). The array of official and semi-official estimates published since 1973 are ill-defined and often contradictory. Moreover, the failure of the labour-receiving states to distinguish between Jordanian and Palestinian sub-populations in their official statistics, and the confusion between de jure and de facto Jordanian citizenship, frustrates attempts to establish the scale of East Bank emigration on the basis of external data sources. The problem of quantifying labour flows has been reviewed in detail elsewhere (Birks and Sinclair, 1978; Kirwan, 1981; Seccombe 1983) and need not be elaborated here. As a benchmark, we will accept here the figure of 139,000 East Bank migrant workers abroad in 1975 provided by the World Bank. (Serageldin et al., 1983).

Despite the confusion over the number of migrants working abroad, the available data confirm the acceleration in out-migration during the mid-1970s. Between 1973 and 1975 the number of trade proficiency certificates issued by the Ministry of Labour (MOL) increased by 186%, rising to over 4,900 at its peak in 1977. In that year the Ministry of Labour and Social Affairs in Kuwait issued more than 4,700 new work permits to Jordanian workers. By 1979 the number of permits issued by the MOL in Amman to Jordanians seeking employment in Saudi Arabia had increased to over 7,300. In the late 1970s, then, annual net labour outflows were almost certainly in excess of 10,000 per annum. To place this in context, a net outflow of 50,000 workers during the period of the five-year development plan (1976-80) represents a loss of more than 35% of the expected growth in domestic labour supply. (More recent trends in labour outflows will be considered below.

EMIGRATION AND THE DOMESTIC LABOUR MARKET

While Jordan was experiencing high rates of labour emigration, domestic manpower demand was also increasing dramatically. Part of that increase was the result of the expenditure of workers' remittances, particularly in the urban residential construction sector, which absorbed a high proportion of remittance earnings (Findlay, 1984; Saket, 1983). In addition, domestic labour demand also received a substantial boost as a result of the increased aid and budgetary support pledged to Jordan following the Arab Summit meetings at Rabat in 1974 and Baghdad in 1978.

Evidence of the growth in domestic labour demand comes, for example, from the 64% increase in local job vacancies advertised in the Jordanian press over the 1974-76 period (MPS, 1977). In addition, crude unemployment data from the Multi-Purpose Household Survey series demonstrate a fall in unemployment to less than 2% in 1976. Substantial wage-rate inflation accompanied the growing labour shortfall; between 1973 and 1976 average daily earnings of males (non-agricultural sector) rose by more than 153% increasing by 24% in 1976 alone. These increases were particularly high in financial services, utilities and the construction sector. Wage inflation and skill shortages were accompanied by high rates of labour force turnover (al-Fanik, 1978) and rising recruitment costs (Alawin, 1978). On the East Ghor Canal Project it was estimated that shortages of skilled operatives and maintenance mechanics meant that heavy-duty construction equipment was inoperative for up to 70% of the working day (Salt and Keely, 1976). Even the dryland agricultural sector reported shortages of unskilled labour as a result of labour emigration (USAID, 1980).

As a result of these developments, the authors of the five-year development plan 1976-80 were faced with a completely different situation to that which had prevailed at the outset of the three-year development plan 1973-75. While the latter had stressed the need to reduce unemployment and under-employment, the National Planning Council (NPC) forecast, in 1976, shortages of manpower supply on demand of 12% at the sub-professional/technical level and 78% at the skilled/semi-skilled manual level. The NPC report concluded that labour shortages were: 'bound to exercise a negative effect on the implementation and management of development projects in general and those of the five-year plan (1976-1980) in particular...' (NPC, 1976).

LABOUR EMIGRATION AND GOVERNMENT POLICY

Prior to the mid-1970s emigration for employment from Jordan can be characterized as a response to a succession of political and economic crises. As such, increases in the rate of labour outflows were regarded by successive Jordanian administrations as an expedient means of reducing the labour surpluses which seemed an inevitable accompaniment to those crises. With limited opportunities for employment expansion in the domestic labour market, Jordan was eager to encourage labour emigration, as was made clear in the Jordan Development Board's seven-year programme for economic development (1964-70). What was initially an individual response to political and economic crises had, by the early 1970s, become an accepted tenet of economic policy. Thus the three-year development plan (1973-75) calls for greater investment in vocational education in order that Jordan might benefit from increased workers' remittances. The government's commitment to emigration is reflected in the increasing number of Jordanians abroad on secondment. The number of secondments from the Ministry of Education to the oil-rich Arab states grew from 271 in 1970 to 810 in 1974 (by 1983 the number of secondments exceeded 2,330).

Any illusions which the Jordanian government may have had regarding the benefits of an unrestricted emigration policy had unquestionably paled by the mid-1970s, with the growing problems of skill scarcity, wage inflation and the apparent incongruity of large inflows of non-Jordanian 'replacement' labour (see below). A more stoical view of labour emigration was reflected in the speech given by Crown Prince Hassan bin Talal to the International Labour Conference at Geneva in June 1977. In that address the Crown Prince called for the creation of an 'International Labour Compensatory Facility' to compensate Jordan (and other labour-exporters) for the negative effects of large-scale labour outflows (ILO, 1977). While this view has been reiterated by other Jordanian officials on a number of occasions (for example, Anani and Jaber, 1980), the government has consistently maintained its commitment to a laissez-faire emigration policy.

This response has been conditioned by several interrelated factors which are worth enumerating here:

Labour Emigration and Economic Development

1. First, one should mention the significance of workers' remittances to the Jordanian economy. The volume of <u>recorded</u> remittances increased from JD 7.4 mn in 1972 to over JD 330 mn in 1983, a level substantially higher than domestic exports and accounting for between 25 and 33% of both imports and GNP. This growth reflects the financial and political stability which has prevailed in Jordan as well as the banking sector's relative success in attracting remittances (see Wilson, 1984). In several years, remittances have been higher than external budgetary support and aid, and are increasingly important as more signatories of the Baghdad Agreement renege on aid payments as a result of the continuing Iraq-Iran war and the Gulf recession. A dramatic fall in Jordan's remittance receipts could transform the positive balance of invisable earnings leading to a substantial balance of payments deficit and debt servicing problems.

2. Second, a decision by the Jordanian government to restrict labour outflows could have had a negative impact on the level of external budgetary support which Jordan receives from the labour-importing, oil-rich states. Although this aid is provided for a host of reasons, a close relationship between foreign aid receipts and the supply of labour has been identified on several occasions in official reports (see Owen, 1983). In similar vein, the five-year development plan (1981-85) notes that:

> Jordan is inextricably linked with the other Arab countries. Relations have been cemented on the one hand by the positive role played by the trained Jordanian labour force in the Arab oil-producing states, and on the other hand by the financial assistance extended by the Arab countries to strengthen Jordan's steadfastness.

3. Although selected sectors of the Jordanian economy and certain occupations in the Jordanian labour market have experienced manpower shortages as a result (in part) of out-migration, it is apparent that domestic labour market expansion <u>alone</u> could not absorb the increasing labour force, given Jordan's limited natural resources. The collapse of agricultural employment, which accounts for less than 10% of the workforce, has been a notable feature of the last ten years. Moreover, with the increasing educational attainment of women, there are likely to be a growing number of

labour market entrants. The rapid increase in output from general secondary education may lead to further pressure on the government to expand public-sector employment (already at more than 40% of the labour force) beyond the level that can either be afforded or is necessary. A fall in either external budgetary support, remittances or labour outflows would have severe implications for the level of employment in general and for the two major employers, the construction and public sectors, in particular.

4. A restrictive emigration policy would be both impracticable to police and politically naive to institute. Jordan would undoubtedly be condemned for preventing Palestinians, who comprise a substantial proportion of the East Bank population, from leaving the country.

Finally, and perhaps most importantly, such a policy would run counter to the consistent *laissez-faire* economic philosophy adopted by successive Jordanian governments over the last 30 years. This is a view strongly expressed in the final report of the *ad hoc* committee on labour emigration (1977), which states:

> No matter how adverse the labour situation may become, we must not resort to the use of police restrictions. Such measures do not conform to the private free-enterprise system to which we adhere.

Jordanian policy towards labour emigration is a direct and logical outcome of Jordan's economic and political history. The combination of the country's internal political structure, together with its economic and ultimately political dependence on neighbouring oil-rich states, effectively precludes alternative strategies. Thus, while maintaining an unrestrictive emigration policy, Jordan has sought to maximize the returns to emigration for employment at the national scale. In doing so, the government has focused on increasing the supply of technical and skilled manpower available to both the domestic and international labour markets. An increased supply of skilled manpower would ameliorate domestic skill scarcity and, through their higher earnings' potential, increase workers' remittances to Jordan. Summarizing this policy, the five-year development plan (1981-85) states clearly that: 'The base of qualified and trained manpower in the vocational and technical categories will be expanded in a manner consonant with the requirements of the development process in Jordan and with the level of growth and development of sister Arab countries.'

In the absence of restrictions on emigration, this clearly amounts to a strategy of training manpower for migration. The government's policies towards remittances have been examined elsewhere (Saket, 1983). The present chapter will briefly consider efforts to increase the supply of skilled manpower.

VOCATIONAL EDUCATION, TRAINING AND MIGRATION

The government's main efforts to increase the supply of skilled manpower have focused on the formal education system, and on vocational secondary enrolments in particular. The expansion of formal vocational education has been a major aim since the early 1970s, when a revision of education priorities was prompted by high rates of unemployment among secondary 'academic' graduates, and the 1970s saw a number of innovations designed to increase the emphasis on vocational education. These innovations have included the introduction of vocational studies into the compulsory grades (at the elementary and preparatory levels) and the establishment of comprehensive secondary schools. Although the declared aim of having 30% of secondary cycle enrolments in vocational education by 1980 has proved elusive (vocational enrolments have risen to 18% of total enrolments), there has been a considerable expansion in vocational facilities and student numbers. In 1982 vocational education received over 20% of the Ministry of Education's (MOE) capital outlay. The number of students in vocational education - including the United Nations Relief and Works Agency (UNRWA) and other authorities - has risen from 6,500 in 1973 to 20,550 in 1982, while the number of teachers has increased from 439 to over 1,000. In addition the MOE trade training centres (two-year vocational courses for preparatory school leavers), first opened in 1971, now have more than 2,000 students enrolled.

Despite the expansion of enrolments, studies of student preferences for secondary education options indicate a continued negative attitude towards vocational education (UNESCO, 1980).

Moreover, tracer studies have shown only limited correlation between vocational secondary enrolments and graduate employment (MOE, 1977), while much of the expansion in enrolments has been in commercial studies.

At the post-secondary level there has been a dramatic increase in the number of community colleges from 7 in 1973 to 44 in 1982, of which 20 are privately run. These private colleges account for more than 18,000 of the 28,200 students enrolled in 1982 (compared to total enrolments in 1973 of under 3,000). Again, however, community colleges have concentrated on commercial courses and teacher training; increased output is unlikely to diminish critical skill shortages at the skilled manual and technical levels. Although technical education is provided at the Marka and Irbid polytechnics (with plans for new polytechnics at Salt, Tafilieh and Jarash), the current intake is less than 1,000 students and the polytechnics have experienced major problems in recruiting and retaining qualified instructors.

Despite the growth in enrolments, the vocational education system is unable to respond efficiently to short-term labour market demands. Recognizing this, the government has established (in 1976) a centralized training organization, the Vocational Training Corporation (VTC), to co-ordinate and promote training activities within the labour market itself. Through a programme of apprenticeships and short-term skill up-grading courses, the VTC is designed to respond directly to employers' needs for skilled manual workers. In its short operating history the VTC has negotiated apprenticeship contracts with an increasing number of firms, with apprenticeships growing from 156 in 1977 to 1,600 in 1982.

It is evident from continuing skill scarcity (Seccombe, 1984b) that government efforts to increase the supply of skilled manpower through formal vocational education have been largely misplaced. At the same time, the VTC programme remains far too limited to meet the shortfalls of skilled manual labour. This problem will become increasingly significant if demands in the international labour market, which are increasingly biased towards skilled manpower, continue. In the short-term, Jordanian employers have responded to labour shortages by importing so-called 'replacement' labour (Birks and Sinclair, 1978). The growth and characteristics of such labour inflows are briefly reviewed here (for a detailed survey, see Seccombe, 1984b).

While the NPC recognized, in the mid-1970s, that labour inflows would be needed to supplement the domestic labour supply, they envisaged a small-scale and controlled inflow to meet specific requirements. During the mid-1970s the number of work permits issued to foreign workers remained small; significant clandestine employment was occurring. In 1975 only 803 work permits were issued while the labour force census (itself only a partial survey) enumerated almost 2,300 foreign workers. Between 1976 and 1979, however, the number of work permits issued increased by more than 450% to reach 26,415. The 1979 census records almost 89,000 non-Jordanians in the country, of whom some 65% were in active employment. Revision of residence permit requirements in June 1980, and the introduction of stiff penalties for violation of work permit regulations, led to a dramatic increase in work permit issues by more than 270% in the second half of 1980. By 1981 recorded immigrant employment had risen to 93,000. Data for 1982 and 1983, which show a decline in work permit issues to 61,280 and 58,441 respectively, reflect the Ministry of the Interior's decision to remove residence permit requirements from Egyptians working in Jordan, rather than a real fall in immigrant numbers. Remittances by non-Jordanian workers have continued to grow, from JD 46 mn in 1980 to JD 73 mn in 1983. The MOL currently estimates that 120-130,000 non-Jordanians are in active employment.

Although the majority of immigrant workers are Egyptian, and despite the priority accorded to Arab workers in the Jordanian labour law, Asians have taken an increasing share of the labour market. In 1983 Asian immigrants, more than half from the Indian subcontinent, accounted for 41% of work permit issues compared to only 35% in the previous year. In addition, there are a large number of Asian workers employed by contracting companies from their country of origin. This is particularly the case with South Korean, Chinese, Filipino and most recently Turkish construction workers (see Seccombe and Lawless, 1984). In addition to the construction sector, a number of contracts have been won by Asian firms in the services sector, particularly in industrial cleaning and hotel services. In this respect the internationalization of the Jordanian labour market reflects wider regional trends in contracting.

A survey of work permits issued in Amman during the period October 1982-January 1983 (Seccombe, 1984b) demonstrates that Asian workers accounted for the majority (69%) of skilled manual and technical employees (although large numbers of Sri Lankans and Filipinos were in the service sector). Less than 20% of Arab immigrant workers were engaged in skilled and semi-skilled occupations; the majority were employed in unskilled occupations, particularly in construction and agriculture (Seccombe, 1981).

'Replacement' migration provides only a partial explanation of labour flows into Jordan and applies primarily to the skilled and semi-skilled workers who receive wage rates similar to those of their Jordanian counterparts. An important factor in the employment of unskilled immigrants is their acceptance of poorer conditions of employment and of wage rates up to 40% lower than the Jordanian workforce. As a result of this labour inflow the total labour supply is increased and employers may choose between alternative supplies. Once established, such 'secondary' labour flows appear to bear little relationship to primary Jordanian emigration. In addition to forming a cheap, mobile and casual labour force, secondary labour immigrants perform low-status service sector tasks increasingly seen as socially demeaning by Jordanian nationals. The growing number of immigrant women (11% of total work permit issues in 1983) are employed in such occupations.

The inflow of replacement labour has helped to ameliorate the problems of skill scarcity caused by labour outflows and the shortfall in output from the vocational education and training programmes. However, such labour inflows have also led to new problems, such as a fall in employers' commitment to on-the-job training for Jordanian nationals. Concomitantly, non-Jordanian immigration has expanded beyond simple 'replacement', with large inflows of secondary manpower. There is evidence of rising unemployment among Jordanian nationals, particularly at the unskilled level, some of which may possibly be attributed to the employers' preference for cheap immigrant labour. The 1979 census recorded some 38,175 (10.4%) of the Jordanian workforce as unemployed, and between 1982 and 1983 the number of <u>registered</u> unemployed doubled from 2,886 to 5,569. While this reflects public expenditure cuts and economic recession resulting from falling aid receipts and the effects of Iraq's cut-back in imports, attention from the General Federation of Trade Unions (GFTU) and others has inevitably been focused on the immigrant workers. In response, the government has introduced legislation requiring employers to give preference to Jordanians over foreign workers and has banned the employment of foreign clerical workers.

EMIGRATION TRENDS AND POLICY IMPLICATIONS

Jordan has always given the impression that its traditional role as a regional labour supplier, and the high quality of available manpower, would continue to guarantee it a significant share of the regional labour market. This view can no longer be sustained. Available evidence indicates a significant fall in emigration for employment since the late 1970s. The numbers of Jordanians receiving work permits for employment in Saudi Arabia, Kuwait and the UAE have fallen by more than 60% since 1978. In 1983 only 3,733 Jordanians received work permits for Saudi Arabia, compared to 7,310 in 1979. Similarly, the number of trade proficiency certificates issued by the MOL to prospective emigrants has declined by more than 40%. A collapse in the rate of emigration to under 6,000 per annum is significant, given that the NPC projected a stable outflow of 8-10,000 migrant workers over the 1981-85 plan period and the MOL's prediction that labour exports would _increase_ during the 1980s.

The falling numbers of Jordanians finding employment abroad is matched by a similar decline among other Arab migrant workers. This is a reflection of changing employment policies in the labour-importing states and in particular a growing preference for Asian workers, who, in addition to cost advantages, are less likely to bring their families to the country of employment and to settle there (Birks and Sinclair, 1981). At the same time, there has been an increasing penetration of Asian companies into the regional contracting market. Few Jordanian firms are able to compete either administratively or technologically with the experienced Asian and multi-national corporations. Finally, despite the government's commitment to emigration for employment, there has been little formalization of labour movements and no attempts to market Jordanian manpower abroad. This contrasts with the aggressive marketing by private agents and public agencies in most South and East Asian countries.

While the number of Jordanians obtaining employment abroad has fallen (indeed, the MOL estimates that more than 10,000 Jordanian workers returned to the East Bank in 1983), available evidence suggests that the decline has been most pronounced among the unskilled and semi-skilled (Seccombe, 1984b). Although the absolute number of Jordanians going to Saudi Arabia has fallen since 1979, the share of professional, technical and skilled manpower in that outflow has increased from 15% in 1978 to 32% in 1982. A similar pattern emerges from a 1983 comparison of current emigrant and return migrant households (Saket, 1983). A trend towards greater skill withdrawal and falling levels of unskilled labour emigration would exacerbate the negative consequences of participation in the international labour market.

Jordan's traditional image as a regional labour supplier is on the wane, for the future Jordan is likely to supply a relatively small, but skilled, labour force to neighbouring oil-rich states while the outflow of unskilled workers continues to decline. If this is not to distort the domestic labour market further, then the export of skilled labour must be secured through a framework of bilateral or multilateral labour co-operation agreements. At the same time, Jordan may need to consider much closer regulation of unskilled labour inflows if unemployment is to be controlled, while expanding vocational training and skill upgrading courses. Furthermore, greater efforts need to be made in directing workers' remittances into productive investment and employment creation. The <u>laissez-aller</u> approach must be replaced by a regulatory policy if the role of regional labour supplier, albeit diminished, is to be accommodated with domestic development priorities.

BIBLIOGRAPHICAL REFERENCES

Alawin, A. (1978) 'The Structure and Performance of the Manufacturing Sector in Jordan and its Reflection on the Economy', unpublished PhD thesis, University of Keele

Anani, J. and T. Jaber (1980) Jordan's Experience and Policies in the Field of Reverse Transfer of Technology, MOL, Amman

Birks, J. and C. Sinclair (1978) Country Case Study - Hashemite Kingdom of Jordan, University of Durham, IMP Working Papers

_____ (1981) 'Demographic Settling amongst Migrant Workers' in IUSSP, International Population Conference Manilla: Working Papers, IUSSP, Liège, pp. 449-69

Al-Fanik, F. (1978) 'Labour Force Turnover in Jordan' al-Amal, vol. 1, no. 2, pp. 20-35 (in Arabic)

Findlay, A. (1984) 'Migrations de travail dans le golfe et croissance des quartiers périphériques d'Amman', Etudes Méditerranéenes, vol. 6, pp. 205-24

Höpfner, K. and M. Huber (1978) Regulating International Migration in the Interest of Developing Countries: with Particular Reference to Mediterranean Countries, ILO, Geneva

ILO (1977) Provisional Record, ILO Sixty-Third Session, Fourteenth Sitting, 10 June 1977, Geneva

Kirwan, F. (1981) 'The Impact of Labor Migration on the Jordanian Economy', International Migration Review, vol. 15, no. 4, pp. 671-95

MOE (1977) Follow-up Analytical Study of Graduates of Educational Institutes in Jordan, MOE, Amman (in Arabic)

MPS (1977) An Analysis of Job Vacancies Advertised in Local Newspapers, NPC, Amman, (in Arabic)

NPC (1976) 'Labour Force in Jordan', paper presented at the Jordan Development Conference, NPC, Amman

Owen, R. (1983) 'Government and Economy in Jordan: Progress, Problems and Prospects' in P. Seale (ed.), The Shaping of an Arab Statesman: Abd al-Hamid Sharaf and the Modern Arab World, Quartet, London

Saket, B. (ed.) (1983) Worker Migration Abroad: Socio-economic Implications for Households in Jordan, Royal Scientific Society, Amman

Salt, A. and W. Keely (1976) Manpower Development in the Hashemite Kingdom of Jordan with

Special Reference to the East Jordan Valley, US Department of Labor, Washington, D.C.

Seccombe, I. (1981) *Manpower and Migration: the Effects of International Labour Migration on Agricultural Development in the East Jordan Valley, 1973-80*, University of Durham, Centre for Middle Eastern and Islamic Studies, Occasional Papers Series, no. 11

―――― (1983) 'International Migration for Employment and Domestic Labour Market Development: the Jordanian Experience', unpublished PhD thesis, University of Durham

―――― (1984a) *International Migration for Employment in the Middle East: an Introductory Bibliography*, University of Durham, Centre for Middle Eastern and Islamic Studies, Occasional Papers Series, no. 24

―――― (1984b) *International Labour Migration and Skill Scarcity in the Hashemite Kingdom of Jordan*, ILO, Geneva

―――― and R. Lawless (1984) 'Some New Trends in Mediterranean Labour Migration - the Middle East Connection', paper presented at the Conference on Migration to the Mediterranean Basin, Marseille

Serageldin, I. et al. (1983) 'Human Resources in the Arab world: the Impact of Migration' in I. Ibrahim (ed.), *Arab Resources: the Transformation of a Society*, Croom Helm, London, pp. 17-36

UNESCO (1980) *Jordan: Education and Training for Manpower Development*, UNESCO, Paris

USAID (1980) *Agricultural Sector Assessment*, USAID, Amman

Wilson, R. (1984) 'The Role of Commercial Banking in the Jordanian Economy', paper prepared for the CERMAC Conference on Economic Development in Jordan

World Bank (1976) *Country Economic Memorandum on Jordan*, World Bank, Washington, D.C.

Chapter Eight

INDUSTRIAL DEVELOPMENT IN JORDAN

Michael B. Sullivan

ECONOMIC OVERVIEW

Jordan's economic planners are basing the country's economic future on its role as a major staging area for supplying goods to Iraq and the Arabian peninsula, as Gulf transit routes remain threatened by war. The country's dynamic local business community and free-enterprise environment offer ample reason to believe that these opportunities will be exploited during the next decade and beyond.
  Of course, the country also boasts some familiar handicaps shared by other developing economies. Population growth is averaging a heady 3.4%. Migration from rural areas and a flow of Palestinian refugees from the Gaza Strip and the occupied West Bank are clogging the cities. At the same time, much of the skilled workforce is migrating to the oil-producing countries, leaving behind the largely unskilled job-seekers. The country will be dependent on imported energy for the indefinite future. Water for both drinking and irrigation is scarce, placing an upper limit on industrialization.
  Nevertheless, industrial development is progressing at a satisfying pace. Structurally, the government's objectives during the current plan are to boost the mining and manufacturing share of GDP to 29.3% from 21.8% during the late 1980s, while reducing the relative importance of the services sector to 54% from 61%. During the period, the critical activity in the electricity and water sectors is expected to rise by 13%.
  Industry already boasts an average annual growth rate of 20% - exceeding the 17% target set in the plan. Over the near term, Jordan's phosphate

Industrial Development

-dominated industrial sector (phosphates account for more than one-quarter of the country's total commodity exports) will be largely engaged in processing raw materials into finished goods for local consumption and exports. The development emphasis will be on expansion of medium- and large-sized enterprises, while upgrading the large number of small firms, in everything from furniture to ready-to-wear clothing and foodstuffs. Medium-sized firms in the $5-25 mn sales range produce pharmaceuticals, iron and steel, paper, paints and batteries. Mining development will aim to improve exploitation of proven reserves of phosphates, potash, copper and oil shale.

Expansion of the food supply will focus efforts on the ambitious Jordan River Valley scheme, aimed at bringing 150,000 people to farm 30,000 ha of land in the lush rift valley running north and south through the country. Though the past three years of fair rainfall following several years of drought have temporarily relieved the water shortage, water resource management will be a principal concern of agricultural planners for the foreseeable future.

The centerpiece of Jordan's hopes for an adequate water supply is the Maqarim Dam project straddling the border with Syria. The dam, on the Yarmouk River in the north, will cost an estimated $150-200 mn, be 125 m high and hold 250 mn cu. m of water when completed. The scheme will provide water, electricity, housing, schools, hospitals and market facilities for small farmers whom the government hopes to attract to the region, possibly through a programme of distributing 4-5 ha plots.

GOVERNMENT ROLE IN DEVELOPMENT

Jordan will remain one of the region's staunchest free-market economies for the indefinite future, in line with the dynamic overall philosophy of the government, business and banking communities. The government's role in the economy is that of a catalyst, stabilizer, supporter, promoter and, only in certain cases, a partner. This role is freeing the hands of the government to build up infrastructural services, pursue the exploitation of natural resources, attend to planning and exercise some measure of control wherever and whenever necessary, whether to stabilize and/or subsidize the prices of essential commodities such as wheat,

Industrial Development

meat, sugar, cooking and fuel oils, cement and others.

The government's role is invariably described as that of a watchdog, to see that prices do not run astray and that large projects demanding significant capital outlay beyond the public's reach do not remain unexploited. This role can be described as neither socialist nor capitalist but as an inbetween course, more or less tailored to create a stable balance between economic and social demands and, for this purpose, between economic development and social welfare.

Through this clear vision, Jordan has been able to gain self-confidence and overcome enormous obstacles. Consequently, the country not only sustains a respected economic policy in the region, but has been able to provide other Arab countries with growing numbers of skilled and professional personnel. Successive Jordanian governments have tenaciously adhered to this line of policy and persistently endeavoured to provide the most favourable conditions for a comprehensive development of an amenable economic climate within the framework of free enterprise.

The state intervenes in the economy to help modify the clash of economic forces. The Ministry of Supply provides basic foodstuffs by importing and distributing wheat, flour and meat, which are subsidized commodities. The ministry buys the wheat crop from farmers at a fair market price if they wish to sell and then provides flour for bakeries to sell bread. The farmer thus receives a good price for his crop and can maintain his family's requirement for bread at a subsidized price. The ministry has also built wheat silos and cold storage for meat.

The National Planning Council (NPC) finances studies of the larger projects, including the exploitation of mineral deposits, large tourist enterprises such as the development of the Zarqa-Ma'an hot springs and modern hotels, and any other project that adds to GDP. After defraying the initial cost, the government either starts the project and then invites subscription to the capital, or declares a proportion of the capital and then invites the private sector to fill the rest of the gap in the capital requirements.

Irrespective of the size of its share in the equity, the government confines its role to appointing directors in proportion to its share, without interference in the election of private-sector candidates for boards. The enterprise is, in all cases, run on a commercial basis as if it were a private enterprise. The chairman may be elected by the board from the private sector at the will of the directors. At the general assembly of public-share companies, the board is freely questioned by the shareholders in the presence of the Controller of Companies. Company boards are elected by secret ballot for four years, and the number does not exceed 12 persons. The remuneration of private-sector directors is restricted to JD 1,000 per annum. The remuneration of government representatives is paid to the Treasury, which later pays awards to these representatives.

The government, through the Ministry of Industry and Trade, controls the import system. Import licences are freely issued, each carrying an automatic foreign-exchange permit. The constraint is limited to the materials relating to public safety and health. No medicines, for example, can be imported without permission from the Ministry of Health, which ensures they are safe for use.

The government may also salvage companies in financial trouble under the Defence Regulations and Economic Security Committee. In one example, a large automatic bakery, which was becoming insolvent in 1975, had its board disbanded, and a committee was appointed to run the bakery for one year with government support when the situation worsened. The government accepted the recommendation of the committee to buy the bakery, make up legitimate losses and refund to the shareholders the nominal value of their shares, i.e. above the market or book value. A few years ago, when the Cairo-Amman Bank ran into difficulties because of excessive dispensation of credit, the Central Bank appointed a committee to run the bank, channelled payments to its coffers and fed it with some loans until it regained a sound standing.

The government grants permits to establish new industries. Automatic approval is granted if the capital layout is not in excess of JD 20,000. If the capital is in excess, a feasibility study has to prove that the project is profitable and satisfies some local need at reasonable prices.

The government is reaping the benefits of free enterprise in opening the way to the private sector to shoulder some of the responsibilities of education and medical care within its general policy and guidelines. A number of private schools, institutes of learning, hospitals and clinics are offering first-class service, the cost being within reach of most citizens.

The government participates in the equity of 44 companies with 31% of industrial shares outstanding. Newcomers in the investment field are the newly formed autonomous funds such as the Pension Fund, the Social Security Fund, the Postal Savings Fund and some provident funds. These funds are allowed to invest in any project or enterprise they may wish. The five-year plan (1981-85) reckons that their investments will total JD 1 bn, or 31% of the total investment allocations of JD 3.3 bn.

One other field in which the government exercises authority and control is public transport (buses) and running Royal Jordanian Airlines as a public utility, though of independent status. The governing rule will be the welfare of the people, without obstructing private initiative.

GOVERNMENT ATTITUDE TOWARDS THE PRIVATE SECTOR

The Jordanian government considers the private sector as a collaborator, supplier, initiator, partner, financier, taxpayer and earner of foreign exchange, and it treats the independent business community with remarkable deference. The private sector is allowed to conduct any legitimate business, subject to regulations obtaining, without any administrative or official hindrances. The government encourages the private sector to show more zeal in developing the economy. It provides tax exemptions under the Encouragement of Investment Law, training for upcoming workers and loans through the specialized credit corporations at reduced rates of interest, and it also rewards the private-sector exporters with special certificates of merit.

During the three-year plan (1973-75) the private sector was supposed to invest some JD 80 mn, but it exceeded this level by almost 60%. In the five-year plan (1975-80) the private sector was expected to invest JD 721.9 mn, and again it exceeded this limit. In the five-year plan (1981-85) private-sector investments are marked at JD 1.3 bn. The private sector includes all companies in which the government is a participant. The government invariably invites the private sector to furnish ideas, advice or participation in decision-making. Representatives of the private sector are appointed to a number of councils, committees and boards, among them the National Consultative Council, the Central Bank of Jordan board, the NPC, the Industrial Development Bank, the Social Security Corporation, the Industrial Estate Corporation and the Royal Jordanian Airlines board. Private-sector representatives also sit on the ministerial committee for determining the ceiling for wage increases. Representatives of workers sit on the same committee. Representatives of the private sector also join delegations that conduct trade talks with other governments.

For its part, the government expects the private sector to meet its tax obligations, to show magnanimity in contributing to special national or charitable funds and to play a role in development; it is therefore accepted as a partner.

DEVELOPMENT IN KEY INDUSTRIAL SECTORS

Chemicals and petrochemicals will continue to play a modest role in Jordan's economy, but some major projects are coming on stream over the near term. The country's most important chemical venture, the Jordan Fertilizer Industry Company (JFIC), is pushing ahead with commercial production of fertilizers at a new facility 20 km south of Aqaba. The unit will use high-grade ore from al-Hasa (later the ore will come from Shidiya) to produce 740,000 t/year of diammonium phosphate from two 1,200-t/day units. The activity will also involve the production of over 100,000 t/year of phosphoric acid and 3,600 t/year of sulphuric acid using imported sulphur.

A unit will be built beside the fertilizer facility with the help of Alusuisse to combine fluosilicic, a potentially damaging by-product of the fertilizer-production process, with imported aluminium hydroxide to make 20,000 t/year of aluminium fluoride. If the Jordan Phosphate Mines Company's (JPMC) tests on phosphates prove positive, the JFIC might well quintuple its output of phosphoric acid. Reportedly, Japan's Mitsubishi will market 40% of the sulphuric acid production, the US firm of Woodward & Dickerson will market 35% and the JFIC will keep the rest for its own use.

Related to the fertilizer venture is the Arab Potash Company's (APC) project to produce 1,200 t/year of potassium chloride at its Dead Sea extraction plant, using a series of solar-evaporation ponds leading to a refinery and granulating unit.

Industrial Development

In plastics, Intermediate Petrochemicals Industries (IPI) is moving ahead with the construction of its first plant 15 km east of Amman on the Zarqa road. The six process lines in the unit's first phase will produce, among other things, 8,000 t of monomeric plasticizers, 4,000 t of unsaturated polyester resin, 9,000 t of dry blends and compounds from polyvinyl chloride (PVC) and 10,000 t of low aromatic solvents. The sixth line will produce 1.4 mn sq. m. of glass-fibre reinforced polyester sheets. IPI's parent company, Jordan Polymers & Intermediate Chemicals, is planning to expand its own PVC plant nearby.

Mining will remain a pivotal sector in Jordan for the foreseeable future as the government seeks to exploit the country's position as the world's third largest phosphates producer after the US and Morocco, as well as to fructify deposits of Dead Sea salts and some copper. Other minerals include gypsum, manganese ore, abundant quantities of glass sand, and the clays and special ore required for ceramics manufacture. During the five-year plan (1981-85, mining and manufacturing combined are targeted to grow by 17.8% annually.

Phosphate production grew from 1.76 mn t in 1977 to 4.24 mn t in 1981, most of it from the main mines at al-Hasa and Wadi al-Abiadh in central Jordan, and is expected to rise to over 7 mn t by 1987. As the beds in Rusaifa (a few kilometres north-east of Amman) near exhaustion, officials plan to move its pits and mill to a site nearer Zarqa, where production is expected to begin in about three years, while maintaining Rusaifa's production at a recent level of less than 1 mn t with a new processing plant. Output at al-Hasa and Wadi al-Abiadh will be raised to 5 mn t over the next two years.

Towards the end of this decade, mining of the huge reserves at Shidiya (in remote south-eastern Jordan near the Saudi border) will probably go into full swing, with an output of some 3 mn t targeted for 1990 and nearly 10 mn t by the end of the century. In January 1982 a French consultant signed a contract to study the exploitation of Shidiya's proven, indicated and probable reserves of 1 bn t. The government will spend nearly $200 mn over the next five years to bring the mine on stream and start producing about 500,000 t by 1987, when the JPMC will take over the mine. Shidiya will benefit from its proximity to the port of Aqaba, from where some 85% of production will be exported. The

Industrial Development

government may allow private-sector participation in Shidiya.

The largest market for phosphates is Asia, in particular India, but sales possibilities are also expanding in Europe. Yugoslavia recently agreed to import 100,000-300,000 t/year. Exports of raw phosphates will rise more slowly than production, as the country shifts over to output of finished products.

The APC formally opened its Dead Sea extraction plant in March 1982 with the aim of bringing production of potash to 240,000 t/year by 1986. The efficiency of the project is threatened by Israeli plans to build a canal connecting the Dead Sea with the Mediterranean, which would dilute the Dead Sea's concentration of brine and render extraction of potash compounds more costly.

Jordan may eventually move to exploit its 50 mn t reserves of copper in Wadi al-Araba south of the Dead Sea. The deposits are said to have a 1.35% content, but the high cost of separating the copper from the magnesium could dampen long-term prospects. For the moment, the Natural Resources Authority (NRA) is moving ahead with a pilot extraction plant that will have a capacity of 3,000 t/year of processed copper.

Non-ferrous metal industries are still limited in scope; they include units making mirror frames, chandeliers, chrome furniture and other articles.

An aluminium-extrusion factory has been built with a capacity of JD 1 mn to supply sections to the local market. Prefabricated houses are made in increasing numbers using aluminium frames. Aluminium wires are imported for electricity transmission lines.

Jordan will continue to import much of its needs in iron and steel products. Japan is the primary supplier, followed by France, West Germany, the UK, the USSR, the US, Romania and Belgium.

Jordan has two mills producing iron rods for construction and a third on the way to produce blocks from pellets. The production of the operating two mills increased from 63,800 t in 1977 to 134,900 t in 1981. This industry is protected by a tariff duty on imports. Branded as a losing venture when it was first established in 1965, the venture has succeeded and is now opening the way for other steel facilities.

The NPC has recommended building steel units to make the following items: foundry and machining of pumps (capital cost JD 8.4 mn), drill bits

Industrial Development

(capital cost JD 2.9 mn), hand tools and implements (capital cost JD 1.9 mn), tools and dies (capital cost JD 1.5 mn), structural steel holloware (capital cost JD 5.9 mn), and wire cables (capital cost JD 4.9 mn). A welded-steel-pipes company currently manufactures pipes that are exported, in particular, to Iraq. Other articles made in Jordan include steel radiators for central heating and boilers.

Jordanian companies, in particular the Arab Pharmaceutical Manufacturing Company, are active in pharmaceuticals. Pharmaceutical and veterinary-medicine manufacturers are flourishing enterprises, and their future looks promising. Their contribution to exports has increased in value from JD 5.2 mn in 1977 to JD 10 mn in 1980. Pharmaceuticals are exported to the Arab countries and beyond to Africa, especially Nigeria. The principal local producer, the Arab Pharmaceutical Manufacturing Company, established in 1962 by the government, had sales of JD 5.44 mn, of which 11.5% were for the local market, 16.5% went to the government and 72% to exports. Production includes antibiotics, syrups and other medicines.

The other pharmaceutical companies are: Jordan Pharmaceutical & Medical Equipment (capital JD 500,000), al-Hikma Pharmaceuticals of Jordan (capital JD 500,000) and Dar al-Dawa Development & Investment (capital JD 1,000,000). The veterinary drugs companies are: United Veterinary Drugs Industrial Company (capital JD 400,000), Veterinary & Agriculture Product Manufacturing (capital JD 225,000) and Arab Veterinary Industrial Company (capital JD 500,000).

Food processing is receiving priority consideration for development. Agricultural earnings are exempt from income tax, and farmers obtain a low rate of interest from the Agricultural Credit Corporation and the Co-operative Bank, both government agencies. The main suppliers of processed foodstuffs are West Germany, the Netherlands, Denmark and France, providing powdered milk, butter and cheese.

The Jordan Valley Authority, created in 1973, is using modern methods of irrigation to exploit the valley twice a year for both seasonal and out-of-season crops. Apart from German, British, US and other technical aid, the Japanese government has prepared an integrated Jordan Valley plan that includes agroindustries, and industrial estate and other facilities. The area is irrigated by the East

Industrial Development

Ghor Canal, which replaces the waters of the Jordan diverted by Israel.

Agroindustries are still in their infancy. There are four dairy-produce companies, two with Danish equity. Two breweries have patent licences with Amstel of Holland and Henninger of Frankfurt, with the Department of Standard Specification and the Health Authorities controlling the quality. A baby-food industry is under study, and the packaging industry is expanding.

Malaysia is considering a joint venture to establish a storage plant in Aqaba for the distribution of vegetable oils for processing in Jordan, Syria, Iraq and even Turkey. The unit would provide ready delivery and save on the cost of shipping small quantities.

Chapter Nine

DEVELOPMENT PLANNING IN A TURBULENT INTERNATIONAL ENVIRONMENT: SOME REFLECTIONS ON THE JORDANIAN CASE

Dieter Weiss

THE FOREIGN POLICY CONTEXT

The development performance of Jordan has been particularly successful in cross-country comparison. Economic growth rates in the past have been exceptional, as compared with both the Arab and the international situation. This is true in spite of the heavy burden of the continuing Middle East conflict and the repeated exposure to military confrontation with Israel, which has occupied the West Bank since 1967. Jordan has a population of 3.5 mn, 2.5 mn of whom live on the East Bank. About 800,000 of them are Palestinian refugees.

The country plays a skilful role in the political and strategic balance of power in the Middle East: it maintains excellent relations with the West, particularly with the US, yet rejects the Camp David Agreement; it relies both on the US and the USSR for substantial supplies of military equipment; it takes a differentiated but workable position towards the PLO after having suppressed the organization's military commandos in 1971; and it is a member of a political axis ranging from Iraq to Saudi Arabia, replacing the former close political and economic relations between Jordan and Syria.

THE SOCIO-CULTURAL CONTEXT

The international political and strategic dimension is one crucial aspect of a complex polygon of forces in which Jordan's development planners are operating. The other is the socio-cultural perception of the people who are to implement this development process: until the end of the First

World War, they were subjects of the Ottoman Empire, bedouin leading a traditional nomadic life, or tradesmen and small-scale traders who - after the territorial partition by the colonial powers - were supposed to consider themselves citizens of a newly created Palestine, Transjordan, responsibility of the Hashemite Kingdom of Jordan, and who were exposed to a new crisis of identity following the establishment of Israel.

The discomfort is portrayed in a thoughtful book by Kamel Abu Jaber:

> I feel sorry for our children having to grow up in such an atmosphere of protracted and seemingly never-ending conflict ... Very few people have been harrassed like we have, whether on the individual or the national level ... Most other people in the developing world have only their internal challenges to meet: how to develop their country, raise their standard of living and achieve a better way of life ... We, the Jordanians, Palestinians, Arabs, we have this, plus having to cope with the daily violent threat to our existence. We had to pick one of the most formidable minority groups in the world for our adversary. A minority that, in one way or another, captured the imagination of the Western world in this century and seems to continue to hold on to it. We cannot admit defeat because of its totality and enormity, and at the same time we cannot let go of the struggle.[1]

The cultural consternation following the confrontation with the West is deep and not yet overcome.

> For Arab society and the Arab individual, Western superiority was shocking. It was all the more shocking since Arab Muslim society, centuries after the glorious day of Islam, still cherished the image of its own superiority. On the level of the state, and in every state in the Arab world, an active search was set in motion to ascertain the factors underlying Western superiority ... On the level of the individual, the process was initially that of imitation of Western manners in dress styles and tastes. Later, however, the process of becoming 'franji'-like became a genuine end in itself.[2]

Development Planning

In general, social change is experienced as crisis unless it can be positively accepted. Kamel Abu Jaber diagnoses the enormous psychic strain:

> Only a generation ago almost four-fifths of Jordan's population lived either a pastoral existence or in villages and small towns. The change one observes today is not only in terms of urban versus rural residence, but in physical as well as psychological terms. Not only have the dress styles changed to become 'Westernized' and 'modern', but changes have also taken place in consumer habits, in food consumption and calorie intake, and also in psychological and attitudinal terms ... A whole life style that existed for millennia is changing ... The goat-hair tent, the camel, the individual independence of the desert bedouin are virtually gone, perhaps forever.[3]
> We may look as though we are living in a state of moral schizophrenia, and for many individuals that, indeed, is the case ... To be a Jordanian, an Arab, now, you have to live not in one world, but in two, and in some cases more than two worlds at the same time. In a way, and because of the transitory nature of change, its speed and intensity, it is like living in a no-man's land. Should you rely on your heritage and inherited values, mores and tools, or should you partake of the present innovations coming from the industrialized world? My father had few such dilemmas; my grandfather had none: for both drank from one well of knowledge, and had only one source. For me and my generation, with our sources and resources, choices are limitless. The familiar attracts me, but innovation attracts me more. Often we go on a shopping spree of values, ideas and tools. Ours has become an eclectic approach, whereby we try to reconcile the old with the new.[4]

The pride in Arab culture and history finds itself humiliated. But the desire to launch a real change is strong:

> outwardly denying its shortcomings and manifesting a belligerent though inadequate stance, while inwardly imposing upon itself a severe process of evaluation and re-evaluation.[5]
> ... The idea of change itself has been

consciously accepted, even welcomed as a fact of life. What is traditional, unless it is fundamental and exceedingly basic, is no longer simply sacrosanct and unquestioned. The idea of development and positive change is no longer feared, except by small pockets of resistance here and there.[6]

The book is an outstanding document of a self-critical survey of what has been achieved so far, and it is of an intellectual integrity which so often gets lost in the highly charged atmosphere of the area. 'I have the feeling that we are misunderstood, and this, in turn, because we often behave in an illogical and contradictory manner. In our frustration and anger, we have lost the ability to communicate clearly with others.'[7] Here, reality is not replaced by wishful thinking but is the starting-point of a solid though painful self-critical analysis. Jordan's development planning reflects this intellectual straightforwardness in its concepts and results.

STRUCTURAL PROBLEMS AND DEVELOPMENT ACHIEVEMENTS IN THE 1970s

Jordan's natural resources are limited. On the East Bank only 500,000 ha are arable, 50,000 ha of which are irrigated. Shortage of water and the poverty of most of the usable soil are predominant bottlenecks in the <u>agricultural sector</u>. An exception is the Jordan Valley, which, owing to its geographic characteristics, is a sort of a natural greenhouse.[8] Here, in the course of an integrated development programme, an intensive horticulture has been established with high-quality fruit and vegetables (especially tomatoes, eggplants, melons, grapes and citrus fruits) and animal products which, for the most part, are exported to neighbouring Arab countries. However, the amount of investments required confirms recent international experience that, due to increasing costs of land reclamation along with increasing shortage of arable land in many developing countries, the capital-output ratios in agriculture have often started to exceed those in manufacturing. On non-irrigated soils the yields vary year by year in line with the irregular rainfall. Several drought periods in the past years have stimulated large investments in irrigation, especially in the Jordan Valley which has the

Development Planning

greatest agricultural potential of the country. By now, most of the available river reservoirs are utilized by irrigation plants. In order to secure the increasing water demand of the crowded urban areas, the possibility of importing water in pipelines from Iraq has been discussed.

In the past, the traditional semi-arid soils were neglected over huge public and private investments in a commercial and predominantly export-oriented agricultural production.

> Perhaps much greater emphasis in the future should be placed on the attachment of the rural population to their land, as the exodus from rural to urban areas has been a major cause for concern to the cities as well as to the farms. To this goal, modern facilities should be made available to the rural areas, ranging not only from tractors but also to efficient transport, electricity, health, communication and recreation facilities.[9]

Jordanian professionals are aware of the necessity to provide stimuli for the rural population by means of a wage and price policy offering a substantial rise in incomes as well as a stabilization of incomes against price fluctuations and bad harvests.[10]

In the energy sector, Jordan depends on imported crude oil. Alternative sources of energy (especially solar energy) have been developed purposefully and successfully but do not play an important role in the total energy balance so far.

In the mining industry, phosphates - which are the main export product - potash and various building materials are exploited. High growth rates have been achieved and are projected for the future.

Since the mid-1970s the manufacturing industry has grown by a real 17% per annum, along with considerable growth rates of exports to the Arab oil countries. With approx. 42,000 employees, its contribution to GDP (19%) is considerable. A modern capital-intensive sector consists of some large raw material processing plants on the basis of crude oil and mining products. In addition, a diversified consumer goods industry has developed, promoted by an economic policy supporting private venture. More than 700 new enterprises, in particular including small- and medium-sized plants, have developed in the fields of food processing, beverages, tobacco products, textiles, garments, shoes, leather goods, wooden articles and furniture, paper and printing materials, building materials, prefabricated building units, sanitary equipment, fittings, pharmaceuticals and chemicals. Some 150 of them were established as joint ventures with foreign partners, partly with the goal of substituting imports, mainly, however, for exports to Arab countries.

The main bottleneck is a shortage of qualified personnel which, in part, is balanced by foreign workers. Furthermore, there is a marked shortage of professional management.[11] Owing to the competing job opportunities in the Gulf states, the Jordanian wage level is relatively high compared with international standards. With wages six times higher than those of Egypt, the leading industrial country in the Arab world, Jordan can no longer be considered as a low-wage country.

Jordan's economists see possibilities for further industrial development, particularly with regard to the Arab Common Market, and favour joint ventures with foreign companies with access to international markets, in order to establish modern plants of a reasonable size and to promote the transfer of technology. The government helps with several measures within a market-oriented economic system that is comparatively free from government intervention.

In 1980 the services sector predominated, with 61% of GDP and 62% of jobs. Government administration and defence had a share of approx. 20% of GDP. Transportation and communication increased the fastest, with a real 17% per annum. This is due, in particular, to the growing role of the transit trade for the Arab oil countries and Iraq after the Iraqi ports were closed because of the war with Iran, and supplies were sent overland via Jordan.

More than 300,000 (out of the total labour force of approx. 1 mn) are working abroad, especially in the Gulf states, whereas there are some 150,000 low-qualified foreign workers working in Jordan (Egyptians, Pakistanis, Filipinos, Koreans, etc.) About two-thirds of the population live in urban areas; about half of the total population live in the urban agglomeration of Amman, with clear symptoms of an acceleration of the agglomeration process. The social problems normally occurring in other countries (development of slums, unemployment) are scarce thanks to the migration of workers to the Gulf states, where

Table 9.1: Economic Indicators for Jordan (million Jordanian dinars)

Indicator	1980	% of GDP	Target 1985[a]	% of GDP
GDP (at market prices)	814.0	100	2,060.0	100
GDP (in 1980 constant prices)	814.0	100	1,377.0	100
GNP	1,011.0	124.2	2,535.0	123.1
GNP (in 1980 constant prices)	1,011.0	124.2	1,695.0	123.1
Investment	320.0	39.3	852.7	41.4
Consumption	999.0	122.7	2,194.7	106.5
PRIVATE AND PUBLIC INVESTMENTS	320.0	39.3	852.7	41.4
Central government	83.5	10.3	287.7	14.0
Government agencies & municipalities	68.3	8.3	235.3	11.4
Private investment (including joint companies)	168.2	20.7	329.7	16.0
FOREIGN SECTORS				
Imports of goods	720.0	88.4	1,369.0	99.4
Imports of services	200.0	24.6	378.0	27.4
Exports of goods (+ re-exports)	16.0	19.7	550.0	39.9
Exports of services	235.0	28.9	505.0	36.7
Net factor income (net investment income + net remittances)	197.0	24.2	318.0	23.1
Net transfer payments	381.0	46.8	250.0	18.2

Table 9.1 (Cont'd)

Indicator	1980	% of GDP	Target 1985[a]	% of GDP
GOVERNMENT FINANCING				
Foreign budget support	214.9	26.3	244.0	11.8
Domestic revenue	224.5	27.6	557.0	27.0
Direct	32.9	4.0	103.0	5.0
Indirect	109.0	13.4	257.5	12.5
Expenditure	517.5	63.6	1,219.0	59.2
Recurrent	325.7	40.0	555.0	26.9
Capital	191.8	23.6	664.0	32.2
GOVERNMENT SURPLUS IN CURRENT ACCOUNT	113.7	14.0	246.0	11.9
POPULATION & LABOUR	1980	% of nat. labour	1985	% of nat. labour
Population	2,234,000		2,693,000	
National labour force	390,750	100.0	518,350	100
Male	336,045	86.0	418,645	80.8
Female	54,705	14.0	99,705	19.2
Foreign labourers	79,566	20.4	149,566	28.9
Jordanians working abroad	280,000 to 310,000		300,000 to 350,000	

Table 9.1 (Cont'd)

Indicator	1980	% of nat. labour	1985	% of nat. labour
Total labour force (including foreign)	470,316	120.4	667,916	128.8
Agriculture	78,945	20.2	92,705	17.9
Mining & industry	49,589	12.7	98,759	19.0
Transportation	43,786	11.2	74,116	14.3
Other services	297,996	76.3	402,336	77.6

Note: a. The target figures for 1985 according to the 1981–1985 Plan are given in 1980 constant prices unless otherwise indicated.
Source: NPC, '1976–1980 Plan Reviewed, 1981–1985 Scheme Outlined' (Amman, 1982) (mimeo).

Development Planning

incomes are up to ten times higher than in Jordan. The remittances of Jordanians working abroad are one of the most important positions in the balance of payments (Table 9.1).

An important prerequisite for the migration of Jordanian workers to the OAPEC countries was their high level of education. The ratio of primary cycle enrolment (ages 6-11) had risen to 97% by 1980. The female literacy rate rose from 14% in 1961 to 65% in 1979.[12] Vocational training lagged behind, partly due to the poor social status still enjoyed by handicrafts. In the Gulf states, too, the majority of Jordanian workers hold well-paid managerial and service jobs.

From 1948 to 1967 GDP in real terms increased by an average of 9% per annum. In the aftermath of the 1967 war, the occupation of the West Bank by Israel and domestic troubles led to negative growth rates in all sectors with the exception of services. The development plan (1972-75) brought a recovery (a real growth rate in GDP of 7%), with considerable achievements in phosphate mining and manufacturing, whereas agriculture suffered from drought and frost.[13]

During the following plan period (1976-80) the real growth rate of GDP increased to 8.5% per annum (target 11.9%). Leading sectors with growth rates far beyond those of the plan were housing (stimulated by workers' remittances), transportation as a result of the rapidly growing transit trade (i.e. due to the Iraq-Iran war), manufacturing and energy. Private investments in small- and medium-size businesses played a more important role than expected, while the government primarily financed capital-intensive large-scale projects in transportation infrastructure, mining, fertilizers, cement and oil refineries. The share of government investment was 75% in transportation and 33% in manufacturing industry, whereas private investments were predominant in the housing sector. Altogether, investments in construction activities reached three times the volume planned.

The social sectors lagged behind the plan targets, in particular as concerns rural development, health and education, mainly as a result of delays in project preparation and implementation. <u>Per capita</u> incomes at current prices increased from JD 185 in 1975 to JD 453 in 1980; this corresponded to an increase of 42% in real terms. Population growth was 3.5%. In 1980 consumption expenditures amounted to 123% of GDP. The gap was closed by transfer payments from abroad.

A chronic, and increasing, deficit in the balance of payments has resulted from the rapid increase of imports and the slower increase of exports. There is, in particular, the problem of food security in view of a worldwide shortage of foodstuffs and rising food prices to be expected in the future.

Regional disparities have increased, in terms of both _per capita_ incomes and the supply of public social services. The rural, semi-arid, sparsely populated low-income areas with infrastructural disadvantages are unattractive for private investments. The diseconomies of an uncontrolled agglomeration are all too apparent in the Greater Amman area, where some 1 mn people live. On the other hand, it is not clear whether and how the economies of regional growth poles like Aqaba, Irbid and Zarqa should be used more effectively, in view of the fact that the potential of the backward rural areas is extremely limited and the total East Bank population is only 2.5 mn.

THE GROWING RESOURCE GAP

The rate of investment increased from 17% of GDP in 1971 to 31.6% in 1975 and 39% in 1980. This exceptional performance was to a large degree financed by foreign resources, in the first place by the Arab oil countries, in the second place by Western donors.

The development plan (1976-80) had aimed at consolidating the budget and reducing the foreign trade deficit. The budget is structurally in deficit. In 1980 only 70% of current expenditures could be covered out of domestic revenues with high and increasing expenditures for defence and social services as well as subsidies for petroleum products and basic foodstuffs. Revenues show a distribution that is typical for many developing countries, with their excess of indirect taxes, especially customs duties, versus an extremely low share of direct income taxation.

Deficits in the current budget as well as public capital expenditures are financed by foreign resources, mainly donations from the Arab oil countries. Between 1975 and 1980 budget revenues increased threefold to JD 225 mn but expenditures increased, too, from JD 205 to 518 mn (JD 326 mn of current expenditures, JD 192 mn of capital expenditures). Foreign aid amounted to JD 215 mn, reaching almost the volume of domestic state revenues and equalling two-thirds of total investments (public plus private = JD 320 mn) representing 25% of the GDP of JD 814 mn.

Simultaneously, between 1975 and 1980 the gap between imports and exports of goods and services grew from JD 173 mn to JD 670 mn,[14] which, in part, was balanced by remittances from Jordanians working abroad, an amount which nearly tripled to JD 200 mn (Table 9.1). In 1980 the remaining resource gap was JD 472 mn, i.e. approx. $1.5 bn. These figures demonstrate the structural dependence on foreign assistance.

To sum up, Jordan's economy is characterized by a dominating services sector, both in output and in exports. Mining, manufacturing and agriculture follow at a considerable distance. Despite the country's geographic situation at a 'nerve centre' of the Middle East conflict, it has succeeded in persuading Western and Arab donor countries to engage in continuous subsidy policies, thanks to the exceptional sober-mindedness, prudence and international prestige of its top leadership. The present domestic resource gap of more than $1.5 bn is due to structural reasons and has grown continuously, yet it is not Jordan's responsibility alone. It is, rather, part of the economic and social consequence of the borders drawn up since the breakdown of the Ottoman Empire after the First World War and their violation following the Palestinian tragedy. The ruling royal family has had remarkable success in activating the strategic self-interests of both Western and Arab countries for this continuing financial support.

Jordan has also enjoyed the exceptional advantage of being able to disregard the social effects of economic strategies, as the Arab oil countries have been prepared to balance any possible social discontent by the admission of Jordanian workers. The relative neglect of the underdeveloped, semi-arid and arid rural areas with low development potential, and of the poorer outskirts of the new metropolitan areas, have thus not led to the usual consequences of political unrest familiar from other developing countries.

In the Arab oil countries there are, however, limits to the absorptive capacity for Jordanian excess labour. In Kuwait, for example, the share of foreign workers has already reached 1 mn, compared to 500,000 Kuwaitis, and this has led to considerable domestic tension. Religious-orthodox countries like Saudi Arabia fear an increasing secularization brought about by well-educated immigrants. The Saudis have recently tended to prefer Asian workers, whose claims are more moderate as regards pay as well as social and political rights or permanent settlement.

Assuming that most Jordanians abroad will eventually have to return, the number of people looking for jobs in Jordan would more than double. This situation seems impossible to plan for, let alone to solve within a reasonable time-span, and can hardly be anticipated in some sort of contingency planning with reasonable economic opportunity costs. Yet it is a real possibility. This is one of the specific problems faced by planners in small countries which are extremely dependent on foreign assistance and which, in practical terms, do not have the option of a mainly inward-looking strategy.

THE DEVELOPMENT PLAN (1981-85) AND ITS IMPLEMENTATION

Basic Strategic Objectives

The aim of the plan was to maintain development dynamics without claiming to solve all the problems in five years. The absorptive capacity for new investments was to be fully used and to manifest itself in a larger volume of investment. The main objectives were the following:[15]

(a) <u>Increase in real per capita incomes</u>. Maintenance of a high growth rate with optimal utilization of available resources, especially of the phosphate and potash deposits and of the agricultural potential; promotion of the raw material processing industry and of tourism.

(b) <u>Improvement in the infrastructural support of backward areas</u>. Strengthening of regional participation in formulation and implementation of programmes; more consideration of the poor rural and urban areas.

(c) <u>A more equitable income distribution</u>. This was to be achieved mainly by new fiscal policies, minimum wages, vocational training programmes for low-income groups, improvement of the social security system, easier access to jobs for women.

(d) <u>Reduction of regional disparities and a better distribution of the population</u>. Development of new decentralized growth centres in various areas; investment incentives outside the urban Amman/Zarqa region.

(e) <u>Strengthening popular participation in the development process</u>. Mobilization of the population by the mass media; education, voluntary services, co-operatives, professional organizations.

(f) <u>Education and vocational training</u>. Technical specialization; improvement of the quality of life and individual capabilities, particularly of youth, including girls.

(g) <u>Initiation of a population policy which is 'consistent with available resources and Jordan's role in the Arab World ...'</u> The country's demographic situation calls for a constant appraisal of population trends and policies to turn the population increase into an active instrument for development.[16] Services, maternity child-health centres, community health and family planning services.

(h) <u>Increase in agricultural production and improvement of food security</u>. Incentives for farmers; provision of agricultural inputs, technology and credit facilities; measures for developing livestock; storage facilities for grain.

(i) <u>Development and economic use of water</u>. Research programmes in this sector.

(j) <u>Reduction of dependence on imported energy</u>. Economy measures, oil exploration, developing of non-conventional energy sources, close co-operation with OAPEC countries.

(k) <u>Utilization of mineral resources</u>. Exploration and exploitation using the latest technologies, development of the respective domestic capabilities.

(l) <u>Advancement of science and technology</u>. Encouragement of domestic research activities in technical, economic and social fields; establishment of a Science and Technology Fund.

(m) <u>Increase of domestic savings and attraction of foreign capital</u>. Development of national financial markets. Mobilization of savings of Jordanians working abroad.

(n) <u>Environmental protection</u>. Elaboration of standards to prevent soil erosion, water and air pollution as well as the regulation of land use, and development of respective management capacities.

(o) <u>Enhancement of the efficiency of public institutions of planning and implementation; improvement of conditions of the private sector</u>. Administrative reforms, training programmes, incentives to encourage qualified personnel to stay in the country.

(p) <u>Continuation of the free market economy, with closer co-operation between the private and public sectors</u>. Enlargement of the scope for joint ventures between government and private business in investment and job-training programmes.

(q) <u>Strengthening of all forms of co-operation with other Arab countries</u>. 'Jordan aims at complete economic unity with other Arab countries by participating in joint Arab economic action and promoting inter-Arab mobility of capital as well as trade.'[17] Unified educational systems and curricula are aimed at.

These strategic guidelines matched Jordan's actual situation. The essential problems were plainly outlined. In contrast to other countries of the region, there was no extravagant rhetoric or visionary projection of objectives. Matter-of-factness and a realistic attitude ranked before formal elegance. The general tendency of the policies aimed at was usually formulated distinctly, yet allowed for flexible adaptation and implementation in view of limited management capacities and the unpredictability of the future international economic and political environment. As a matter of fact, Israeli troops marched into Lebanon a few months after the new plan had been published.

Basic Economic Data of the Plan
GDP was supposed to increase at an annual growth rate of 11% (from JD 705 mn in 1980 to JD 1,193 mn in 1985 at constant 1980 prices). Annual sectoral growth rates were indicated as follows: productive sectors 14.9% (agriculture 7.5%, mining and manufacturing 17.8%, electricity and water 18.7%, construction 12.6%); services sectors 8.4% (trade 10%, transport and communications 11.1%, public administration and defence 3.5%, other services 9%). <u>Per capita</u> incomes were planned to increase by 6.8% per annum.[18] Overall targets were comparatively high, yet not unrealistic as compared with the country's efficiency developed during the past.

Change in Sectoral Composition
The predominance of services was supposed to diminish in favour of the commodity-producing sectors by increasing the latter's share from 39%

Development Planning

to 46% of GDP, with a corresponding decline of services from 61% to 54%. Mining plus manufacturing were supposed to become the leading sectors, with a rise in share of GDP from 22% to 29%. In view of the limited possibilities of agriculture; it was expected that its share would drop from 8.5% to 7% in spite of various promotional measures.[19]

Reduction of the Balance of Payments Deficit
An increase of 18% was projected in exports as a result of the diversification of export goods and services, the promotion of tourism and an increase of workers' remittances. An increase in imports by 13% was anticipated. Thus, the balance of payments deficit was expected to drop from 52% of GNP in 1980 to 41% of GNP in 1985.[20] Even with such a reduction of the resource gap, the high foreign aid requirements would still persist in the second half of the 1980s.

Basic Needs and Regional Balance
Regional disparities were supposed to be reduced by decentralization of public services and infrastructural supply. In view of the extremely limited development potential of marginal areas and of the high attraction of the new growth centres, however, it was clear that the chances of these endeavours succeeding were not to be overestimated.

Labour Force and Employment
Until 1985 the share of vocational training in total secondary enrolment was supposed to expand to 30%. The capacity of the technical training centres was to be increased to 8,000 industrial apprentices and to provide more female participation in the labour force. The system of social security was to be improved.[21]

The plan remained vague as regards a long-term concept for dealing with the employment situation, apart from the indication that 254,000 additional workers were required to implement the plan. According to the plan, 184,000 new jobs would be created, another 40,000 would become vacant due to emigration and a further 30,000 would have to be filled because of retirement and death. Furthermore, it was not clear how many of the extra workers were supposed to be domestic or foreign and what additional problems might be brought about by the

Development Planning

latter.[22]

Investment and Financing

The planned total of investments was JD 3.3 bn at current prices, 61% of which were in the public sector. Investments were allocated in the following main sectors: mining and manufacturing 23%, transportation and infrastructure 17%, irrigation and water sewerage 16%, housing and government buildings 9%, and agriculture 7%. A total of 53% of the planned investments were related to commodity-producing sectors and tourism, the rest to infrastructure, social projects and other services. This distribution was based on the following criteria.[23] The first priority was given to commodity-producing sectors and related infrastructural facilities, with the aim of reducing Jordan's dependence on the services sector. Further priority was given to infrastructural and social projects linked with regional development policies. Furthermore, projects were emphasized that would strengthen Arab co-operation. In general, emphasis was laid on the completion of projects which had been held up due to difficulties in implementation, and on projects for which feasibility studies and tender documents had already been presented (project gap).

Of the planned total of investments of JD 3.3 bn, public-sector projects were supposed to amount to JD 1,760 mn.

Financing was planned as follows:

foreign aid	JD 1,162 mn
current account budget surplus	JD 921 mn
internal borrowing	JD 150 mn
total	JD 2,233 mn

Capital expenditures:

government investment projects	JD 1,760 mn
repayment of foreign loans	JD 98 mn
repayment of domestic loans	JD 50 mn
government credits and contributions to non-government institutions	JD 325 mn
total	JD 2,233 mn

More than half of the total amount, including government contributions to projects of the private sector (1,760 + 325 = JD 2,085 mn), was to be financed by foreign aid (JD 1,162 mn). This amount would increase to the same extent that the planned budget surplus did not materialize.

Administrative Problems
The plan emphasized the need to improve the performance of public administration, which is suffering from a continuous decline in productivity due to uncontrolled quantitative expansion and to the emigration of skilled manpower to the Arab oil countries. With considerable frankness, the plan mentioned the weak points in the existing administration, such as vagueness of objectives, too much centralization of decision-making, duplication of functions, overstaffing, unattractive salaries and terms of employment, inadequate on-the-job training, and inefficient budgetary control.[24]

Formulation of Policies, Programmes and Projects
In the process of transforming the objectives into policies, programmes and projects, Jordan's planners were acting in an unusually straightforward and pragmatic way. They methodically abandoned the pretentious planning rituals based on the voluminous analytic tools of the 1950s and 1960s, thus appreciating realistically their limited applicability for small, outward-looking countries exposed to extreme economic and political uncertainty. Nor did they overstrain the administrative and political steering capacity. Instead they focused on an amazingly plain outline of the main problems of each sector, then deduced relevant policy recommendations and proposed respective projects.

Plan Implementation, 1982-84
The development plan (1981-85) was published in spring 1982. A few months later Israeli troops marched into Lebanon, marking the beginning of another round of military confrontation in the area. The same year marked the beginning of Jordan's economic recession, which continued throughout 1983 and 1984. Capital inflows from abroad declined. Arab aid resources were cut, too, though maintaining their leading role in financing the Jordanian structural deficit (Table 9.2).

Table 9.2 Foreign Aid Contributions, 1982-83 (million Jordanian dinars)

Donors	1982	1983
Budget aid of Arab countries	184.5	130.0
Capital assistance	61.5	101.5
United Kingdom	0.2	0.3
Fed. Rep. of Germany	3.4	3.9
Kuwait	3.4	16.8
USAID	3.5	7.5
Saudi Arabia	9.3	10.2
Denmark	0.9	0.2
Arab Fund for Economic and Social Development	1.2	1.2
Iraq	3.2	-
Japan	4.1	5.4
Others	32.4	56.0
Total	258.9	331.5

Source: Central Bank of Jordan (CBJ), Monthly Statistical Bulletin (Amman), vol. 20.

manpower rather than from a lack of capital. During the final few years, however, the financial resource gap was increasingly being felt. Public investment programmes had to be cut or stretched over a longer time-span, and there were major delays in project implementation.

GDP growth rates in real terms fell from 19.6% in 1980 to 10.7% in 1981, 5.5% in 1982, and 4.5% in 1983. (Table 9.3) Estimates for 1984 assume a rate in the magnitude of 3.5%[25] which would still be a remarkable performance by international standards.

The commodity-producing sectors did not develop homogeneously. Agriculture suffered from low rainfall and a major drought in the winter of 1983-84. Grain production in 1984 fell from the last ten years' average of 62,000 t/year to 10,000 t/year.[26]

Various industrial sub-sectors suffered from shrinking markets and sales problems. Export demand had been declining during the last few years, and there were delays in establishing production capacities. Nevertheless industrial and mining production increased by 7.1% in 1983 and 8.4% in 1984.[27]

Table 9.3: Macro-Economic Performance, 1981-84

Indicator	1981	1982	1983[a]	1984	Annual rate of growth (1980-83) at current prices (%)	Annual rate of growth (1980-83) at 1980 prices (%)
GDP at factor cost (mn JD)	1,059.4	1,201.2	1,318.0		14.0	6.9
Real growth rate (%)	10.7	5.5	4.5			
GDP per capita (JD)	430.0	440.0				
Composition of GDP (mn JD)						
Agriculture, forestry & fishing	76.6	83.8	99.1		15.3	8.1
Industry	208.3	230.3	256.8		15.4	8.1
Electricity & water supply	21.0	25.3	28.5		18.6	11.2
Construction	110.6	121.9	126.8		9.1	2.3
Wholesale & retail trade, restaurants & hotels	196.7	220.5	233.7		12.0	4.9
Transport & communications	102.7	123.5	146.3		22.4	14.7
Producers of government services	191.2	218.5	232.9		11.0	4.0
Other services	152.3	178.4	194.0		15.7	8.3

Table 9.3 (Cont'd)

Indicator	1981	1982	1983ª	1984	Annual rate of growth (1980-83) at current prices (%)	Annual rate of growth (1980-83) at 1980 prices (%)
Budget (mn JD)						
Receipts	638.3	765.0	762.0	759.0		
Expenditures	638.3	765.0	775.4	770.2		
Surplus/Deficit	–	–	– 13.4	– 11.2		
Total public debt	231.7	278.2	307.7			
Total foreign debt (mn JD)	561.2	620.1	766.7			
Net national product at factor cost (mn JD)	1,312.2	1,462.6	1,577.4		14.7	7.4

Sources: CBJ, Monthly Statistical Bulletin, vol. 20, and Twentieth Annual Report 1983.

Tourism, too, showed a number of structural weaknesses, in addition to its high vulnerability to external political circumstances. Nevertheless, it has remained one of Jordan's major income-generating sectors. Hotel capacities were extended, but foreign tourists declined from 2.03 mn in 1982 to 1.75 mn in 1983 and 1.59 mn in 1984. Arab nationals made up nearly 80% of the 1.59 mn. Of these, Syrians accounted for almost one-quarter and Egyptians one-half. Revenues dropped from JD 184 mn in 1983 to JD 172 mn in 1984.[28]

Services in general maintained their dominant role in Jordan's economic structure, although their share in GDP declined from 61% in 1981 to 54% in 1984, due mainly to an increase of manufacturing and mining from 20% to 29% during the same period.

Foreign trade experienced a downward trend in 1983, with regard to both exports and imports. The EEC was Jordan's major supplier, with JD 330 mn in both 1982 and 1983. Jordan's exports consisted mainly of phosphates. Its major clients were the Arab countries, led by Saudi Arabia with an increase from JD 28 mn to JD 35 mn between 1982 and 1983, followed by Iraq with a decline from JD 67 mn to JD 27 mn.[29] In 1984 the situation improved again because of a growth in phosphate sales and a good performance by the manufacturing sector. Principally as a result of a recovery in exports to Iraq, the trade deficit dropped by 17% in 1984.[30] The political arrangement with Egypt is expected to stimulate industrial exports further. But it is obvious that there is no possibility of closing the structural gap between imports and exports during the next few years.

Part of the deficit is financed by remittances. Migration of skilled Jordanian manpower to OAPEC countries has declined since 1982, following the overall recession in the oil-producing countries. Fortunately, the number of returning migrants has not yet overcompensated for the declining outflow. The overall remittances of Jordanians working abroad, including those outside the banking system, continue to be substantial. They are estimated at JD 450-500 mn per annum, three times the amount of exports and twice the amount of industrial production. On the other hand, about 150,000 foreigners, mainly unskilled labour from Egypt and other low-wage Arab countries, and from the Far East, transferred JD 62 mn in 1982 and JD 73 mn in 1983.[31]

Jordan's overall performance has been amazingly

robust, and clearly more successful than in several other non-oil Arab countries, let alone in the large number of low-income countries in Asia and sub-Saharan Africa. Key ingredients have been the outstanding development commitment of Jordan's political leadership, linked with political stability, the competence and skill of its entrepreneurial and professional cadres, and the availability of substantial foreign financial support mainly from Arab donors.

It is obvious that dependence on foreign aid will persist for many years. Considering the declining receipts of the OAPEC countries, however, it remains to be seen whether foreign finance will come forward to the extent required within the strategic development perspectives of Jordan's planners. In addition, a continuing high level of remittances will be instrumental in financing import requirements.[32] Non-Arab donors will probably maintain their aid commitment, although - as in the past - at a level much below OAPEC contributions.

OPEN QUESTIONS CONCERNING A LONG-TERM DEVELOPMENT STRATEGY IN AN ENVIRONMENT OF INCREASING INTERNATIONAL TURBULENCE

Efficiency of the Institutions

As distinct from many developing countries, Jordan's planners clearly link the macro, sector and project levels. Overall strategic concepts, sectoral goals, policies and institutions, and transformation of the sector policies into investment projects are interconnected. Thus, many mistakes made by other developing countries have been avoided, such as disconnection of planning levels, lack of concentration on projects as essential building blocks of development (thus creating the 'project gap'), and neglect of the administrative-institutional framework.

The planners are aware of priorities. Objectives and policies are clearly indicated. In the institutional field, however, difficulties may continue. Contrary to conventional growth theories, the critical bottleneck of development is not due so much to the shortage of physical resources but lies, rather, in the institutional field: there can be no policies without institutions in charge of formulating and implementing them. Development of efficient institutions and continuing strengthening

of their professional standards despite adverse
influences of (personnel-) policies is, in fact,
the most difficult task and usually beyond the
political competence of economic planners. It
requires, above all, the 'development commitment'
of the political leadership[33] along with continuity
in handling institutions and personnel. Countries
with frequent changes in government, combined with
frequent replacement of their professional staff,
do not satisfy this condition, irrespective of the
best intentions or varying ideological proclamations.

Jordan belongs to the small group of
developing countries which enjoy both the continuous
development commitment of their political leaderships
over many years, and considerable administrative
stability, despite ongoing political confrontation
from the outside. The efficiency of Jordan's
institutional set-up is significantly higher than
that of most other Arab countries, and - along with
a liberal economic order - has been manifested in
an outstanding economic growth rate in the past.

Realism of Objectives
The objectives of the development plan (1981-85)
were ambitious yet not unrealistic, considering
past performance as well as the policies,
programmes and projects suggested. Each forecast is
necessarily bound to be uncertain, and particularly
so if a country is small, outward-oriented and
exposed to increasing turbulence in the international
markets of goods and factors. Besides, in the case
of Jordan, there are extreme political risks due to
the ongoing Middle East conflict.

In spite of the unusually big resource gap of
$1.5-2 bn per annum, financing seems possible as
long as the Arab oil countries, being the most
important donors, are able to maintain domestic
stability. Jordan's absorptive capacity will
continue to depend on its institutional ability to
prepare and implement feasible projects.

Regional and Social Balance and Employment
Jordan's planning is primarily oriented and
organized into sectoral categories. Considerations
regarding domestic political stability play an
important role. Programmes designed to balance
regional differences in development tend to be
considered only if they accord with the criteria
of: (a) undisputed political control by the central

government; and (b) economic viability. In remote areas with an ethnic and tribal heterogeneity, the first criterion may not always be met; fulfilment of the second criterion is difficult, due to the extreme underdevelopment and to the low development potential of the remote semi-arid and arid areas.

Regional development processes are concentrating on the integrated Jordan Valley development programme, on the port of Aqaba along with new industrial capacities, and on the activation of a few zones around Amman. A further centre is developing in the north around Irbid, with its new university.

These efforts, however, are unable to balance the unplanned and uncontrolled agglomeration process in the Greater Amman area. Planners are aware that the economics of agglomeration in the Amman area are extremely attractive from the individual entrepreneur's point of view, whereas its diseconomies from the overall point of view have not yet surpassed the threshold of public sensitivity. For the city of Amman an effective, long-term planning of infrastructure does not exist. Nor is there any concept as to what a more balanced regional development process might look like, or how the advantages and disadvantages of decentralized development poles in the context of Jordan's overall strategies might be balanced. This question would be particularly relevant to marginal, semi-arid rural areas with extremely poor development potential. Elements of a sensible compromise could include a selection of four or five development areas outside the Greater Amman area, deliberately accepting continuing migration from several semi-arid areas, in combination with special programmes for extremely disadvantaged areas and for social groups which would be kept in their hereditary regions for general political reasons (tribal loyalty, preservation of traditional ways of life and of significant elements of cultural identity, domestic stabilization, strategic considerations etc.). For some bedouin tribes in arid zones such programmes are already in operation.

In Jordan's political reality, there exists not only the conflict between 'territory and function' (Friedmann) - i.e. the conflict between territorial (= regional) and functional (= central) points of view - but also group-specific considerations with regard to individual tribes with traditionally varying loyalties to the royal family, and to the Palestinian population (traditional residents as well as refugees inside and outside the UNRWA camps), a problem that has complex links with the history of the PLO and its demand for the creation of a Palestinian state as well as with the question of its location.

An additional socio-political problem is the partial exchange of the workforce. More than 300,000 Jordanians are working in the Gulf states, whereas 150,000 foreign workers are working in Jordan. In recent years the Jordanian government was in the comparatively comfortable situation of being able to balance any possible social discontent by the option for emigration - an opportunity which was seized by the Palestinians in particular. As mentioned before, this possibility will, before long, be restricted, due to limits in capability and willingness of the host countries to admit more immigrants, even if the domestic situation in the Gulf states remains stable.

Policies to Secure Natural Resources
The country's extreme external dependency is a main starting-point for any development strategy. It is the greatest challenge to those who formulate policies which, in the light of increasing international turbulence and impending military confrontation in the Middle East, aim to ensure survival. Food security is one of the predominant problems. In bad crop years, as for instance 1979, domestic wheat production met only 5% of Jordan's consumption. In 1980 Jordan consumed 400,000 t of wheat, 133,000 t of which were produced by Jordan itself; yet wheat production dropped to 57,000 t in 1981 and 10,000 in 1984.[34] Urgent problems are the shortage of water and the dependency on irregular rainfall in the rain-dependent agricultural areas (with small-sized farms being predominant there), efficiency gaps in the use of existing irrigation systems, and inefficient methods of cultivation and soil preservation as well as the low yields resulting therefrom. Co-operative and marketing policies could be improved substantially.

A problem closely linked with food security is the shortage of water. Within the next few years, the question of the physical availability of water will become still more urgent. The water reservoir of rivers is largely utilized by hydroplants. On the other hand, the demand for agricultural irrigation, municipal drinking water and industrial water is increasing exponentially along with development measures. The <u>per capita</u> water consumption is now one-fifth of the international average. (The possibility of conveying fresh water by pipelines from Iraq has been discussed.)

In the energy sector, Jordan depends on the importation of crude oil. Expenditure on oil imports has risen continuously. Transport consumes about half of the total refinery output; industry and electricity are other large absorbers.[35] Subsidies on oil products at prices far below the international market, with no discrimination as to needy groups, have delayed economy measures. Hopes have been placed in successful domestic oil exploration, as well as in alternative energy sources in the solar and wind-power sectors where there has been considerable technical success, but which, in absolute figures, cannot be of noticeable relief in the next decade.

Development of Adaptation Potential and Flexibility in a Turbulent Environment

Considering the unpredictability of future events, yet facing the possibility of critical developments in the socio-political environment, a small country's problem is how to develop suitable precautionary policies. The established planning theories of the 1950s and 1960s have neglected this problem. Until the mid-1970s the planning concepts advanced were based on the idea that, first, future conditions can be predicted within a reliable margin, and, second, an optimal programme can be formulated. Ever since the mid-1970s it has become obvious that, due to the increasing speed of change, such assumptions are less and less realistic and that new paradigms are required.

Since the 1970s there has been a growing realization, even in the larger economies, that, along with the increase of internal complexity of socio-economic systems, the role assigned to comprehensive national development planning (articulating itself in the formulation of consistent four- or five-year plans drawn up with great analytical engagement) had decreased; nor were political decision-makers able or willing to bear its cost in terms of time, limited professional resources, analytic effort and decision-making capacity.[36] Internal structures characterized by increasing differentiation, partly as a result of the development process, can less and less be

Development Planning

planned by bureaucratic institutions such as planning commissions or ministries of planning, even as far as the political-administrative process within the public sector is concerned. With increasing complexity and differentiation it becomes essential to shift the emphasis from direct government intervention and resource allocation to more indirect incentive systems.

In addition, small developing economies are facing the problem of an almost inevitable external dependency which calls for outward-looking strategies, as actually practised in the development policies of most of the successful small countries (e.g. Taiwan, Singapore, Hong Kong, Malaysia, Tunisia, Cyprus). Small countries need to ensure that their internal economies can adapt quickly to foreign commodity and factor markets. Here, economic policy primarily and typically is foreign-trade policy (and often foreign policy), whereas domestic economic policy becomes adaptive policy.[37] In the small Middle Eastern countries the primacy of foreign policy considerations is extremely strong.

From the empirical analysis of development processes in a large number of semi-industrialized countries during the last two decades, two major elements of successful strategies can be derived. The first is the concept of development as an evolutionary process towards increasing complexity and differentiation (and not primarily quantitative growth) in all sectors and on all levels as an universal principle,[38] and its appreciation and application in formulating economic and social policies. The second is the establishment of management systems and decision-making structures that permit the utmost openness for this principle, in particular allowing for learning-processes, flexibility, variety, adaptive potential and self-organization.

The ongoing increase of turbulence can, for a large part, be regarded as a consequence of blocked evolutionary processes of change. The necessary structural transformation is retarded by political as well as administrative tendencies of inertia. The short-term maxim of preserving power is ranked before the medium-term maxim of development. Continuously flowing and comparatively unperturbed processes of adaptation to new conditions are blocked, and inevitable changes take a turbulent form. There is an increasing realization that we are indeed beyond the 'stable state' which, in a totally dynamic universe, never actually existed.

Development Planning

Hence, all attempts to achieve 'stability' are ultimately bound to fail. This insight is not translated sufficiently into policy design. Large bureaucracies, in both the public and private sectors, tend to cling to established patterns of operation. Turbulence as the characteristic feature of all systems and their environment is, for the most part, caused by the institutions themselves. In any case, it has become the dominant boundary condition of economic policy.

A sensible strategy which suggests itself in a turbulent environment is to build <u>potential</u>: if future situations and processes are unpredictable, rational action will switch away from the attempt to formulate optimum programmes with regard to expected future environmental conditions and towards the establishment of possible responses to unforeseeable situations rapidly, efficiently and from a position of relative strength.[39] This implies the capability of fast analytical comprehension of new environmental situations, i.e. the ability to learn. It also calls for: the ability and readiness to adjust, i.e. flexibility and adaptability; institutional permeability for new tasks, along with a high degree of self-organization in decentralized structures; and the ability to mobilize and to create resources. Potential in this sense does not only consist in immediately accessible financial and physical resources (the traditional way of making provision for the future). In a dynamic perspective, it means analytical management potential in the widest sense, the know-how and technological skills of the labour force, scientific research capacities, standing in international capital markets, and, last but not least, political goodwill in donor countries. For Jordan, the latter factor has been pre-eminent in securing economic survival, and is closely linked to King Hussein's international prestige.

Small countries often have no specific comparable advantages. Jordan has neither considerable capital resources nor a cheap workforce. In such circumstances it is essential to create specific competitive advantages.[40] Such policies can start from already existing, relatively strong economic features, such as the agility and entrepreneurial skills of a trade-oriented population with an unusually high level of general education; proximity and cultural affinity to promising markets, both in the Arab oil countries and in the industrially advanced Mashrek countries,[41] and the possibility of taking over a still larger share of Lebanon's traditional transit function in the Middle East in view of the continuing Lebanese crisis.

In addition to the efforts to strengthen the commodity-producing sectors of mining, manufacturing industry and agriculture, Jordan has the potential of an effective services economy with transit-trade and service functions for the Arab world. An important feature in this concept is the level of technology, not only with regard to industrial activities, but particularly with regard to a sophisticated services sector. The traditional trade component can be upgraded and extended through technological consulting services, such as market research, identification of feasible production techniques, participation in plant layout, construction and operation, as well as in adapting and implementing internationally available technologies, processes and products to the specific demand profiles of Arab customers. These would be elements of a policy to create potential in the sense mentioned above.

There are components of such policies in Jordan: the development of the universities' technical faculties and the establishment of scientific and technical research centres[42] as well as an activation of their consulting function.[43] These features can be integrated into a coherent, clearly defined policy to strengthen Jordan's potential to prepare for an uncertain future which, in view of the ongoing political and military tension as well as increasing socio-cultural and religious conflicts in the Middle East, will continue to challenge the country's viability.

Development Planning

NOTES

1. Kamal Abu Jaber, The Jordanians and the People of Jordan (Amman, 1980), pp. 28-9.
2. Ibid., pp. 31-2.
3. Ibid., p. 34.
4. Ibid., p. 44.
5. Ibid., p. 39.
6. Ibid., p. 40.
7. Ibid., p. 1.
8. Rami G. Khouri, The Jordan Valley: Life and Society below Sea-Level (Longman, Harlow, 1982).
9. Bassam Saket, Bassam Asfour and Gazi Assaf, The Economy of Jordan over the '70s and 1979 - A Bird's Eye View (Royal Scientific Society (hereafter RSS), Economics Dept., Amman, 1980), p. 3.
10. Ibid., p. 27.
11. Ibid., p. 3.
12. Jordan, National Planning Council (hereafter NPC), Summary of the Five Year Plan for Economic and Social Development 1981-1985 (n. p., n. d.) (hereafter quoted as Summary).
13. See also Michael P. Mazur, Economic Growth and Development in Jordan (Croom Helm, London, 1979), pp. 145ff.
14. The debt service ratio (interest and redemptions as a percentage of exports) increased from 23% in 1978 to 35% in 1980. See Bassam K. Saket and Bassam J. Asfour, Jordan's Economy: 1980 and Beyond (RSS, Economics Dept., Amman, June 1981), p. 15.
15. Summary, pp. 14-17.
16. Ibid., p. 16. The natural growth rate of the population is 3.8%, thus being one of the highest in the world. Including the movements of refugees, Jordan's population increased by an average of 4.96% per annum between 1960 and 1979.
17. Summary, p. 17.
18. Ibid., p. 18. Considering Jordan's strong external links, GDP and not GNP was used as a frame of reference. (See also Tables 10.3 and 10.4).
19. Summary, p. 19.
20. Ibid., NPC, A Brief Review of the Previous Plan and the Main Features of the Plan for 1981-1985 (Amman, Sept. 1981) (hereafter quoted as NPC).
21. Summary, pp. 20-1; NPC.
22. NPC, Plan for Economic and Social Development 1981-1985 (Amman, 1982), pp. 283-4 (in

Arabic) (hereafter quoted as Plan 1981-1985). See also Table 9.2. AN earlier version of the plan did not contain any indication of employment outlook either; see Social and Economic Development of Jordan 1981-1985, summary and translation by Muhammad A. Tijani (Amman, Dec. 1981).

23. Summary, p. 22.
24. Ibid., pp. 23-4.
25. International Herald Tribune (hereafter IHT), 25-6 May 1985; Mitteilungen der Bundesstelle für Aussenhandelsinformation, March 1985, Weltwirtschaft am Jahreswechsel 1984/85 - Jordanien.
26. Middle East Economic Digest (hereafter MEED), (29 June 1984).
27. Mitteilungen.
28. Ibid.; IHT, 25-6 May 1985.
29. Mitteilungen.
30. IHT, 25-6 May 1985.
31. Mitteilungen.
32. Arab Gulf states have failed to honour in full their pledges made at the 1978 Baghdad Summit. Financial transfers have declined from a promised $1.2 bn to $500 mn, with only Saudi Arabia honouring its commitment in full and Kuwait in part. In 1984 Qatar and the UAE failed to meet their commitments. On the other hand, remittances have kept up at $2 bn/year.
33. I. Adelman and C.T. Morris, 'Performance Criteria for Evaluating Economic Development Potential: An Operational Approach', Quarterly Journal of Economics (1968), p. 272.
34. Saket, Asfour and Assaf, Economy of Jordan, p. 9; Saket and Asfour, Jordan's Economy, p. 28; 'Plan Implementation, 1982-84', pp. 160-5 of the present chapter.
35. Saket and Asfour, Jordan's Economy, pp. 32-3.
36. D. Weiss, book review of W. von Urff, Zur Programmierung von Entwicklungsplänen (Berlin and Munich, 1973), Zeitschrift für die gesamte Staatswissenschaft, no. 131 (1975), pp. 189-92; H.-H. Taake, 'Das Ende der Planungseuphorie in der Entwicklungspolitik' in Neue Elemente in den Beziehungen zwischen Industrie- und Entwicklungsländern (German Development Institute, Berlin, 1975).
37. See also: D. Weiss, D. Kampe, Ch. Schmidt and J. Wagenseil, 'Consequences of the EC South Enlargement on Industrial Strategies of Third Mediterranean Countries - The Case of Cyprus', Konjunkturpolitik, vol. 26 (1980), pp. 129 ff; W.

Hillebrand, 'Probleme der Industrieentwicklung und der Industrieplanung in kleinen Ländern - Der Fall Irland', in V. Timmermann (ed.), <u>Beiträge zur Industrialisierungs und Handelspolitik der Entwicklungsländer, Schriften des Vereins für Socialpolitik</u>, NF, vol. 110 (Berlin, 1980), pp. 65ff.

38. D. Weiss, 'Some Reflections on Outward-looking Economic Management in a Turbulent International Environment', <u>L'Egypt Contemporaine</u>, no. 385 (1981); D. Weiss, 'Culture, Perception of Reality, and the Newly Emerging Planning Paradigm, <u>Social Indicators Research</u>, vol. 16 (1985)

39. A.J. Katsenelinboigen, 'Constructing the Potential of a System', <u>General Systems</u>, vol. 19 (1975), pp. 27ff.

40. H.G. Grubel and P.J. Lloyd, <u>Intra-Industry Trade</u> (Macmillan, London and Basingstoke, 1975), pp. 147-8.

41. It is noteworthy that most of the larger Arab non-oil countries have pursued an import-substituting strategy during the last decades. None of them, however, has successfully moved towards laying the foundations for a successive orientation towards international markets in industrial products such as consumer goods, semi-finished industrial products, basic industrial commodities and engineering industries. Egypt is a striking example. Having started the process of industrialization as early as 1830 under Mohamed Ali, several new attempts have been made during the 1930s, the 1950s and the reforms and counter-reforms since 1974. However, Egypt has not been able to join the group of Newly Industrializing Countries so far. Instead, it still belongs to the lower third of the developing countries in terms of industrial output and <u>per capita</u> income.

Some of the Arab non-oil countries have benefited from the OAPEC markets. Engineering industries offer particularly interesting prospects, which might partly be used by Jordan. Promising branches are fabricated metal products (builders' hardware, kitchen utensils, hand tools, wire products, structural products), consumer durables (refrigerators and water coolers, washing machines, water and space heaters, air conditioners), industrial electrical products (electrical cables, transformers, switchgear, relays, capacitors, electric motors, accumulators) and transport products (railway wagons, medium-sized buses, components for cars and buses, road and agricultural trailers).

Development Planning

Some of these might be efficiently manufactured in Jordan. They have good export prospects, particularly in regional markets in neighbouring African and Arab countries over the medium term.

Trade in engineering goods among developing countries increased from $455 mn in 1970 to $7,057 mn in 1980, with an annual growth rate of 31.5%. Arab and African countries have been the fastest growing markets for engineering goods, and they could offer substantial prospects for Jordanian exports in several carefully selected product lines.

42. Jordan belongs to the few developing countries where leading policy-makers in education and research are committed to excellence. Technology is applied science, and science can neither be bought nor given. It means creative participation in the international scientific process. Its output is information, and information has increasingly become the prime input factor replacing the traditional factors of production like capital, labour and natural resources. The future industries will be knowledge industries.

43. *Summary*, pp. 74-82.

Chapter Ten

TARGETS AND ACHIEVEMENTS OF JORDAN'S LAST FIVE-YEAR PLANS, 1976-1980 AND 1981-1985: A SUMMARY

Bichara Khader

During the last decade, Jordan has succeeded in completing two five-year plans (1976-80 and 1981-85) with investment of some $9,600 mn, and in maintaining a relatively rapid rate of economic development. This has been achieved despite five major handicaps: being in the eye of the Arab-Israeli conflict, being poorly endowed with natural resources, relying heavily on foreign aid for its annual budget, seeing its highly skilled manpower in great demand throughout the Arab oil states, and having its West Bank occupied and colonized by the Israeli Army.

Jordan's remarkable performance has lain in its ability to 'turn constraints into pillars of the development process', thus realistically exploiting the country's geographic, demographic and political position within the broader Middle Eastern context. Thus, although the energy bill has been substantial, the sudden upsurge of oil prices which began in 1973/74 and the resulting boom in the oil economies have been the driving force behind Jordan's economic and social development.

This led to an increase in regional demand for Jordanian exports, to the exodus of more than 350,000 skilled Jordanians who departed for jobs in Arab oil-producing states, to the inflow of migrant workers' remittances, and finally to budget aid from the Arab oil states. Since 1973 much of Jordan's growth has been financed by income generated abroad, while domestic revenues, despite continuous attempts to increase them, have remained consistently below government recurrent expenditure. A rapid glance at the aims and achievements of the last two five-year plans will reveal the complex reality of Jordan's economy, with its limitations and trump cards.

Targets and Achievements

THE FIRST FIVE-YEAR PLAN (1976-80)

Table 10.1: Sectoral Projections of the Five-Year Plan (1976-80)

	Average annual 1975-80 growth rate (% per annum)	Share in GDP 1975 (%)	Share in GDP 1980 (%)	Share in total growth of of GDP 1975-80 (%)	Share in total investment 1976-80 (%)	Gross ICOR 1976-80
Agriculture	7.0	10.3	8.3	5.5	14.7	9.3
Mining & manufacturing	26.2	15.5	28.3	45.5	30.0	2.3
Water & electricity	17.1	1.7	2.2	2.8	8.9	11.3
Transport & communications	10.6	9.0	8.5	7.8	18.3	8.2
Trade	7.2	19.0	15.4	10.6	0.5	0.2
Ownership of dwellings	12.0	5.9	5.9	6.0	10.8	6.4
Others	7.4	38.6	31.5	22.0	16.8	2.7
Total	11.9	100.0	100.0	100.0	100.0	3.5

Note: All figures here are derived from projections in constant-price dinars. Investments in irrigation are included in the agricultural sector.
Sources: National Planning Council (NPC), Five-Year Plan (Amman), pp. 109, 122, 292, 681; Michael P. Mazur, Economic Growth and Development in Jordan (Croom Helm, London, 1979), p. 250.

The targets set in this first five-year plan were as follows:

    (a) a 12% annual real growth of GDP;
    (b) a 16.5% annual real increase in domestic revenues, increasing their share of total revenues from 51% in 1975 to 68% in 1980 and their proportion to current expenditures from 61.5% in 1975 to 91.5% in 1980;

(c) a reduction of the trade deficit from JD 153 mn in 1975 to JD 131 mn in 1980;
(d) a balanced development of all regions.

As is apparent from Table 10.1, the projected growth rate is deliberately too high. Investment was to be heavily concentrated on agriculture and industry (Table 10.1). The plan on the whole is a high-investment plan. Over the plan period, gross domestic investment was scheduled to average 32.3% of GDP at market prices - compared to about 18% for Jordan in 1979-86. The plan also revealed something of a 'big-projects' strategy. As Table 10.2 shows,

Table 10.2: Major Investment Projects in the Five-Year Plan (1976-80)

	Planned Investment (mn JD)	Share in total plan Investment (%)
Maqarim Dam	25.35	3.3
Phosphate expansion	24.00	3.1
Petroleum refinery expansion	39.00	5.1
Chemical fertilizer industry	61.00	8.0
Potash extraction	25.00	3.3
Cement factory in southern Jordan	21.30	2.8
Central thermal power station at Zarqa	21.89	2.9
Amman International Airport	25.50	3.3
Total for eight projects	243.04	31.8

Note: Total plan investment was JD 765 mn.
Sources: NPC, Five-Year Plan, pp. 122, 267, 355, 420; Mazur, Economic Growth, p. 253.

only eight projects (five in the industrial sector) accounted for almost one-third of projected investment during the plan period. The reasons behind such an option probably lie in the ready availability of foreign assistance, which was expected to equal 86.3% of gross domestic investment during the plan period.

The plan projected a marked decline in the

relative importance of government outlays over the course of the plan period, primarily due to slow growth in government investment and government expenditures on defence and public security. Over the same period, government current domestic revenues were to rise from about 24% to 36% of GDP (Table 10.3).

Table 10.3: Projected Government Outlays of the Five-Year Plan (1976-80)

	Share in GDP (%) 1975	1977	1980	Average annual growth rate (%, per annum)
Total current expenditures	36.7	33.7	30.8	7.6
Central government	35.3	32.4	29.7	7.7
Defence & public security	14.9	13.1	11.4	5.5
Other	20.4	19.4	18.3	9.1
Municipalities	1.4	1.3	1.1	7.0
Gross capital formation	14.4	18.1	9.9	3.5
Loans & grants to private sector	4.9	6.7	3.2	2.1
Debt payment	2.7	2.7	2.4	8.4
Total	58.7	61.3	46.2	6.3

Sources: NPC, Five-Year Plan, pp. 109, 112, 114; Mazur, Economic Growth, p. 255.

The plan put the emphasis on several other measures: promotion of co-operative societies, development of modern financial instruments and institutions, financial liberalization, vocational training, and so on.

Achievements

The ambitious five-year plan (1976-80) fell short of its objectives in several respects. Real annual growth of GDP averaged about 9.6% instead of the 11.9% forecast. The total figure of investment spending exceeded the planned targets by 10.3%, although the distribution among sectors was very uneven. The targets set for a number of industrial sectors, as well as for mining, electricity and water supply, were not met as a result of lower

Targets and Achievements

than expected growth in phosphate production and the delays incurred in the fertilizer project. Construction and agriculture, on the other hand, performed better than anticipated (Table 10.4).

Table 10.4: National Accounts (million Jordanian dinars)

	1977	1978	1979	1980	% change in 1980
GDP at factor cost, of which:	406.7	508.1	627.6	762.4	+21.4
Agriculture & fishing	41.7	58.6	43.6	58.5	+34.2
Manufacturing	65.1	74.4	88.5	108.4	+22.5
Mining & quarrying	19.9	22.9	27.5	34.3	+24.7
Construction	27.0	35.0	60.5	75.6	+25.0
Trade & tourism	66.3	83.0	110.0	133.0	+20.9
Financial services	47.0	65.5	90.3	103.8	+15.0
Transport & communications	35.9	59.3	62.9	75.3	+19.7
Government services	84.4	95.0	129.1	155.8	+20.7
GDP at market prices	481.0	589.1	712.0	869.0	+22.0
Plus net factor income from abroad	145.9	150.0	157.0	190.0	+21.0
= GNP at market prices	626.9	739.1	869.0	1,059.0	+21.8
Disposable income =	781.7	858.7	1,219.9	n.a.	n.a.
Private final consumption	420.2	517.4	681.7	752.4	+10.4
+ Government final consumption	156.6	190.0	235.3	260.5	+10.7
+ Saving	204.9	151.3	302.9	n.a.	n.a.
Of GDP at market prices:					
Compensation of employees	179.0	208.7	269.4	324.2	+20.3
Operating surplus	221.7	286.7	337.8	410.2	+21.4
Consumption of fixed cap. for.	11.0	13.7	20.4	28.0	+37.3
Net indirect taxes	74.0	81.0	84.4	106.6	+26.3

Sources: Jordan, Dept. of Statistics, (May 1981); Bassam K. Saket and Bassam J. Asfour, <u>Jordan's Economy: 1980 and Beyond</u> (Royal Scientific Society (RSS), BS, BA/Economy/14/6-80, Amman, June 1981), p. 2.

Targets and Achievements

The growth rate of domestic revenues in the government budget did not exceed 9% per annum and total domestic revenues reached only JD 129.5 mn.

Table 10.5: Industrial Production, 1978-80 (million Jordanian dinars)

	1978	1979	1980	% change in 1980
OVERALL INDUSTRIAL PRODUCTION INDEX (1975 = 100)	159.2	188.0	232.1	+ 23.5
Food, drinks & tobacco	141.8	186.4	218.7	+ 17.3
Textiles & clothing	119.8	148.7	172.3	+ 15.9
Construction materials	114.2	137.5	163.0	+ 18.5
Chemicals	275.3	266.9	345.3	+ 29.4
of which				
Pharmaceuticals	(139.5)	(161.3)	(274.0)	(+ 69.9)
Plastics	(541.4)	(341.8)	(308.3)	(- 9.8)
Petrol refining	172.9	197.6	210.3	+ 6.4
Phosphates	172.1	209.9	290.4	+ 38.4
Electricity & batteries	144.7	177.8	216.3	- 21.7
Fodder	124.9	124.6	115.3	- 7.5
Paper & cardboard	110.3	170.1	209.5	+ 23.2
Leather	94.7	79.3	85.3	+ 7.6
OUTPUT OF MAIN INDUSTRIES				
Phosphates (mn t)	2.3	2.8	3.9	+ 39.3
Petroleum products (mn t)	1.4	1.6	1.8	+ 12.5
Cigarettes ('000 t)	2.6	3.4	4.2	+ 23.5
Electricity (mn Kwh)	571.5	774.1	938.8	+ 21.3
Iron ('000 t)	65.3	31.0	86.2	+ 6.4
Cement ('000 t)	553.0	623.2	912.7	+ 46.5

Sources: Central Bank of Jordan (CBJ), Monthly Statistical Bulletin (Amman) (Dec. 1980); Saket and Asfour, Jordan's Economy, p.7.

Targets and Achievements

The trade deficit, instead of being cut back, expanded during the period to reach approximately JD 500 mn, again partly attributable to the shortfall in phosphate output (Table 10.5 and 10.6); while the uneven distribution of per capita

Table 10.6: Industrial Origin of Gross Domestic Product: Growth Rates, 1976-80

	GROWTH RATES: ANNUAL REAL	
	Plan	Actual
Agriculture	7.0	7.4
Industry & mining	26.2	16.0
Electricity & water	17.1	11.9
Construction	4.1	13.1
Services	8.5	7.7
GDP at factor cost	11.9	9.6

Sources: NPC; Saket and Asfour, Jordan's Economy, p. 39.

Table 10.7: Government Revenues, 1975-80

	1975	1976	1977	1978	1979	1980
DOMESTIC REVENUES (mn JD)						
Plan	82.6	107.8	125.4	144.1	160.6	189.2
Actual[a]	82.6	96.5	111.4	116.0	118.7	129.5
TOTAL REVENUES (mn JD)						
Plan	199.4	262.8	290.4	357.1	293.6	292.2
Actual[a]	199.4	173.7	252.9	242.4	280.0	278.1
RATIO %: DOMESTIC REV. / TOTAL REVS.						
Plan	41.4	41.0	43.2	40.4	54.7	64.8
Actual[a]	41.4	55.0	44.0	47.3	42.4	46.6

Note: a. Constant prices: 1975 = 100.
Sources: NPC; CBJ, Monthly Statistical Bulletin; Saket and Asfour, Jordan's Economy, p. 39.

Targets and Achievements

Table 10.8: Some Indicators of the Regional Distribution of Income, 1973

	Average Factor Income For Earners (JD)		Ratio to Average Income In Urban Amman (%)	
	Urban	Rural	Urban	Rural
Amman Gov.	603	381	100	63
Irbid	561	373	93	62
Balqa	428	308	71	51
Karak	333	291	55	48
Ma'an	487	276	46	46
East Bank	572	362	95	60

Notes: Income share of bottom 10% of East Bank earners: Rural 2.4%/Urban 2.0%. Income share of top 10% of East Bank earners: Rural 27.3%/Urban 35.8%.
Sources: RSS, Economics Department,'1973 Income Distribution Survey' (Amman, unpublished); Saket and Asfour, Jordan's Economy, p.42.

incomes (between rural and urban areas, and between the southern parts and the rest of the country) has not been corrected (Tables 10.7 and 10.8).

Thus 'the five-year plan 1976-80 seemed clearly over-optimistic in its aggregate economic projections and, a little less certainly, over-ambitious in its investment programme'.[1]

THE SECOND FIVE-YEAR PLAN (1981-85)

The second five-year plan embodied quite similar development objectives to the first one (1976-80), but targets were readjusted to more realistic levels, profiting from experience gained in the 1970s. The following targets were envisaged:

(a) a 10.4% annual GDP growth rate;
(b) a rise by 7% per annum of value-added in agriculture;
(c) a rise by 17% per annum of value-added in industry and mining, following the completion of projects like the Gulf of Aqaba fertilizer complex;

(d) an increase of the productive sectors' share in GDP from 38.8% in 1980 to 44.8% in 1985;
(e) an increase in domestic revenues to cover at least current expenditures. The ratio of domestic revenues to GDP was set to rise from 22.2% in 1980 to 35.4% in 1985;
(f) imports of goods and services to grow only by 11.9% annually, to a forecast JD 653 mn in 1985; a planned growth figure of 19.8% was established for exports.

According to the plan, total investment expenditure would amount to JD 2.8 bn during 1981-85, of which 53.4% was earmarked for production sectors and tourism and the remainder for infrastructure and social services (Table 10.9).

Table 10.9: Planned Distribution of Investment, 1981-85 (million Jordanian dinars)

	Central government	Public & autonomous institutions[a]	Private & mixed	Total
Agriculture & co-operatives	52.6	-	181.9	234.5
Water & irrigation	275.6	246.1	-	521.7
Manufacturing & mining	23.0	19.0	716.8	758.8
Electricity & energy	-	124.3	39.1	163.4
Tourism & antiquities	16.9	-	48.8	65.7
Sub-total: commodity-producing sectors & tourism	368.1	389.4	986.6	1,744.1
Trade & supply	25.5	6.0	5.5	37.0
Transportation	246.1	239.4	60.0	545.5
Communications	3.6	103.2	-	106.8
Culture & youth	9.8	-	-	9.8
Information	7.9	-	-	7.9
Education	120.0	86.3	20.0	226.3
Health	80.7	-	20.0	100.7
Social development	9.4	-	5.8	15.2
Labour & manpower	1.0	6.5	1.7	9.2

Targets and Achievements

Table 10.9 (Cont'd)

	Central government	Public & autonomous institutions [a]	Private & mixed	Total
Housing & government buildings	17.9	123.1	167.1	308.1
Municipal, rural & environmental affairs	10.7	164.9	-	175.6
Al-Awqaf	2.5	-	3.9	6.4
Science, technology & statistics	1.2	-	6.2	7.4
Sub-total: services sector	536.3	729.4	290.2	1,555.9
Total investment	904.4	1,118.8	1,276.8	3,300.0

Note: a. Autonomous public institutions include the following: Telecommunications Corporation (TCC), Royal Jordanian Airlines (Alia), the Ports Corporation, the Jordan Valley Authority (JVA), the Industrial Estate Corporation, Amman Municipality, Aqaba Railway, Free Zones Authority, public transportation, housing and vocational training authorities, municipal and village councils, universities. Sources: NPC; Economist Intelligence Unit (EIU), <u>EIU Regional Review: The Middle East and North Africa 1985</u> (Economist Publications, London, 1985), p. 121.

  The plan was obviously founded on at least two main assumptions: first, the maintenance of a mixed economy with a strong private sector, the public sector's role being to create the basic infrastructure for private business and to promote the larger-scale productive projects too great to be supported by private investment alone; and, second, the continuation of Arab financial support and the promotion of Arab co-operation.
  By and large, the focus of the new plan was very much on large industrial and mining projects, including: the $465 mn potash plant on the Dead Sea (completed in March 1982), the $230 mn Portland cement plant at Rashidiyeh, and the massive new phosphate mine at Shidiya near the Saudi border to be inaugurated in 1986. But the plan did not neglect medium-sized industries or agriculture.

Targets and Achievements

Further, a process of regionalization was envisaged, dividing the country into planning regions within which social and economic development would be on the basis of indigenous resources and manpower.

Unfortunately for Jordan, there was an accumulation of unfavourable factors which prevented the plan from achieving its main targets. It is worth mentioning here the most salient negative factors:

(1) The loss of Iraq as an export market. In the early months of the war, Iraq could still pay for large imports and Jordan prospered: its exports to Iraq rose from JD 12.7 mn in 1979 to JD 63.5 mn in 1981, accounting for 37.5% of total exports. By 1983, however, they had dropped to JD 26.9 mn. The manufacturing sector was the hardest hit by this slump in exports: the value of industrial exports dropped from JD 42.7 mn in 1982 to JD 13.5 mn in 1983.

(2) Less income from phosphates than expected. Although total production of raw phosphate rock jumped from 2.83 mn t in 1979 to 3.91 mn in 1980, 4.24 mn in 1981, 4.39 mn in 1982 and 4.75 mn in 1983, these exports earned Jordan JD 47.2 mn in 1980, JD 54.8 mn in 1981, JD 57.1 mn in 1982 and only JD 51.6 mn in 1983.

(3) A dramatic decline in budget aid (Table 10.10). Until 1981, foreign loans and grants constituted over 50% of Jordan's government revenue. However, not only has Jordan's support for Iraq in the Gulf war deprived it of Libyan aid, but also the drop in oil revenues has led the other oil states to reduce their aid to Jordan since 1982. Thus, the share of foreign grants and loans in total revenues dropped from 55.4% in 1980 to a mere 36.8% in 1983. From a high point of over $1.1 bn in 1981, this figure had dropped to nearly $725 mn in 1983 and only $644 mn (or JD 253 mn) in 1985.[2]

(4) A decrease in the level of remittances. The level of remittances has risen to over $500 bn in 1979, $1.1 bn in 1983 and $1.299 bn in 1984.[3] But while Jordan exports manpower, with over 350,000 of its best-qualified workers employed in the Gulf states, it also imports about 120,000 workers to fill mainly unskilled technical jobs, thus resulting in a reverse outflow of capital. Although thousands of Jordanian expatriates are returning home because of the general recession in the Gulf, remittances still constitute the largest single source of foreign exchange.

Targets and Achievements

Table 10.10: Government's Foreign Receipts (thousand Jordanian dinars)

Source	1978	1979	1980	1981	1982	1983[a]
Total	172,396	247,926	280,869	282,043	245,991	231,547
Budget Support	81,699	210,302	202,834	206,312	184,500	130,000
US	12,405	10,695	-	-	-	-
Arab	69,294	199,607	202,834	206,312	184,500	130,000
Economic & Technical Assistance	-	-	2,000	-	-	-
Development Loans	90,697	37,624	71,566	75,731	61,491	101,547
UK	2,100	1,500	2,348	4,327	151	283
West Germany	8,874	3,442	4,695	5,689	3,381	3,946
Kuwait	8,200	10,304	11,717	8,389	3,421	16,762
IDA	5,166	4,430	8,760	9,459	-	-
USAID	13,930	2,703	17,513	5,147	3,515	7,529
Saudi Arabia	35,250	2,461	5,001	7,036	9,277	10,199
Other	17,177	12,784	21,532	35,684	41,758	62,828

Note: a. Preliminary.
Source: Arab Petroleum Research Center, <u>Arab Oil and Gas Directory 1985</u> (Paris, 1984), p. 188.

(5) The aggravation of Jordan's outstanding debt, which soared to JD 762.8 mn in 1983 from JD 602 mn in 1982, rising as a percentage of GNP from 35% in 1982 to 41.3% in 1983.

Thus, by 1983, the recession in the region had filtered through to Jordan and it was clear that the 1981-85 plan's target of an 11% growth in the real value of GDP was hopelessly over-ambitious. In fact, the real value of GDP rose by approximately 4.5% in 1984 and 5% in 1985, according to Finance Minister, Hanna Odeh.[4]

The Jordanian budget for 1985, published on 13 December 1984, projected a 49% increase in the deficit from JD 11.2 mn in 1984 to JD 16.7 mn in 1985. Expenditure was budgeted to increase by 9.1% (although spending on defence and security was held at 1984 levels), while income was to rise by 8.4% over 1984. Table 10.11 gives details of the budgets

Targets and Achievements for 1984 and 1985.

Table 10.11: Jordanian Budget, 1984 and 1985 (million Jordanian dinars[a])

	1985	1984	Change (mn JD)	Change (%)
Total Expenditure	811.2	770.21	+ 41.0	+ 5.3
Locally funded expenditure	724.6	664.2	+ 60.4	+ 9.1
Current expenditure	487.5	452.5	+ 35.0	+ 7.7
o.w. Defence & security	206.0	204.6	+ 1.4	+ 0.6
Capital expenditure	237.1	211.7	+ 25.4	+ 11.9
Foreign funded expenditure	86.6	106.0	- 19.4	- 18.3
Total Revenues	707.9	653.0	+ 54.9	+ 8.4
Local revenues	479.9	449.0	+ 30.9	+ 6.9
Arab aid	183.0	183.0	0.0	0.0
Investment income & foreign loans[b]	45.0	21.0	+ 24.0	+114.3
Deficit	16.7	11.2	+ 5.5	+ 49.1

Notes: a. One JD = $2.54 at current exchange rates.
 b. In 1985 investment income accounted for JD 27 mn of the total.

For 1986 the projected deficit was expected to jump to JD 37.8 mn, but projected revenues were to cover as much as 88.3% of current expenditure (80.2% in 1985), as indicated by Table 10.12.

Jordanians are not particularly alarmed at this sudden downturn in their economy. They usually regard it as a cooling-off period after the boom years, a period that can be used to perform the necessary tasks of increasing domestic revenues and reducing external dependence. They point out that, although they failed to achieve a high peak of 11% growth in their GDP, they had a minimum of 4.5% growth in 1984 and almost 5% in 1985, which is still a good performance when compared to percentages of GDP growth in the industrialized and developing countries.

Targets and Achievements

Table 10.12: Projected Budget for 1986 (million Jordanian dinars[a])

Total Expenditure	923.7
Locally funded expenditure	825.5
Current expenditure	563.8
Capital expenditure	261.7
Foreign funded expenditure	98.2
Total Revenues	787.9
Local revenues	497.9
Foreign aid	253.0
Investment income & foreign loans	36.9
Deficit	37.8

Note: a. One JD = $2.55.
Source: Minister of Finance, Hanna Odeh, in Al-Rai', 5 Dec. 1985.

During 1985 much time was spent in preparing the five-year development plan (1986-90). It appears, from the publication of the plan, that development spending will concentrate on making the best use of such natural resources (phosphate, potash, etc.) as exist in the country. A big push to attain food security, with investment in upland agriculture as well as the Jordan Valley, is envisaged. Oil drilling and testing will be allocated a larger slice of resources. On the whole, the plan properly focused attention and investments on those portions of the economy best suited to rapid growth and to easing balance-of-trade deficits.

LOOKING AHEAD

Any serious attempt to assess Jordan's economic performance must take into account the inescapable fact that, since 1967, its West Bank has been 'amputated' and occupied by the Israeli Army. This entails a reduction of receipts for the Jordanian government, although the cost to the country is still high, in terms of defence requirements and the subsidies granted to West Bankers. It would be useful if a research team could one day estimate the cost of Israel's occupation of the West Bank and its threat to Arab security for Jordan's economy. In this brief summary it has not been possible to tackle such a thorny question.

Jordan's economy is labouring under a number of constraints, such as the shortage of water and energy, and the brain drain of its highly skilled workforce. Nevertheless the country has undeniably been able, during the last decade, to step up its expenditure on infrastructural projects, to mobilize public and private capital, to exploit better its raw materials, to intensify its regional links, and on the whole to engage in a massive development scheme, both locally and regionally oriented.

In the light of the general recession in the region, the main tasks of Jordan's economic planners (for the coming years) will be challenging: to reduce the ravages of inflation and the cost of living, to be more cost-conscious, to attract Arab investments, to encourage Jordanian money to stay at home, to reduce unemployment and to promote further Jordan's regional role. The country cannot afford for long to live on Arab charity and Western loans. Such a dependence could, in the long run, put its national security in jeopardy. The time is now ripe for Jordan to cut its suit according to its cloth.

NOTES

1. Michael P. Mazur, *Economic Growth and Development in Jordan* (Croom Helm, London, 1979), p. 266.
2. *Al-Rai'*, (Amman), 5 Dec. 1985, p. 11.
3. Ibid., 8 Dec. 1985, p. 6: JD 475 mn.
4. Ibid., 5 Dec. 1985, p. 11.

Chapter Eleven

JORDAN: A DISTURBING DEPENDENCE ON A DETERIORATING REGIONAL SITUATION

François Rivier

Jordan's exceptional growth throughout the second half of the 1970s was the result of a careful adjustment to the Gulf countries' sudden increase in wealth after the first oil boom. This success was nevertheless fragile, as revealed by the effects of the deteriorating regional situation since 1982. In the middle term - in other words, up to the end of the 1980s - this situation is likely to remain depressed, or even get worse. At the same time, the large new Jordanian industries, aimed at a world market, cannot alone act as a relay station providing an adequate substitute for regional capital flows.

Even if a crisis scenario cannot be dismissed, it seems extremely improbable. Jordan has nevertheless embarked on a new phase of slower growth, and the measures of adaptation adopted since 1983 will have to be tightened up. This necessary shift in economic policy is desirable, first, to put Jordan in a position to participate in a subsequent phase of recovery and, second, to give its economy a wider productive base and thus reduce its excessive dependence on the regional economic climate.

1974-81: THE REGIONAL REDISTRIBUTION OF OIL WEALTH

From 1974 to 1981 Jordan was able to take advantage of its position in the regional channels of redistribution of oil wealth. After the destabilization following the loss of the West Bank in 1967 and the events of 1970-71, the country regained control of its economic orientation at the same time as the first oil boom and the sudden unprecedented increase in wealth of the region's oil-producing countries.

Jordan was thus able to take full advantage of the repercussions of the increased oil revenues: over the period 1974-81 its GDP rose at an average annual rate of 13.7%, a remarkable result for a country with no oil whatsoever. This performance was obtained without excessive indebtedness. The external public debt only increased from 29% to 37% of GNP between the end of 1973 and the end of 1981, and the ratio of debt servicing over the same period kept within the extremely reasonable limits of 4.9% and 6.3% of GNP.

Space does not permit an analysis of the nature of this growth. A brief look at the structure of the balance of payments is nevertheless revealing.

Table 11.1: Jordan's Balance of Payments, 1974-81 (million dollars)

	Cumulative total
Exports (FOB)	2,770
Imports (FOB)	- 11,244
Visible trade balance	- 8,474
Balance on services	- 540
Private transfer payments (net)	3,642
Government transfer payments	5,480
Current balance	108

Source: International Monetary Fund (IMF), International Financial Statistics.

Over this eight-year period, the balance in the current account was essentially obtained through: (a) remittances from emigrant workers (private transfer payments); and (b) government grants (official transfer payments). These compensated for a growing structural trade deficit (on average, total exports covered less than 25% of imports) which increased from $218 mn (or 33% of GDP) in 1973 to $2,082 mn (58% of GDP) in 1981.

Thus the two sources of external revenue

which play a major role in the financing of growth are directly linked to increases in the region's wealth.

Remittances from Jordanian-Palestinian emigrants rose from $55 mn in 1973 to $922 mn in 1981.[1] The majority of these workers, who numbered more than 300,000 at the beginning of the 1980s, live in the Arab oil-producing states.

Government transfer payments - which amounted to $186 mn in 1973 and reached their highest level of $1.3 bn in 1980 - also bear a marked relationship to the redistribution of oil revenues. Whereas US aid was important for Jordan between 1972 and 1973, subsequent government transfer payments have come mainly from the Arab countries. This was particularly true after the Baghdad Summit Conference of 1978, at which seven oil-producing countries undertook to provide Jordan with annual aid worth $1,250 mn. [2]

When compared with these two main sources of external revenue, the other inflows in foreign exchange are less important over this period. Their development is none the less significant as it reveals the government's systematic determination to encourage activities likely to help the Jordanian economy share in the regional increase in wealth.

This is true, first, for transit and re-export operations, in particular those destined for Iraq: these operations have been encouraged by the expansion of the port of Aqaba and the setting up of free zones. Thus re-exports increased dramatically from $12 mn in 1973 to $223 mn in 1981. Since 1977 their share in Jordan's total exports has been higher than that of phosphates.

The development of the manufacturing industry[3] is envisaged within the framework of the expansion - throughout the Middle East - of the policy of import substitution. This is designed to take advantage of the boom in demand experienced by markets in neighbouring countries. Thus between 1970 and 1978 exports of manufactured goods rose from 29% to 45% of total domestic exports, and from 4.5% to 21% of total industrial production - clear evidence of the increasing openness of the Jordanian economy. This progress has been exclusively registered in goods exported to Arab countries: more than 99% of exports of manufactured goods were geared to these markets. Nevertheless, in order to put the situation in its proper perspective, it should be pointed out that exports of manufactured goods (taking 1980 as an example) represent a mere 12% of the foreign exchange receipts linked to government transfer payments.[4]

Financial and service operations are also conceived within a regional perspective, aiming, in particular, to develop Amman's position as a financial centre. This policy helps to maintain a balance on services.

Progress in the mining industry[5] (meaning exclusively phosphates in this initial period) is not linked to the regional situation, even though Morocco was able for a short period in 1974-75 to increase the price of phosphates in the wake of the quadrupling of oil prices.

Throughout this period the government used part of the country's external transfer payments for three main purposes: to increase the country's phosphate and potassium extraction capacities; to build the necessary infrastructure (roads, railways, ports) to export these products; and to set up new industrial installations designed to exploit these raw materials locally (e.g. the fertilizer complex at Aqaba).

1982-84: THE GULF WAR AND THE DECLINING OIL MARKET

Jordan is now suffering from the impact of the continuing Gulf war and the turn-around in the oil market. From the beginning of the 1980s two events were to have a major impact on the entire region: the outbreak of the Iran-Iraq war in September 1980 and the continued drop in oil production by the OPEC countries, aggravated in March 1983 by a drop in the reference price of a barrel of oil from $34 to $29.

Table 11.2: Total OPEC Production, 1977-83 (million barrels)

1977	1978	1979	1980	1981	1982	1983
31.2	29.8	30.9	26.9	22.6	19.0	17.0

Source: *Middle East Economic Survey*, 17 Dec. 1984.

The economic consequences for Jordan are

A Disturbing Dependence

clear. The drop in the producer countries' oil revenues has a direct bearing on the share of their surplus earmarked for bilateral and multilateral aid. At the same time, the slowing down of activity in the oil economies has had repercussions on the employment of workers, on the level of remittances (which is stagnant) and on the outlets provided by these markets.

What has had the most severe impact on Jordan, however, is the fact that the negative trend in the oil sector has coincided with the prolongation of the Gulf war. Engulfed in a disastrous war, Iraq was soon unable to honour the commitment it had made to Jordan ($200 mn) at the Baghdad Summit: it even started to compete for aid itself. The support which Iraq receives from Saudi Arabia and the other Gulf states is massive (over $30 bn between 1981 and 1984) and takes priority: aid for countries on other 'battlefronts' has been reduced accordingly. Thus only Saudi Arabia and Kuwait continue to pay Jordan the full amount as agreed (and in 1984 even Kuwait fell short of its commitment). This means that the level of Arab aid to Jordan has dropped from $1,200 mn in 1981 to $950 mn in 1982, $700 mn in 1983 and below $600 mn in 1984. Moreover, in 1983, faced with growing financial difficulties and the depletion of its external assets, Iraq undertook adjustments which were the more dramatic for having been put off for so long: Iraqi imports dropped sharply from $19 bn in 1982 to $9 bn in 1983. As Iraq had become a major outlet for Jordanian re-exports, as well as for agricultural produce and industrial goods, Jordan's exports were severely hit. In 1983 they dropped by 20% in relation to their 1982 level (for re-exports, the drop was nearly 40%).

The combination of these unfavourable circumstances led to a slowing down of growth - although not to the extent of creating major external imbalances. Due to the levelling off of direct investment and the limited amount of soft loans, Jordan has over the last two years had to resort to the international capital market for a total amount of $310 mn in 1983 and $309 mn in 1984. The conditions attached to the Kingdom of Jordan's latest Euroloan, in July 1984, are none the less favourable: $150 mn and 15 mn Kuwaiti dinars (KD) (a total of $200 mn) spread over seven years, with a three-year grace period, and a spread over Libor (or Kibor) of 0.5%. This is evidence of continued confidence on the part of the banks.

A Disturbing Dependence

Table 11.3: Key Indicators, 1982-84

	1982	1983	1984[a]
Growth in GDP (%)	5.7	6.1	2.4
Budget surplus or deficit (as % of GNP)	- 7.6	- 7.8	n.a.
Exports	752	580	650
Imports	2,879	2,700	2,550
Visible trade balance	-2,127	-2,120	-1,900
Balance on services	- 172	- 10	
Private transfer payments (net)	933	924	1,600
Government transfer payments	1,033	795	
Current balance	- 333	- 391	- 300
(as % of GDP)	(- 8.7)	(- 9.4)	(- 7)

Note: a. Estimated
Source: IMF, International Financial Statistics.

External reserves (excluding gold) have dropped dramatically - from nearly $1.1 bn at the end of 1981 to some $500 mn at the end of 1984, equivalent to two months' exports. Finally, two other factors are clear evidence of an extremely tight cash-flow situation: first, the marked increase in 1984 of clearing agreements for phosphates (in order to limit the constraints on the balance of payments, tied to infrastructural development projects): and second, Jordan's recourse, in January 1985, to the mechanism of compensatory IMF financing[6] amounting to 57 mn SDRs.

PROSPECTS IN THE MEDIUM TERM

The Situation in the Region
The regional situation is likely to remain unfavourable (it could even deteriorate) up to the end of the 1980s.

<u>The Iran-Iraq War</u>. The Gulf war is now in its sixth year. The present flare-up in the fighting,

and the noticeable shift in Iraq's favour, might lead one to hope that a negotiated end to the conflict was in sight. Unfortunately such hopes have already been dashed in the past and the prospect of a war of attrition, with disastrous consequences for both countries, is a hypothesis that cannot be ruled out.

Above all, it must be stressed that even if the fighting were suddenly brought to an end, Iraq would then be exhausted by the war and very heavily in debt. The massive reconstruction effort required would continue to mobilize (to Jordan's detriment) a considerable proportion of Arab aid. In this context, outlets for Jordanian goods will remain limited.[7] In a word, post-war Iraq is in danger of no longer being the motor force behind Jordan's growth that it was up to 1981. Moreover, a return to 'normal' levels of oil production by Iraq would merely accentuate the downward trend in the price of oil.

Oil Prices. To predict the price of oil is an extremely risky business. As the experience of the years 1973/74, 1978/79 and 1982/83 has shown, such predictions are very inaccurate. Nevertheless, we will venture so far as to predict that, during 1985, the price of 'Arabian light' will continue to drop below $20/barrel.

Space does not allow us to provide detailed arguments in support of this conclusion. Nevertheless we will opt for a hypothetical price of $20/barrel, while stressing that a drop to around $15/barrel is a scenario that cannot be totally dismissed. Thus for 1985 and the next few years, there will be a noticeable decrease in the revenues of the oil-producing countries of the Middle East.

Jordan's Large Export Industries
The development of major, export-oriented phosphate and potash industries geared to a world market cannot provide a substitute for regional revenues. Two points should be made at the outset. The first concerns potash: major technical problems have apparently arisen in the SAFICO plant at the south of the Dead Sea and it is very unlikely that the projected increase in productivity will be realized.

As far as phosphates are concerned, the Aqaba

complex (which produces phosphoric acid, monoammonium phosphate and diammonium phosphate) was constructed with the aim of exploiting locally a raw material found in Jordan. But since the time of the feasibility studies, the cost structure of the plant's end-products has been considerably modified, taking particular account of the steep increase in the price of sulphur.[8] At present, the net gain in foreign exchange derived from exports of phosphoric acid or DAP/MAP, when compared with exports of natural phosphate, can no longer be taken for granted.

The last comment forms the basis of the following estimates which attempt to evaluate (in relation to 1983) Jordan's additional revenues from exports of phosphates and potassium or their by-products in 1987 and 1990.

Table 11.4: Additional Revenues from Phosphates and Potash, 1983-90

	1983	1987[a]	1990[a]
Phosphates			
Estimated level of production (mn t)	4.75	7	9
Price (in constant 1983 $/t)	37	41	45
Additional export revenues, 1983 (totals rounded up in mn $)	-	100	200
Potash			
Estimated level of production (mn t)	0.3	0.7	1.2
Price (in constant 1983 $/t)	75	96	100
Additional export revenues, 1983 (totals rounded up in mn $)	-	50	100
Total additional export revenues, 1983 (total rounded up in mn $)	-	150	300

Note: a. Estimated
Sources: World Bank and government sources.

These rough estimates are given simply in order to establish orders of magnitude: thus for 1987 the additional export revenues derived from phosphates and potash are likely to be in the order of $150 mn, and for 1990 about $300 mn. The projected prices and production levels for these products lead one to suspect that the estimates are somewhat over-optimistic.

A comparison of this figure of $300 mn (over a five-year time-scale) with the level of transfer payments (government and private) coming from the Middle East (approx. $1.6 bn in 1983) shows that the development of Jordan's major export industries can provide only a very partial substitute for regional revenues.

A Crisis Scenario?
Even if a crisis scenario appears very unlikely, it cannot be dismissed out of hand. In the (admittedly very pessimistic) event of a fall in the price of oil to $15/barrel and the continuation of the Gulf war, the prospect of a collapse of 50% in government transfer payments and emigrants' remittances cannot be totally ruled out.[9] Compared to the 1983 level, this would represent a drop in external revenues in the order of $800 mn. This loss could only partially be compensated for by revenues from major exports (as we have seen, for 1987 the maximum will be $150 mn) and by the positive effect of the drop in the price of a barrel of oil on the cost of oil imports (of the order of $200 mn). All in all, the current balance of payments deficit would more than double. In this event, the banks' confidence would evaporate fast (and long before 1987). Jordan would then experience a financial crisis.

As previously mentioned, this scenario seems unlikely. Not only is the oil hypothesis extreme; Jordan's geopolitical importance would lead other countries (notably the US) to fill the gap left by the drop in Arab aid. Above all, the Jordanian authorities would probably strengthen the policy of restraint in force since 1983, and thus prevent the current deficit going beyond what is considered an alarming threshold.

A Phase of Slower Growth
Jordan has now entered a phase of slower growth, characterized by a policy of restraint which still needs reinforcing and by attempts to expand the economy's productive base.

Even if we discard the crisis scenario and

opt for the hypothesis of a moderate fall in oil prices, Jordan will inevitably suffer from an unfavourable regional situation that might well continue to the end of the 1980s. In order to cope with this transition period, whose duration is extremely difficult to calculate, the measures taken over recent years must be tightened up.

Since 1983 the government has been trying to put a brake on the increase in current expenditure in the state budget and to increase its domestic revenues, and is adopting a restrictive monetary policy. The 1985 budget was an attempt in this direction: for example, there were heavy increases in customs duties on luxury goods, a reduction in fuel subsidies and a parallel rise in the price of electricity and oil products (within the general framework of an energy-saving campaign). Nevertheless the level of investment - particularly by the state - remains very high (40% of GDP in 1983). And for the moment, there are no apparent signs of a change of direction: the projected 1985 budget provides for a further increase of 11% in capital expenditure. Due to the country's limited domestic savings and the present declining and uncertain nature of non-debt-generating sources of external finance, a slowing down in government investment expenditure seems inevitable if the Jordanian economy is to reduce its domestic and external deficit.

Needless to say, because of the level of government expenditure (45% of GDP), the measures mentioned above will have a noticeable impact on the growth rate of the economy. But it is clear that the era of double-figure growth rates is (provisionally) over, and that Jordan has entered a phase of slower growth. Thus investment priorities must be rigorously defined.

Since the productive base of the Jordanian economy is limited, attempts to expand it are clearly one of the above-mentioned priorities, although aspirations in this area should not be overestimated.

In recent years the deficit in the food balance has stood at around $400 mn. This underlies the importance of initiatives in the agricultural sector. Dry-farming is at the mercy of unpredictable climatic conditions, as revealed by severe fluctuations in cereal production. Irrigated agriculture would appear to have better prospects and the schemes undertaken in the Jordan

A Disturbing Dependence

Valley since 1973 are truly remarkable. Nevertheless, if these products are to become competitive on the external market, there must be major improvements in productivity, costs[10] and commercialization.

Jordan's oil bill stands at around $600-650 mn. In the light of the recent oil finds, optimism over future research activities and hopes for significant progress in meeting internal demand are justified. But, for the moment, production in the Azraq zone - a total of 2,300 barrels/day - is neglible compared to the level of imports of crude oil, which amounted to some 700,000 barrels/day in 1984. This underlies the importance of an energy-saving programme designed to reduce the too rapid increase in domestic consumption (+14% in 1984).

In addition to the major export industries based on raw materials, possibilities still exist in the area of medium-sized industries. Jordan's previous experience of Iraqi outlets has revealed the danger and fragility of a market in which good political relations were more important than competitive products. Progress still needs to be made in this area.

Even in a depressed overall climate, however, the Gulf states will still need to maintain their recently created infrastructure, equipment and industrial installations. Here Jordan enjoys a double advantage: its geographic proximity and its highly qualified labour force. It should thus be able to develop both its industrial activities and its service industry.

In conclusion, although Jordan derived substantial benefit up to 1981 from the oil wealth of its neighbours, it has also been 'contaminated' by certain deformations typical of <u>rentier</u> economies. The down-turn in the oil market has led to a phase of austerity which will last for several years. However, it will also provide an opportunity for the economy to expand its productive base, thus allowing it to become more competitive and consequently less dependent on the vagaries of the overall regional situation.

A Disturbing Dependence

NOTES

1. These are actually net private transfer payments, after deducting remittances abroad made by foreign workers in Jordan. The latter became important from 1976.

2. The total can be broken down as follows: Saudi Arabia $350 mn, Iraq $200 mn, Kuwait $200 mn, UAE $170 mn, Libya $150 mn, Algeria $100 mn, Qatar $80 mn. In fact, Algeria and Libya have never fulfilled their commitments, but up to 1981 their share was partly covered by the other states.

3. For a more detailed treatment of Jordanian industry, the reader is referred to the author's Croissance industrielle dans une économie assistée; le cas jordanien (CERMOC-PUL, Beirut, 1980).

4. This is true even without taking into account the import requirements of export-oriented industrial ventures.

5. Export revenues from phosphates rose from $12 mn in 1973 to $61 mn in 1974 and $166 mn in 1981. The corresponding rise in the volume of production was 1 mn t, 1.7 mn t and 4.2 mn t respectively.

6. This is the first time (apart from the exceptional period 1971-73) that Jordan has had recourse to IMF loans. It was forced to take this step because of the increased cost of cereal imports from June 1983 to June 1984, following the exceptional drought during the cropping season 1983/84.

7. The most important sectors for the Iraqi economy will correspond only very approximately to those of Jordanian industry.

8. Taking the production of DAP as an example, it is estimated today that phosphate represents scarcely more than 30% of total production costs, the rest being spent on products which Jordan must import: sulphur (to obtain the sulphuric acid needed to produce phosphoric acid) and ammonia.

9. The 'adjustment' in the oil-producing countries of the Middle East has so far been moderate. A sharp drop in oil revenues would inevitably affect the amount of aid they give, and the extent to which they rely on an immigrant workforce. The period of drawing on external assets seems to be over, as indicated by Saudi Arabia's 1985/86 budget.

10. Water is provided free by the state.

Chapter Twelve

RENTIER OR PRODUCER ECONOMY IN THE MIDDLE EAST? THE JORDANIAN RESPONSE

Michel Chatelus

INTRODUCTION

Analysing the Jordanian economy is an exciting yet perilous exercise. Paradoxes and contradictions abound, and the international context is decisive. The present chapter will not present an exhaustive balance-sheet; better qualified authors have already undertaken this task.[1] Rather, it will aim to put Jordan's economic development in some sort of perspective, in the light of some considerations about the major trends in the Arab economies since the 1960s.[2]

Jordan faces endless challenges and its economic situation - like that of most Arab countries - is to some extent 'overdetermined' by political constraints. Like several other states in the region, the country's structures are undergoing change and are subject to such a 'dynamic of disequilibrium'[3] that observers may reach widely differing conclusions, depending on their point of view. Some stress the country's buoyancy and capacity to react to successive crises. Others point to persistent foreign dependence and a sluggish production sector. Still others point to Jordan's precarious situation and the inability of its rulers to control the main factors influencing the economy. Each of these 'readings' has some justification but none alone can adequately encapsulate such a complex and often contradictory situation.

Jordan's is a 'subsidized'[4] economy, perched along the Middle East circulation channels of direct or indirect oil revenues. It is an indirect rentier state, living far above its means. According to World Bank figures, domestic demand (public and private consumption plus investment)

Rentier or Producer Economy?

exceeded GDP by 57% in 1982.[5] The country's relatively high standard of living (a <u>per capita</u> income of $1,700 in 1983) puts it in the upper bracket of medium-income countries in World Bank tables and largely depends on the influx of funds linked to oil, whether directly (grants and aid from oil-producing states) or indirectly (emigrants' remittances).

The country's foreign dependence is thus considerable, and both the current drop in oil revenues and neighbouring Iraq's growing involvement in an all-out war will inevitably aggravate the precarious nature of Jordan's economic situation. Nevertheless the average annual growth rate since the beginning of the 1970s has often exceeded 10%, there has been industrial investment in major projects that function well and produce goods for export, several financial ventures have registered success, and a dynamism and spirit of initiative have led to the significant development of small and medium-sized enterprises.

It is a contradictory picture, whose essential features are sometimes difficult to pick out and above all to interpret. The present chapter will seek to identify and illuminate some of them and to place them in the economic development of the region. The discussion will turn on three basic hypotheses:

1. Like all Arab Middle East states, Jordan is linked into the circulation of oil revenues. It therefore shares features common to most <u>rentier</u> economies.
2. Economic development is heavily dependent on the regional politico-military situation. The unstable environment leads to abrupt upheavals which frequently alter the conditions in which the Jordanian economy operates.
3. Faced with these multiple and repeated challenges, Jordan has managed to find particular responses that solve these problems only in part.

JORDAN IN THE MIDDLE EAST CIRCULATION OF OIL REVENUE

Widespread dependence on oil revenue, and an outlook that sees the allocation and redistribution of this revenue as more important than production, would seem to characterize all the countries of the

Rentier or Producer Economy?

Middle East.⁶ The frequently made distinction between the _rentier_ states (until recently, surplus oil-exporters) and the others may well be pertinent for some analyses (those relating to foreign trade or financial policy, for example). But in examining how the Middle East economies function, the important distinction is between direct and indirect _rentier_ economies, the former being the oil countries, the latter all the others. Without going into all the possible interpretations of _rentier_ income and the _rentier_ state, it may still be useful to specify the exact sense in which these concepts are used here. They apply to situations in which a major role is played by revenues of external origin whose size and flow are not linked to the productive activity of the recipient; these revenues depend on decisions and an environment over which the recipient has little, if any, control. It is in this sense that Jordan, like Saudi Arabia and Kuwait, and even Syria and Yemen, can be defined as a _rentier_ state. In all the states of the region we will find common features related to the _rentier_ economy. In Jordan, as elsewhere, these features are objective, but they also concern attitudes and behaviour.

Jordan exhibits, sometimes in a very pronounced form, the basic imbalances characteristic of the _rentier_ state. A first prominent trait is a major disequilibrium in the trade balance. (In _rentier_ states with surpluses, this disequilibrium is registered as a surplus; in the others it is a deficit). While not exclusive to _rentier_ states, this deficit situation is particularly pronounced in them. Jordan's trade deficit - which was just over $1 bn in 1978 - increased to more than $2 bn in 1982 and, in spite of a slight drop in imports, rose still further in 1983. For 1985, the last year for which we have figures, exports ($581 mn) covered only 21% of imports ($2,701 mn).⁷

A second feature shared by Jordan and other indirect _rentier_ states is a large budget deficit. In 1982 government spending stood at JD 671 mn, while income was no more than JD 344 mn, and tax receipts JD 250 mn. Tax receipts therefore covered only about 36% of expenditure, the balance being made up by grants and transfer payments (about JD 200 mn, or 30%) and by cash operations.

In itself this dual deficit (foreign-trade and budget) is not remarkable (most developing countries find themselves in a similar situation), but its scale is. Outside the Middle East it is

Rentier or Producer Economy?

very unusual to find such low export/import ratios. It is this that produces the previously mentioned revenue deficit,[8] which in some sense sums up the dependence of the indirect rentier state. In 1982 spending exceeded income by more than 50%, which means that public and private consumption alone exceeded domestic product (savings of -11%), and all investment (46%) was financed by revenue of foreign origin. The trade deficit reflects and is a measure of this savings deficit in relation to need, and shows the degree to which the country is living beyond its means. This is just what happens in a rentier state. Domestic labour and production cover only a small part of national expenditure.

External revenue thus permits a level of consumption and investment well above the country's GDP. Between 1980 and 1983 unrequited transfers – which record in the balance of payments revenue of foreign origin not accounted for by invoices (in other words, which are not paid in exchange for goods or services or for investment) – came to about $2 bn a year, or nearly 40% of GNP and 50% of GDP. The two main components of these transfer payments depend directly on oil revenue and thus represent the means of redistributing this revenue from the region's producer countries (direct rentier economies) to the others (indirect rentier economies). The first item (emigrants' remittances), of scant importance before 1973, grew very rapidly between 1975 and 1981 and stabilized (temporarily) at around $900 mn officially registered in 1982 and 1983. The second item was grants and government aid from the oil states (and a limited amount of aid from other countries). These transfer payments peaked in 1981 and 1982, when they exceeded $1,200 mn. They have fallen since then, but are still decisive in financing the budget deficit and reducing the trade deficit.

The decisive role of transfer payments for both the rentier state and its inhabitants leads to attitudes and behaviour related to those payments. They are found throughout the Middle East, with only slight variations.

Inasmuch as a significant section of the population depends for its living on income for which nothing is given in exchange, behaviour is powerfully influenced in ways not calculated to encourage the sort of creative activity required by a diversified, productive economy. The link between income and activity is frequently quite tenuous, and it is often more important to be well placed in

Rentier or Producer Economy?

'income allocation channels' than to be an efficient producer. Economic agents (individuals, groups, businesses, and so on) tend to play down the importance of real economic results in favour of revenue-allocation strategies, which leads to anti-productive inclinations, or at the very least, to inclinations that do not encourage production. Although such behaviour is probably less systematic in the Jordanian economy than in others of the region, it is none the less significant.

The tendency for much of the labour force to emigrate (a majority according to some estimates) is a prime expression of the influence of rentier income on behaviour. The number of emigrants (in 1981-82) has been put at around 330,000 in a labour force of fewer than 600,000. The emigrants go mainly to Iraq and the Gulf states, but also to some Western countries. This emigrant labour force is rather highly skilled (25% are technicians or in skilled trades in construction and industry, and nearly 20% are teachers).[9] The high skill-level may raise the value of remittances sent back to Jordan, but it deprives the country of talent whose absence can compromise development efforts. Moreover, many positions left vacant by Jordanians who have gone to the Gulf are filled by foreign workers. It is estimated that 120,000 immigrants (75% of them Egyptian) thus account for a 'second cycle' circulation of the income earned by Jordanians in the oil states. Revenue transferred out of Jordan in this way stood at $200 mn in 1983.

The ambiguities of massive state intervention in an economy that preaches free enterprise is another aspect of the influence of rentier income on attitudes and behaviour. The state is the inevitable intermediary in the collection and redistribution of foreign revenue of public origin (state transfer payments), which it hands out to domestic economic agents. It is also responsible for the infrastructure, for basic investment and for the creation of general conditions which encourage the investment of emigrants' savings in the production sector. The state also acts to redistribute income, to varying degrees, among the various sectors of the population in the form of social spending and subsidies, especially for housing and basic consumer goods. Food subsidies are widespread throughout the region (accounting for one-third of Egypt's public spending), and attempts to reduce subsidies have encountered violent opposition: the regimes in Morocco, Sudan,

Rentier or Producer Economy?

Tunisia and Egypt have all been shaken by bread riots. In 1980-81, Jordan managed to suspend some subsidies (on sugar, rice and petrol) without provoking too much opposition, while the most essential ones (on flour and bread) were maintained. Compared to the other countries of the region, state redistribution activities in Jordan are relatively limited, but they do exist.

The attitudes induced by the size of external revenue undermine attempts to diversify and expand the production sector. Official targets - as expressed in particular in successive development plans - reveal two overriding concerns: to reduce food dependency and to increase industrial output for the domestic market and for exports alike. A very high rate of investment (up to 40 or 45% of GDP) and the introduction of incentives have registered significant success (see pp. 213ff).

But the role of foreign revenue remains primordial, and reveals the constraints on production in a rentier economy. In 1982, for example, $2 bn came into the country from abroad, while value-added was only $233 mn in agriculture, $500 mn in industry and $130 mn in mining. Any rise or fall in foreign revenue therefore has much greater consequences for the Jordanian economy than a sharp increase in agricultural or industrial output. Food imports account for two-thirds of consumption (85% in the case of grain, imports of which rose from 171,000 t in 1974 to 668,000 t in 1982).[10] Although some noteworthy progress has been made, the index of per capita agricultural production stood at 70 in 1980-82, based on 100 in 1969-71.[11] The poor performance of the production sector is not caused solely by foreign revenue, but it seems clear that this revenue, while providing resources, also generates obstacles to the effective use of these means.

A striking example of the contradiction between stated objectives and behaviour as influenced by foreign revenue is provided by land speculation and the westward spread of urban centres which are now absorbing an increasing amount of good cultivable land suitable for dry-farming. The state has been unable to control this penchant for land-grabbing by the greater part of the rentier capital sent back by emigrants, even though it is in complete contradiction with the stated goal of agricultural growth. On the whole, the objectives of economic diversification and a reduction in the service sector's share of GDP have

209

Rentier or Producer Economy?

not been met: the service sector accounted for 65% of GDP in 1976 and 68% in 1982. But the regional environment is one of the important reasons for this failure, which cannot be attributed to the role of foreign revenue alone. An encouraging trend in 1980-81, for example, was interrupted by a change in the regional situation.

THE IMPACT OF AN UNSTABLE ENVIRONMENT

The Jordanian economy is a good example of how important it is to treat cautiously concepts which, although in frequent use, are loose and imprecise - concepts such as economic viability (or lack of it) and dependence. If by viable is meant an economy which is balanced, complex and broadly based, then there are scarcely any viable economies anywhere in the world, and none at all in the Middle East. It is more important to analyse the nature and weight of the imbalances than simply to state their existence. It must also be recognized that, since all countries are dependent to some degree, any investigation must focus on what constitutes this dependence and, above all, the stability or instability of the environment and the impact of external crises. In understanding Jordan's situation, extreme environmental instability is thus more important than the country's 'dependence' or the 'artificial nature' of its economy.

The regional instability results, first, from the incessant political and military conflicts since the Second World War. The military conflict with Israel, whether open or latent, has had a profound influence on Jordan ever since the creation of the present state. The multiple costs of this conflict are both direct and indirect.[12] Not only has Jordan had to bear the costs of the destruction wrought by war and the transfers of population, in 1967 considerable areas of territory were 'amputated', thus depriving the country of its richest part. These facts are so widely known that it is not necessary to go into them here.

In the long term, the most harmful consequence for the Jordanian economy is the permanent uncertainty affecting the basic parameters within which it operates: uncertainty over its territorial boundaries, uncertainty over its relations with the West Bank, uncertainty over its labour force, over population flows, and so on.[13] In addition, military constraints determine where industries are

Rentier or Producer Economy?

located, interfere with irrigated agricultural projects and periodically cast doubt over prospects in the medium term. The six-year development plan (1964-70) was a classic example: it was interrupted in the middle by a war which ended up cutting the country in half. It is extremely difficult to direct a country's economy efficiently and rationally when the future is permanently uncertain.

The burden of defence expenditure, or expenditure tied to strategic considerations, is a major component of the costs imposed by the conflict with Israel. Defence spending has accounted for up to 40% of total budgetary spending in recent years, tending to stabilize at around 25% of total expenditure in 1981 and 1982. This figure was 3.5 times higher than the percentage spent on education; according to World Bank figures, it is three times the average percentage defence spending of countries with similar levels of income.[14]

The permanent state of war with Israel is only one source of uncertainty for the Jordanian economy. A second major source is the state of relations with the Arab countries of the region - while directly influenced by the conflict with Israel, these relations nevertheless operate under their own logic. For the last 30 years economic relations have come second to political considerations. This has led to a series of devastating external crises.

First, one should mention the sometimes drastic changes that may affect the external financial revenue on which, as we have seen, the country's survival in its present form and under its present regime depends. The private remittances transferred by emigrants depend on the oil situation, at both the regional and the international level. The ceiling reached after the 1979-80 oil price rises is problematic in the new situation in which the oil-exporting countries find themselves (their revenues have been dropping since 1982) and in the light of the restrictions on immigration that they are introducing or considering tightening up. Jordan's future revenues in the form of emigrants' remittances will thus depend heavily on being granted 'special treatment' by the oil states. Such treatment is itself dependent on these countries' opinions of Jordan's policies. When one considers the importance of the Palestinians in emigration from Jordan, the role of remittances sent by Palestinians working outside the Arab countries, developments relating to the Palestinian

Rentier or Producer Economy?

question and the resulting state of intra-Arab relations, the country is up against a risky situation which is highly political and therefore almost impossible to control.

The same is true of grants from certain Arab states which make a decisive contribution to covering the country's imports and public expenditure. At the 1978 Baghdad Summit a number of Arab countries pledged an annual contribution of $1,250 mn as the price of Jordan's break with Egypt and refusal to associate itself with the Camp David accords. Several of these countries reduced or ended their payments after the drop in oil revenues; they contributed less than $700 mn in 1982 and under $600 mn in 1983. The recent re-establishment of economic relations with Egypt may compromise this vital contribution still further.

Similar risks threaten economic activities, particularly those that depend on outlets for agricultural and industrial products. Jordan is the only country in the region (apart from Lebanon until recently) to direct most of its exports towards the neighbouring Arab states; in 1982 over 65% of Jordan's exports went to Arab countries. Exports of processed goods are almost entirely dependent on markets in neighbouring countries. In a favourable overall climate, these outlets can increase dramatically - as happened with sales to Iraq in 1981 and 1982 (in the latter year they are estimated to have reached $200 mn). But such gains are fragile and in 1983 the Iraqi market collapsed due to the war, forcing the Jordanian government to intervene massively to save local producers.[15] Trade relations with Jordan's supplier and natural client, Syria, have long been promising and have resulted in joint ventures, yet they are dependent on the state of political relations between the two countries. Today they have sunk to a minimal level. Jordan's industrial growth is thus heavily dependent on fluctuations in the regional situation. The situation of international public works companies (notably Turkish and Taiwanese) provides a good illustration, if one were needed: having lost their traditional markets due to the recession in the oil states, these companies are now falling back on Jordan, where they would be prepared to undercut local companies in order to obtain contracts.[16]

A similar logic can be applied to the activities of income-generating services: transit, banking, insurance and tourism, all of which

Rentier or Producer Economy?

fluctuate according to the overall climate. For example, the gains made at the expense of Beirut, which have turned Amman into a local financial centre, due to its geographic location and infrastructure, may be wiped out at a stroke by a deterioration in the regional situation. The transit trade with Iraq, which had partly compensated for the drop in trade with Syria and Lebanon, had led to an extension of the port of Aqaba and to the development of a communications network and a fleet of lorries. These activities have nowadays slowed down considerably.

THE CHALLENGES FACING JORDAN - THE POSSIBILITIES AND LIMITS OF AUTONOMY IN THE ECONOMY

The influence of the environment and a rentier economy has not led to a spirit of fatalism in Jordan. Through specific responses, the country has managed to recover from some of the challenges it faces. Although far from overcoming all these difficulties, the Jordanian economy has made good use of the margin of autonomy it enjoys. In unstable conditions, a country without great weight must be permanently adaptable to fluctuations in the environment. A particular form of internal political and structural stability has allowed a flexible policy to be followed. Jordan has thus been able to profit from favourable situations as and when they arise.

The first element in the Jordanian response is the particular interrelationship between the private and public sectors.[17] Jordan's economy sees itself as liberal; the overriding keynotes are a spirit of enterprise and regulation by market forces. Nevertheless, as in all Arab economies, the presence of the state is considerable. A particular feature of Jordan's economy is that this state presence finds a reciprocal, if limited, dynamism in the private sector.

The state plays the major role in the economic system; its intervention is not justified by dogmatic concepts or any particular ideological stand, but by the need to occupy an area which would otherwise remain empty. Its role is, first, to spell out overall objectives and select the means by which economic policy will be implemented. In an economy that by no stretch of the imagination could be called planned, we therefore find a succession of development plans which spell out economic perspectives, provide key indicators (overall growth rate and growth rate by sector, aims of diversification, siting of activities, and so on) and consider methods of financing them. The six-year development plan (1964-70) was interrupted by the 1967 war and a three-year plan (1973-75) took account of the changed environment: it provided for investment of JD 179 mn, some 45% of which was to come from the private sector (for construction, mines and industry). In the following two plans, investment was shared in almost equal part by private sources and public funds. The 1976-80 plan was very ambitious (it had been drawn up at the time of the massive hike in oil revenues); it envisaged an overall annual growth rate of over 12%, the rate for industry being 26.1% in current JDs. Actual investment exceeded all forecasts - which had predicted a level of around JD 843 mn. This was largely due to the high level of private investment, 60% above what was expected. The average annual growth rate reached 8.5%, that of industry reaching 13.6% in real terms. Even if the goals were not achieved, such results cannot be dismissed.

The 1981-85 plan, drawn up at the time of the second hike in oil revenues, was also very ambitious. It envisaged investment of JD 3.3 bn, 23% going to factories and industry, which were expected to grow at around 17.2% per annum. The accent was laid on providing for basic needs, but at the same time the service sector's contribution to GDP was to be reduced in relation to that of the production sector. External capital was expected to make a substantial contribution in all fields other than health and construction.

Although the results are still provisional, the development plans have undoubtedly contributed to a growth in public investment by proving its effectiveness and the way it complements private-sector investment. The latter has frequently exceeded expectations, revealing at one and the same time a favourable set of circumstances and a buoyant, confident climate. In fact, most large public enterprises are mixed, part of their capital being held by the public and quoted on the stock exchange. Privatization of capital is pursued whenever favourable conditions appear. On the other hand, the state has minority holdings in a large number of private companies. A law passed in 1972 and amended in 1984 encourages private investment by granting tax exemptions and fiscal advantages.

Rentier or Producer Economy?

In times of crisis, the state's pragmatic attitude leads it to increase its intervention in order to protect what it sees as the national interest. Recent circumstances have led to two forms of state intervention. First, the state came to the aid of Jordanian producers threatened by the drastic reduction in Iraqi outlets in 1984: it did this both through a loan to the National Bank of Iraq to finance part of its sales and through buying back goods to resell on the domestic market. Second, as previously mentioned, measures have recently been introduced to protect local contractors from excessive competition from companies involved in public works which have lost markets in the Gulf. All contracts worth less than JD 2 mn are reserved for local firms. Moreover, in order to fulfil its promise to create 250,000 jobs, the government has instituted a process of 'Jordanianization' - this applies even to the banking sector, where obligatory Jordanian participation in the capital of not less than 51% is envisaged.

Since it is met by a reciprocal dynamism in the private sector, this state intervention is reasonably effective. In Jordan (as in Lebanon and other Arab countries) it is easy to dismiss misleading questions as to the lack of a spirit of enterprise and whether such a thing as the 'Arab entrepreneur' exists. In the Arab countries, as elsewhere, such a spirit of enterprise is usually just waiting for the appropriate policies and a favourable climate.[18] There is a fairly large number of new businesses in Jordan; tradesmen turned industrialists rub shoulders with engineers accumulating sufficient capital to launch a productive company. Whereas the minerals sector is dominated by the big companies with majority public capital, small and medium-sized private-sector companies provide the bulk of manufactured goods.

Between 1970 and 1982 the number of companies registered rose from 2,305 to 12,439. From 1976 to 1980, 670 medium-sized companies and 2,300 craftsmen's workshops were granted licences.[19] Some 180 new industrial companies were registered in 1981 and 650 the following year. Even in agriculture, where state investment in irrigation and soil protection is essential, private enterprise and the efforts of individual producers are playing an increasing role. Irrigation schemes in the Jordan Valley, with the Ghor Canal, have encouraged farmers to produce on an industrial scale, adopt more up-to-date management techniques and export a

Rentier or Producer Economy?

major part of their crop.[20]

Even if the private sector's response to state encouragement should not be overestimated, it nevertheless represents one of the most effective aspects of the way Jordan is facing up to the economic challenges.

Due to this interrelationship between the private and public sectors, the productive sector has scored some noticeable successes. In the first place, the 'Big Five' companies are the showcase of Jordan's industrial success. They have been successful in exploiting the country's limited mineral resources and, while not all necessarily achieving a perfect financial equilibrium, they function satisfactorily, particularly when compared with the regional norm. We will briefly mention the main characteristics of these companies, in which state participation ranges from 51% to 92%.

The Jordan Phosphate Mines Company (JPMC) makes Jordan the world's third largest exporter of phosphates (exports were expected to reach 7 mn t in 1985 and go to 27 countries). The strategic location of Aqaba has allowed Jordan to export phosphates, fertilizer and potassium derivatives to Asian markets.

In 1983 the Jordan Fertilizer Industries Company (JFIC), with its $400 mn factory, started to export phosphoric acid (over 100,000 t/year) and concentrated fertilizer (a capacity of 700,000 t/year).

Since December 1982 the Arab Potash Company (APC), with its $450 mn factory (constructed on time and within the estimate), has been exporting potash extracted from the Dead Sea; production is estimated at 1.2 mn t when the plant is working at full capacity.

The fourth large industrial installation is the Jordan Cement Factory Company (JCFC). Its capacity has recently (1982) been brought up to 2.2 mn t and a new extension is envisaged. A second cement plant, producing 2 mn t/year, is to be built in the south (Rashidiyeh) at a cost of $235 mn.

The last of the Big Five is the recently enlarged oil refinery at Zarqa. Its capacity of over 4 mn t/year is in excess of the country's needs. The oil processed here comes from Saudi Arabia.

In addition to the five star performers of Jordanian industry, there is a mass of industrial companies producing consumer goods. They have made

Rentier or Producer Economy?

a decisive contribution to the growth of industrial output - from JD 46.8 mn in 1975 to JD 154 mn in 1980 (in current-price dinars) - while the number of people employed in industry rose from 27,000 to 40,000. Moreover, it is these companies that are expected to ensure that the growth targets set in the 1981-85 plan are reached: 27.8% per annum for an industrial output amounting to JD 350 mn in 1980. Once the resources of the major mineral-based industries have been exploited, hope for the future lies in the production of consumer goods. These will use local resources as far as possible and be destined for a regional market, thus permitting the exploitation of economies of scale. The recent opening up towards Egypt is in line with this policy. Over and above the political hazards, producers face the major obstacles of water and energy.

We have mentioned above the encouraging response by 'new-style' farmers to the efforts to bring agriculture up to date. Overall results have been positive, with a growth rate of 18% (5.7% at constant prices) between 1976 and 1980; production rose from JD 26 mn to JD 60 mn. At the price of massive investment (estimated at $1.5 bn), Jordan's plans - in which the government has entered into partnership with 14 international organizations - will lead to 30,000 ha being irrigated and create tens of thousands of jobs. Growth in the agricultural sector is expected to register 7.5% per annum from 1980 to 1985 (from JD 60 mn to JD 86 mn); state investment will go to the infrastructure, and private investment to activities that are directly productive. Particular success has been registered in the fruit and vegetable sector, notably in out-of-season crops (winter crops).

Income-generating services have registered some growth, benefiting from upheavals in the region. Since 1975 there has been rapid growth (around 20% per annum) in the banking sector, a partial staging-post after Beirut. Six investment banks have been set up and a financial market has developed, specializing in shares and bond issues of the 'Big Five'. Turnover on the Amman Financial Market (AFM) rose from JD 4 mn in 1978 to JD 128 mn in 1982, with growth continuing in 1983. These developments enable productive activities to be financed by domestic sources, by allowing immigrants' remittances to be channelled to the needs of industry and agriculture. We have already mentioned the extension of services linked to transit activities, an area particularly subject to the hazards of the regional situation.

The foregoing achievements reveal the Jordanian economy's capacity to adapt to an unstable environment and to overcome some of the biases and constraints of the _rentier_ economy. It is thus possible to speak of the country's economy as 'lean and well managed'[21] and the overall situation as 'economically healthy, thanks above all to external aid and remittances'.[22] The fundamental constraints still exist, however, and Jordan's control over the fundamental parameters influencing its standard of living and level of activity is still very limited. In spite of spectacular growth in industrial exports and a significant rate of growth in agricultural production, the external debt is larger than ever. Moreover, the goal of diversification has not been achieved, since the service sector's contribution to GDP still represents more than two-thirds. After the high growth in the 1970s and at the beginning of the 1980s, 1985 was heading towards a zero growth rate. Thus the country has suffered the full effects of the drop in oil revenues and has had to borrow more than $500 mn on the international capital market in the space of two years. The external debt corresponds to about 50% of GNP ($2,137 in 1983, or two and a half times the 1978 level). The short-term bank debt stands at $460 mn. Debt-servicing is at a low level, however, absorbing a mere 6% of the value of exports in 1983.

Thus there are no permanent gains in an economy that remains heavily dependent on its position in the regional system of _rentier_ income and subject to environmental hazards. The achievements are far from negligible, however, and the essential steps have been taken on the road towards establishing the structure of a productive economy. Over the last two decades Jordan has shown its capacity to adapt. Relying on these gains and the skills of its population, it is better placed than most of its neighbours to respond to the challenge of the regional situation. Nevertheless the autonomy of the economic system is only relative. Political storms could at any moment sweep everything away.

Rentier or Producer Economy?

NOTES

1. See in particular the classic work by Michael P. Mazur, Economic Growth and Development in Jordan (Croom Helm, London 1979). For sources in French, see: the standard work (although published some 20 years ago) by A.M. Guichon, Jordanie reelle, 2 vols. (1967 and 1972); F. Rivier, Croissance industrielle dans une économie assistée, le cas de la Jordanie (CERMOC, Beirut, 1980); and P. Rondot, La Jordanie (PUF, Que sais-je? series, Paris, 1980).

2. The reader is referred to several GRESMO studies (by both individuals and groups) in which these hypotheses are spelled out: GRESMO, Industrialisation du bassin méditerranéen (PUG, Grenoble, 1983); M. Chatelus, 'L'Economie des pays arabes 20 ans apres', Maghreb-Machrek (Oct. - Dec. 1983): M. Chatelus and Y. Schemeil, 'Towards a New Political Economy of State Industrialisation in the Middle East', IJMES (April 1984); and M. Chatelus, 'Attitudes toward Public Sector Management and Reassertion of the Private Sector in the Arab World', paper presented at the meeting of the Middle East Studies Association (MESA), San Francisco, Dec. 1984 (the text has not yet been published, but is available from the author).

3. The author adopted this expression as the heading for a study of the Syrian economy that appeared in A. Raymond (ed.), La Syrie d'aujourd'hui (CNRS, Paris, 1980). It would appear to be equally applicable, mutatis mutandis, to Jordan.

4. See Rivier, Croissance industrielle.

5. For the terminology and ways of calculating the revenue deficit, we will be using in particular the annual World Development Reports produced by the World Bank. External revenue makes up for the difference between expenditure and domestic product (GDP). If consumption exceeds this product, the saving is negative and external revenue must cover all investment plus this negative saving. The external deficit is the measure of this revenue deficit.

6. See, in particular, Chatelus and Schemeil, 'Towards a New Political Economy'.

7. In general, we have used statistics provided by the IMF and the World Bank, the two organizations which have the best access to national income statistics. Not all the data are equally reliable, however.

8. See note 5.

9. See, for example, 'Big Income from Expatriate Labour' *Financial Times* (hereafter *FT*), 13 Aug. 1982, and Odone and Roberts, 'Jordan', *Middle East Review* (1984).

10. A. McDermott, 'Plan Aims to Quadruple Investment', *FT*, 13 Aug. 1982.

11. World Bank, *World Development Report, 1984*.

12. The author suggested a methodology for analysing the costs of the conflict in a paper presented at a day's seminar organized by CERI in Paris in October 1984. The paper is due to appear in a forthcoming issue of *Maghreb-Machrek*.

13. In this respect, see the accurate analyses by F. Rivier in *Croissance industrielle*.

14. World Bank, *World Development Report, 1984*. The upper bracket of countries with middle-range incomes includes those with a *per capita* income of $1,600 or more in 1982. These countries' average defence spending amounts to 8.8% of public expenditure, which itself represents, on average, 20.6% of GNP (compared with 35.8% in Jordan). Only Syria (with more than 11%) and Israel (31.2%) spend a higher percentage than Jordan. By means of comparison, South Korea allocates 6.5% of its GNP to defence.

15. P. Robbins, 'Industry Review, Jordan' in *Arab Industry Review* (Inter Crescent Publications, Dallas, 1984).

16. *Le Monde*, 6, 7 July 1984.

17. The relationship between 'public' and 'private' is a particularly important issue for the Arab economies. The author tackled this problem in the MESA paper cited in note 2. M. Bader's doctoral thesis (due to be defended at the University of Grenoble in 1985) throws some interesting light on this subject.

18. On this issue, see Yusif Sayigh's classic work, *Entrepreneurs of Lebanon. The Role of the Business Leader in a Developing Economy* (Harvard University Press, Cambridge, Mass., 1962) and O. Penef, *Industriels algériens* (CNRS, Paris, 1981).

19. *FT*, 13 Aug. 1982.

20. In an investigation by *Le Monde* (2 Dec. 1984), E. Jarry described a visit to this area of the valley and spoke of the 'gentlemen farmers' who were running 'full-blown industrial enterprises'.

21. 'Lean and well-managed economy', according to an American banker quoted by Odone and Roberts in *Middle East Review*, 1984.

22. *FT*, 13 Aug. 1982.

Chapter Thirteen

SOME REFLECTIONS ON THE FUTURE ISSUES CONCERNING ECONOMIC DEVELOPMENT IN JORDAN

Adnan Badran, Elias Baydoun, Kapur S. Ahlawat and Siva Ram Vemuri

During the last three decades, a number of important lessons have emerged from Jordan's experience. This experience is continuously being examined and re-examined, with a view to providing insights as to whether development, and deliberate attempts at it through the planning process, have succeeded or not. There is an increasing plethora of material on this question.

The present chapter is an attempt to provide an outline sketch of future directives, to enhance and strengthen the development process in transforming the Jordanian economy.

Our explicit concern in this chapter is with regard to what lies ahead for overall economic management of the country. Any such futurology depends upon ingredients from the past and interpretations of the future. As a result, the chapter is structured as follows. In the first part, issues concerning future development perceptions, as a result of the introspections, will be dealt with. The observable future is interpreted in the light of the economic challenges emanating from the experiences of the past. In the second part, it will be argued that the development processes and policies must be discussed in the light of appropriate development perceptions and a clearly defined development strategy. The discussion centres around the view that the appropriate implementation of the policies is related to the achievement of a proper planning framework and evaluative perspective. Finally, a case-study approach will be followed, involving the health and education sectors, to highlight the methodology to be used for meeting the development challenges of the future.

Future Issues

THE OBSERVABLE FUTURE

For the followers of development literature, it is becoming increasingly clear that the traditional dichotomy between the developed and developing countries on the one hand, and planned and market economies on the other hand, is not as striking as was thought in the late 1950s. As Brookfield (1973) suggests, research in the Third World should lead only to an enrichment of our understanding of the First and Second Worlds, where the same phenomena of dualism, centres and peripheries exist and, above all, the institutional and behavioural contrasts that underly varying receptivity and reaction in the face of change. The only real difference is the more striking degree to which the Third World exhibits these things. In similar vein, the purpose of observing the future in all the world's economies, both developed and developing, is the same. Whatever the interpretation of future perspectives, it remains true that development issues and their various manifestations such as employability, social and economic mobility, regional equitability, etc., as in all economies of the world, are all variants of the same theme - to provide a better future and, in our case, to provide a better future for Jordanian society.

Jordan's future depends upon past data (information), present expectations and future achievements. One striking issue with regard to the economic development process is that Jordan, like many of its counterparts, has been unable to benefit from any one single theory that could provide the 'golden key' to economic development. The complicated processes of economic development, on the other hand, were (and are) strewn with numerous anxieties and external uncertainties. In spite of this, the country has attempted to utilize, to the best of its ability, its human and natural resources, by preparing and attempting to implement its economic and social development programmes.[1] Although development efforts suffered a severe setback as a result of the Israeli occupation of the West Bank in 1967, Jordan's efforts to provide for a better future were made possible through the successful completion of the three-year development plan (1973-75) and the first five-year development plan (1976-80), as well as the implementation of the second five-year plan (1981-85), thereby enabling Jordan, once again, to resume its economic and social momentum.

Viewed in this light, there seems to be every reason for optimism as to the potential for economic development in Jordan. It is becoming increasingly obvious that Jordan possesses no inherent disadvantages in natural or human resources compared with any other developing country. This holds true both quantitatively and qualitatively. To suggest, for instance, that Jordan does not have sufficient economic potential, or that Jordanians have a relatively low innate capacity for participating in the more complex forms of social and economic reforms needed for development - all such views are rejected. Whereas there are difficulties in the understanding and utilization of the resource base for Jordan's development process, these difficulties stem from lack of information, co-ordination, experience and training, and are therefore not of the kind to inhibit Jordan's economic development permanently.

Further grounds for optimism about Jordan's future development are provided by a recognition of the relative adaptability of the appropriate and deliberate policy mixes hitherto put forward since the 1973-75 plan. Such an optimistic view can be justified, on the one hand, by an examination of the performance of the economy since the 1973-75 plan in the trade sector, budget deficits and the related issue of debt servicing, and, on the other hand, by evaluating whether the future challenges are within reach of the country's economic potential.

It must explicitly be understood why we choose to evaluate the performance and past management practices of the Jordanian economy on the basis of the following variables: foreign trade, balance of payments, foreign aid, debt servicing and budgetary deficits. The paramount importance of these variables in Jordan stems from the significant role of the foreign sector, especially due to the problems of economies of scale related to small domestic markets in Jordan. As a result, economic issues in Jordan can never be understood, let alone be tackled, out of the context of the world economy within the international political, financial, administrative and trade arenas.

Foreign Trade and Balance of Payments

Foreign and domestic trade plays an important role in Jordan's economy. The one sector that contributes the largest share of GDP is trade.[2] Jordan has experienced and continues to experience an increasing value of imports since its creation. For instance, the value of imports increased from JD 67.7 mn in 1969 to JD 1,103.3 mn in 1983. It is true that Jordanian exports also increased from JD 11.9 mn to JD 160.1 mn during the period 1969-83. But its exports have never paid for its imports. How, then, can one rationalize such an increase in the trade imbalance and be optimistic about the future? It is important to note that no country in the world, ceteris paribus, can expect a dramatic shift in the balance of trade in the relatively short time-span of a decade. Therefore, in order to justify future optimism, it is essential to focus attention on how Jordan has influenced trade patterns, activity and financing since the 1973-75 plan period. Although the value of imports has been on the increase from 1969 to 1983, the average value of imports during the different plan periods reveals an increasingly moderate rate, from 68.3% of GNP per annum in the 1973-75 plan to 80.12% of GNP per annum in the 1976-80 plan and 87.12% of GNP per annum (based on three years) during 1981-83, thereby reflecting the efficiency of imports. At the same time, average propensity to import increased from 56.5% in 1973 to 79.4% in 1983.

It can be seen that not only have imports been growing during the plan periods but also the level of GNP. It is therefore important to compare Jordan's imports and the levels of GNP. A comparison of rates of growth of GNP and imports reveals that, since the plan periods 1973-75, increasing levels of imports can be attributed to increases in GNP.

This means that not only has the rate of growth of GNP outstripped the rate of growth of imports during the plan periods, but also the gap between GNP and imports narrowed from the 1973-75 plan to the 1981-83 plan period. In order to continue to narrow this gap between GNP and imports, Jordan should concentrate not only on import substitution policies but also on export promotion activities. Jordan's bottleneck hitherto has been the smallness of the domestic market. This has hindered private initiatives to indulge in production activity that is cost-effective and of sufficient scale. As a result, there was a need for large infrastructural imports (that were not readily forthcoming from the domestic markets) but also large imports of consumer goods (to meet small but increasing need). The increases in imports of

Future Issues

production-based commodities have led to increases in output of goods and services, which necessarily need to be marketed both domestically and abroad.

Table 13.1: Comparison of Rates of Growth in Imports and GNP during Plan Periods (percentage)

Plan period	Rate of growth (%)	
	Imports	GNP
1973-75	48.65	8.88
1976-80	111.78	91.095
1981-83	28.13	81.62

As a result, there is a need to see whether commodity patterns of trade activity have changed and how domestic exports have performed in the recent past, both with regard to commodities as well as export markets.

The second reason for optimism as to future trade activity concerns how the pattern of imports has changed since the 1973-75 plan period. It has been asserted in the past[3] that Jordan's imports of consumption goods have always outpaced its imports of capital goods. But an examination of the composition of commodity patterns reveals the start of a reverse trend: while the average percentage of capital goods and raw materials since the 1973-75 plan period has slightly increased, the average percentage of imports of consumer goods has, in fact, been falling, from 45.4% in the 1973-75 plan period to 32.6% during the 1981-83 plan period.

This changing pattern of composition of imports is further evidenced by examining the average value of propensities to import by economic function. Since the plan period 1973-75, the average value of raw materials and capital goods has revealed large increases, from 11.6 to 21.0% and from 14.8 to 22.5% of GNP per annum respectively. The average value of imports of consumer goods, on the other hand, has revealed a marginal decline, from 23.2 to 21.0% of GNP per annum during 1981-83.

Future Issues

Table 13.2: Average Percentage of Type of Imports to Total Imports during the Plan Periods 1973-1983

Plan Period	Capital goods	Raw materials	Consumer goods	Total
1973-75	31	23.6	45.4	100
1976-80	35	29	36.0	100
1981-83	34.4	33	32.6	100

The third reason for optimism stems from the realization that Jordan is not only an importer but also an exporter of raw materials, consumer goods and capital goods. Indeed, average exports as a percentage of imports, by type of goods, for the plan periods since 1973 reveal that, while consumer goods exports as a percentage of imports are steadily increasing (thereby reflecting the export potential for Jordan's consumer goods), there has been a decline in both raw materials and capital goods exports as a percentage of imports.

Table 13.3: Average Exports as a Percentage of Imports by Plan Period, 1973-1983

Plan period	Average exports as % of imports		
	Consumer goods	Capital goods	Raw materials
1973-75	17	8	44
1976-80	20	5	20
1981-83	24	3.5	21

The fourth reason for optimism with regard to future trade potential in the international markets stems from Jordan's ability to shift and further exploit its trade relations both with the socialist bloc and with the Arab Common Market (ACM) countries. An examination of the geographic distribution of domestic exports during the plan periods since 1973 reveals that, while the percentage of domestic exports to other Arab countries (other than those in the ACM), EEC and Asian countries has fallen, there has been a steady

Future Issues

increase in exports to the ACM and socialist countries.

Table 13.4: Geographic Distribution of Domestic Exports by Plan Period, 1973-1983 (percentage)

Plan period	ACM	Other Arab countries	EEC	Socialist countries	Asian countries	Other countries
1973-75	18.5	30.0	3.0	9.3	17.3	22.6
1976-80	28.8	32.6	0.8	10.2	9.7	16.6
1981-83		36.0	27	12.9	10.0	11.3

The future challenge for the economic manager in Jordan is to examine ways and means of expanding the export market more than substituting for its imports. As stated earlier, the problem of the small size of the domestic market makes it imperative to explore hitherto unexploited marketing channels, not only in Third World countries but also in terms of financing the higher levels of imports. It is here that barter forms of trade (goods for machines) need to be fully explored, especially as Jordan is facing a small market potential. Jordan's import capacity and ability to import are restricted by export expenditures, aided and unaided capacity and foreign exchange reserves, as shown in Tables 13.5 and 13.6.

The fifth reason for future optimism stems from the observation that although imports and category of import capacity moved in line with each other, having an upward trend, the growth rates increased from 1973-75 to 1976-80 and then declined in the period 1981-83.

The unaided import capacity is much more realistic, in the economic sense, than the other two categories.[4] Although there is a fall in the percentage rate of growth of unaided import capacity from 31.6% (1976-80) to 10.5% (1981-83), it is important to note that this is the largest percentage among all the categories of import capacity. It could thus be inferred that Jordan's real import capacity has been growing in the plan periods under observation, that the growth has not kept pace with import volumes and the deficit has been offset by aided import purchasing power.

227

Future Issues

Table 13.5: Average Propensity to Import and Imports by Economic Function by Plan Period, 1973-85[a] (averages in percentages)

Plan periods	Imports	Import by economic function		
		Consumer goods	Raw materials	Capital goods
1973-75	68.3	23.2	11.6	14.8
1976-80	80.12	22.0	17.4	21.8
1981-83	87.13	21.0	21.0	22.5

Note: a. Data available in CBJ vols. until 1983 only.
Source: Compiled from Central Bank of Jordan (CBJ), vol. 21, no. 1, (Jan. 1985)

Table 13.6: Percentage Growth Rates of Imports by Economic Function by Plan Period, 1973-85[a]

Plan periods	Consumer goods	Raw materials	Capital goods
1973-75	21.16	36.66	59.24
1976-80	12.48	20.00	16.57
1981-83	3.88	7.00	- 9.12

Note: a. Data available in CBJ vols. until 1983 only.
Source: Compiled from CBJ, vol. 21, no. 1.

Table 13.7: Average Annual Growth Rates of Jordan's Import Capacity by Plan Period, 1973-83 (percentage)

Plan period	Aided import capacity	Unaided import capacity	Import capacity of export proceeds
1973-75	12.3	25.7	21.3
1976-80	25.2	31.6	29.2
1981-83	2.8	10.5	7.4

Future Issues

Jordan's growth of import capacity has steadily been declining in the plan period, and at the same time the foreign exchange reserves equivalent to imports have also been declining.

This strengthens the argument for heavier restrictions on imports than those in existence, through the regulations either of the Ministry of Supply or of the Ministry of Industry and Commerce. As tariff policies have a protective role as well as an objective, it is increasingly becoming evident that tariff rates should be reviewed to bring them into line with their overall impact on Jordan's development potential. This is very much in the spirit of the import system No. 81/1971.[5] The challenge for the future lies in devising appropriate administrative and tariff restrictions in line with the use to which the imported goods are put, and evaluating their short-, medium- and long-term impact on the Jordanian economy. In the past, increases in tariffs have been advocated on consumption goods rather than on capital goods and raw materials, for the following reasons:

1. They distort production, due to an increase in marginal costs.
2. They have a negative effect on export competitiveness.
3. They distort domestic demand, by making domestic market price higher than the world price.

Jordan has neither enjoyed price competitiveness for its exports nor has it been able to protect its domestic markets by relaxing tariffs on capital goods and raw materials. Tariffs and other restrictive measures on imports must be considered in line with the problems of smaller economies of scale.

Table 13.8: Average Annual Growth Rates of Months of Import Capacity and Foreign Exchange Reserves (fer) Equivalent to Imports, 1973-1985 (percentage)

Plan period	Months of import capacity	Fer equivalent to imports
1973-75	6.8	56.4
1976-80	5.1	42.3
1981-85	3.6	30.0

Future Issues

Financing the Development Process: Foreign Aid, Debt Servicing and Budgetary Deficits

The provision of aid, whether financial, in kind or in technical assistance, has undoubtedly played an important role thus far in the development process of Jordan. The impact of foreign aid has increasingly come under the scrutiny of both the 'armchair' economist and the economic practitioner. Even the briefest survey of a discussion of the role of foreign aid would open up a Pandora's box of questions such as 'Is increasing foreign aid good or bad for the economy?' 'How much further foreign aid should the economy accept?', 'What development projects should foreign aid assist?', and so on. If we were to consider all these issues, a brief outline such as being attempted in this chapter, would be transformed into a treatise.

Suffice it to note that, in the foreseeable future, the Jordanian economy needs to focus attention on two interrelated issues in the field of financing development projects. The obvious consequence of increasing foreign aids and loans is the problem of debt servicing, partly resulting from loans and aid being obtained under the auspices of the public sector. The other interrelated issue is the role of the private sector in financing development projects. Jordan's debt-servicing capacity, and the extent of its external debt burden in relation to its balance of payments in the plan years since 1973-75, reveal another of the future challenges facing the country.

The short-term indicators of the debt-servicing capacity, as shown in Table 13.9, indicate that increasingly over the plan periods there is considerable short-run rigidity in the balance of payments position in Jordan. This implies, as theory suggests, that Jordan may be experiencing in the short-run a weakening of debt-servicing capacity and needs to cut down on imports. However, the picture is not as bleak as some would like to suggest. Although the short-term indicators of debt-servicing capacity are showing warning signals, the solution does not necessarily lie in cutting down on imports. In a more pragmatic sense, it is a matter of changes in attitude in the evaluation of imports. It is not a question of imports of capital goods <u>vis-à-vis</u> imports of consumer goods. The traditional argument for supporting imports of capital goods has been based on the grounds that if imports of capital goods and raw materials decline, then the investment ratio

Future Issues

Table 13.9: Plan Averages of Jordan's Debt Service Ratio and Ratio of Debt Services to GNP, 1973-1983

Plan periods	Debt service ratio			Ratio of debt service & GNP
	Using export of goods only	Using total exports of goods & services	Exports of goods and non-factor services	
1973-75	17.6	5.7	7.8	1.7
1976-80	25.1	6.4	16.0	2.36
1981-83	41.4	11.0	27.3	4.2

Source: Adapted from Riad al-Momanie (1985).

declines leading to lower levels of GNP, which in turn result in a reduction in import capacity. No longer is this justification realistic or appropriate in the case of Jordan. Table 13.2 suggests that capital goods and raw materials have been given preferential treatment in comparison to consumer goods, in spite of this, during the same plan periods. Table 13.9 suggests a deterioration in debt-servicing capacity.

The reasons for such a trend stem from the fact that Jordan will necessarily be in a position to pay back capital imports as well as consumer imports only after market transactions have taken place. Capital imports contribute to the production of goods and services, which in turn must be sold in order to generate funding capacity of Jordan's imports. It is here that the traditional argument in support of capital goods imports at the expense of consumer goods does not hold water. Comsumer goods imports are based on demand estimates, which have more 'realistic' transmitting signals for the planners. Moreover, the elasticity of substitution of consumption goods, in the light of absence of competitive consumer goods, is high. On the other hand, capital goods imports are based not only on expected demand but also on expected export market potential and anticipated international competitive suppliers. Due to the small size of Jordan's market, and the interest of financing the imported capital goods from external sources, projects are invariably taken up of such a scale of operations that they can cater for the demands of external markets. When these markets do not materialize in the future, for whatever reason, debt servicing of these projects becomes a burden.

As a result, the challenge for the future lies not so much in trying to build an infrastructural base by importing capital goods and raw materials, but in attempting to alleviate the problem of scale economies of production relevant to a country like Jordan. This requires at least a two-pronged strategy of, first, making barter trade agreements between Jordan and other countries and, second, mobilizing domestic initiatives.

Table 13.10: Average Growth Rates of Deficits and Savings, and Average Percentage Rate of Deficit to Savings by Plan Periods, 1973-1983

Plan periods	Average rate of deficit	Average rate of savings	Average rate of % deficit to savings
1973-75	- 1.75	100.57	-1.74
1976-80	-25.1	697.43	-3.60
1981-83	-18.7	1,367.95	-1.38

Source: Compiled from CBJ, vol. 20.

It is becoming apparent from the various official documents, including the development plans, that efforts are underway to increase the contribution of domestic savings to the development process. This can be seen, first, from the increases in average percentage growth rates of savings to deficits (Table 13.10).

Second, the contribution of the private sector (self-financing and mixed loans) to the development financing of projects has steadily been increasing.

There have been further attempts to 'Jordanianize' both the capital and labour markets to meet the present needs of the development process. Local and domestic financing of development projects are therefore essential, as they result in the following three-fold effect:

Future Issues

1. The mobilization of local financing leads to multiple accelerator effects, that have a longer-term influence than development projects based on aid and loans.
2. Such increases in private-sector participation involve the sharing not only of development benefits but also of costs, thereby enhancing the accountability of development appropriated funds.
3. They provide the financial discipline needed to achieve higher levels of development.

Table 13.11: Project Financing by Type of Finance (percentage)

Plan period	General budget	Private sector
1973-75	30.89	31.05
1976-80	15.7	26.8
1981-83	25.94	37.5

Apart from Jordanianizing the labour and capital markets, a perhaps even more critical need is to find a clearer development perspective for the future.

Future Aspects of Development
A cursory examination of the observable future emanating from past experiences provides insights into some of the economic challenges facing Jordan. These potential challenges need to be met by providing a proper planning frame for considering future aspects of development processes, perceptions and policies.

Popularist studies of development processes reveal a traditional dichotomy between balanced, self-equilibrating methodologies and unbalanced growth strategies. In the past, a country's development processes were dictated by an examination of the type of sectors that can provide the necessary impetus for growth. Increasingly, a different method of evaluation is being adopted by developing countries.

On the basis of two theoretical assumptions -

Future Issues

i.e. that development can be measured by levels of GNP and that there are various combinations of Social Overhead Capital (SOC) and Direct Productive Activity (DPA) that yield the same level of GNP (as described by the Iso GNP curves) - the development processes of any economic system hitherto depended upon the given required factors responsible for development. For example, if an economy had fixed-capabilities in the short-run to contribute effectively to the sectors of the DPA in comparison with those of the SOC, then the development process to be followed was path A shown in Figure 13.1.

Figure 13.1: Theoretical Development Paths

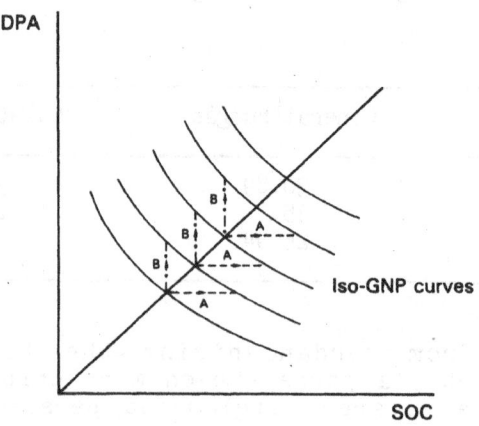

If, on the other hand, the country had the natural advantage of certain raw materials in abundance, and could contribute to the growth much more than SOC, then the country was expected to benefit most by following development path B.

Table 13.12: Average Rates of Return on Investment in Physical Capital, Selected Developing Countries[a] (percentage)

Economic sector	1975	1976	1977	1978
Transportation				
Highways	11.9	15.7	13.9	17.6
Railways	16.0	7.0		13.6
Ports	27.0	12.0	19.5	18.5

Future Issues

Table 13.12 (Cont'd)

Economic sector	1975	1976	1977	1978
Others				32.0
Agriculture	13.5	16.2	16.7	13.1
Industry			18.3	17.0
Public utilities				
Telecommunications		22.0		22.5
Water supply			11.5	8.5

Note: a. Includes Botswana, Ethiopia, Madagascar, Uganda, Central African Empire, Congo, Ivory Coast, Niger, Nigeria, Senegal, Togo, Papua New Guinea, Thailand, Brazil, Ecuador, Trinidad and Tobago, India, Karachi, Colombia, Malawi, Cameroon, Gambia, Dominican Republic, Ghana, Bolivia, Mexico, Sierra Leone, Chile, Indonesia, Nepal, Pakistan, Iran and Jamaica.
Source: World Bank estimates (various issues).

Jordan seems to be no exception to this case, when one attempts a careful analysis of the emphasis laid in the national plans since 1964-70. The country's development process concentrated heavily on expanding SOC in the post-1973-75 plan periods, as shown in Table 13.13, thereby attempting to traverse development path B.

Past studies on other developing countries[6] have revealed that the rate of return to investment in physical capital, at the initial stages of development, is invariably higher in SOC projects than in DPA projects.

But there seems to be a dramatic change in emphasis in the 1981-85 planned expenditure patterns. According to the second five-year planned expenditure patterns, much more emphasis seems to be laid on projects related to DPA rather than SOC. The reason for such a dramatic shift seems to be a case of short-run (immediate) response to the differences between actual and audited rates of return.

If development projects are funded from foreign sources (in the form of loans and assistance), these rate of return calculations play an important role in the allocation of development

Future Issues

Table 13.13: Contribution of Planned Expenditures on DPA, SOC (percentage)

Plan period	DPA to total planned expenditures (%)	SOC to total planned expenditures (%)
1973-75	13.3	86.7
1976-80	28.8	71.2
1981-85	76.2	23.8

Source: Compiled from various National Plans of Jordan by computing sectoral project allocations.

funds. Unfortunately, the reality of project financing and investment decisions is that they have to be based on audited rate of return calculations, while debt servicing and effective development performance are judged on actual rate of returns from project investment. Thus, in the absence of opportunities for marketability and employability, the actual rates of return do not meet the expectations of the audited rate of returns. As such a trend continues, it becomes necessary to increase the funds obtained from DPA; as a result, more funds become diverted towards DPA, on the assumption that markets for DPA continue to exist at least equivalent to the effects of increases in investible funds.

Although the development process appropriate to Jordan is described by path B in Figure 13.1, the fundamental issue is when and by how much the SOC sector should contract in order to compensate for and divert development expenditures to the DPA sector. Moreover, rates of return on various projects should be calculated in line with differing degrees of probability of availability of market potential.

It is also necessary to evaluate the consequences of a dramatic shift in emphasis along the development processes from SOC to DPA. In order to minimize the risk and uncertainty factors of realizing effective demands (both domestically and internationally), it is important to analyse and incorporate the development perceptions of the Jordanian people into the decision-making process. Two case studies involving the predominant sectors of SOC - health and education - will be considered later (see pp. 239-42), to examine the importance

Future Issues

of development perceptions.

There has been a great emphasis on development perceptions in Jordanian plans. Not only has this concern for perception resulted in increasing the domain of issues related to man and space (region); it has also led to an investigation of grass-roots initiatives and grass-roots specifications of development perspectives. The case study involving the health sector discusses one such methodology to be adopted in an attempt to incorporate development perceptions within the development policy options.

The traditional economic justification for proposing investment in a development-related project stems from consideration of the effects of the project on the basis of efficiency, equity and employment. However, if increasing numbers of people are exposed to development projects, the satisfaction of social demand or the freedom to choose becomes a very important perception of development and must necessarily be taken into consideration when evaluating development options. This will be discussed further when we consider the case study of education.

Such considerations of development processes and perceptions warrant a frame of reference that is flexible enough to consider different development policy options and provide timely predictions of future eventualities. In general, the frame of reference suggested here is the behavioural structural model relevant to Jordan. It consists of the following schematic representation.

In general

$$D_t = A_t E_t$$

where D_t : is an n vector of development units at time t

A_t : is a nxn matrix of socio-economic coefficients at time t

and E_t : is a n vector of socio-economic elements on which developmental units depend at time t.

It is important to distinguish between two specific orders of developmental units, namely natural and induced. Natural developmental units are those that are innate to the Jordanian economic system, such as smallness of the market, problem of scale efficiency of production, and so on. Induced developmental units are those that can be induced through varying policy options. As a result, D above will be partitioned into two specific orders:

$$D = D_I : D_N$$

Thus the planned development function becomes a functional form indicating the mix of D_I and D_N respectively and will be described as:

$$P_D = f(D_I, D_N).$$

It should be pointed out that such a schematic model needs to be estimated through a simulation procedure, as the technique of simulation has the advantage of fitting into planning institutions a 'dialogue' between policy-makers.

Although there are other reasons for following the simulation approach (flexibility of handling non-linearities, discontinuities, etc.), the most important feature of simulation is the ease with which a policy laboratory can be proposed. The powerful tool of evaluating development policy options and its short-, medium- and long-term impact are all necessary for a better future based on the proper policy perspectives of today.

Indeed the future developmental perceptions and challenges detailed in this chapter ultimately need to be linked within the frame of reference of 'A' and 'E', as stated above, to provide a general model for planning. The importance of the model becomes more imperative as Jordan's role in the international arena is recognized. The varied problems and different influences of international organizations such as WHO and UNICEF on Jordan add a further dimension to the case study.

CASE STUDIES

We have seen that there has been a shift in strategy in Jordanian planning from SOC to DPA. Two sectors involving SOC, and which play a significant role in influencing the quality of life vis-à-vis development, are the health sector and education. Because of the importance of the shift from SOC to DPA in the plan period 1981-85, it is imperative to consider the role of health and education in the development process.

Future Issues

The fundamental question for the future planner is how much further planned expenditures should be allocated to sectors like health and education, in the light of a shift from SOC to DPA. More importantly for the purposes of the present chapter, it is necessary to shed light on methodological issues related to the future perspectives of Japan. The case study involving health considers the way in which the health issue must be perceived. The case study involving education, on the other hand, considers the role of education in the development process of Jordan.

Health
It is reasonable to assume that a people's standard of health will directly or indirectly affect the quality and quantity of human capital and development. Besides the noble aim of achieving human happiness, the recognition of the influence of health on economic productivity seems to be reflected in the 1978 International Conference on Primary Health Care, at which the WHO member states pledged to co-operate with one another to attain the goal of a standard of health, for all the people of the world by the year 2000, that would permit them to lead a 'socially and economically productive life'.[7]

Jordan, being an active member of WHO and UNESCO, has taken determined steps to improve the health standards of its people. Public awareness through community health education, and the introduction of health education as an integral part of educational curricula in the national school system, are all parts of the more comprehensive health education policy.

In view of the fact that a health education curriculum should be based on the needs of the students, a recent study[8] investigated perceptions of the concept of health among different groups of high-school students in rural and urban areas. The interesting aspects of their findings lie in the cross-national and intra-national comparative interpretations of the results. Jordanian high-school students were found to have a happiness and normal biological function oriented positive view of health. Moreover, psychological, social and spiritual aspects of health were particularly pronounced in the Jordanian students' conceptualization of health. At the intra-cultural level, interesting differences were observed among groups

239

of students defined by age, sex and area of residence. Depending upon age, sex and rural or urban environment, high-school students were found to differ in their understanding and conceptualization of health.

The findings of this study have several implications:

1. The meaning and understanding of the word health may differ not only among different cultures but also among different groups within the same culture.
2. In the field of the behavioural and social sciences, the generalizability of research findings is usually limited and the recommendations most appropriate for one country may not be applicable for another.
3. Health education needs differ not only from country to country but also from group to group, even among such a tightly defined homogeneous population as high-school students.
4. To achieve the maximum objectives of a health education programme, it may be advisable to design differential curricula according to the needs of the students in different areas.

Thus to define health policies, whether to expand the health sector or otherwise, requires a thorough understanding of the interrelated issues. This is possible only through the overall planning frame perspective.

Education
Sceptics of educational expansion programmes point to increases in unemployment of school-leavers, graduates and the like. We would like, however, to approach the issue of higher education from a different perspective: i.e. a demand exists for higher education in Jordan. Because of the skewed age pyramid of the population, educational needs in Jordan will continue to exist. In the light of this, marketability - unlike other goods and services - is not a constraining factor when it comes to education.

Table 13.4 reveals that total expenditures by Jordanian students abroad followed an S-shaped distribution for the years 1979-82.

Future Issues

Table 13.14: Total Expenditures of Jordanian Students Abroad, 1979-1982 (Jordanian dinars)

Year	Expenditure
1979	66,942-886
1980	66,509-005
1981	77,561-482
1982	76,955-532

Source: Compiled from Statistical Educational Year Book (various issues)

Such an increase in the expenditures of Jordanian students is only a part of the opportunity cost foregone by the Jordanian economy. The 'quality of life' factor, influencing the overall national development process, needs to be fully evaluated. The impact of the existence of Yarmouk University on Irbid, and hence on Jordan, is by no means restricted to the number of graduates the university produces. The market structure and level of both goods and services, as well as factor markets, has increased both actually and potentially. The activities of continuing education, 'on the job' training programmes and evening education programmes have all contributed indirectly to the development process of Jordan. The expansion of educational services has also had a positive effect on the number of newspapers and magazines in circulation, the number of publishing companies and the number of computer-based establishments.

Thus, from the point of view of providing services for educationally motivated social demands, if cut-backs in the educational sector occur due to the fear of producing unemployable graduate populations, more and more Jordanians will leave for further studies abroad. In most of these countries, the cost structure of education is such that further education in them is an extremely attractive economic prospect compared to studying in Jordan, even if the opportunities in Jordan were to exist.

The direct consequences are losing a healthy Jordanian market and foreign exchange reserves. The indirect effects also need to be considered: for example, no longer having the accelerator and multiplier effects of further expansion of the educational sector. Moreover, the reorientation cost of student or graduate returnees adds further to the social cost calculations.

Because of these different and varying impacts on the education sector, an educational development planning model is needed in order to calculate all the policy options prior to any implementation.

NOTES

1. Jordan, Ministry of Information, Economic Development in Jordan (Amman, 1978).
2. Central Bank of Jordan, Yearly Statistical Series, vol. 20: 1964-1983, special issues, table 44: Industrial Origin of GDP.
3. Royal Scientific Society (Amman, Dec. 1977).
4. Ibid., p. 27.
5. Official Bulletin, No. 2322.
6. World Bank estimates.
7. World Health Organization, Primary Health Care (Geneva, 1978), 'Health for All' series, no. 1.
8. K.S. Ahlawat and E. Baydoun in International Quarterly of Community Health Education, vol. 5, no. 2 (1985), pp. 129-47.

Table 1.A: Geographical Distribution of Domestic Exports, 1973-83 (million Jordanian dinars)

Year	Total domestic exports	Arab Common Market	Other Arab countries	EEC	Socialist countries	Asian countries	Other countries
1973	14.0	4.4	5.7	0.20	0.3	1.9	1.7
74	39.4	5.9	12.5	0.6	2.0	10.4	8.5
75	40.1	7.0	9.9	2.0	6.4	3.9	10.9
76	49.5	10.1	13.8	1.5	7.3	3.6	12.2
77	60.2	13.6	22.4	0.3	4.2	6.5	12.6
78	64.1	16.4	26.2	0.3	6.4	5.3	8.4
79	82.6	25.9	29.8	0.1	5.3	9.0	11.3
80	120.1	42.4	30.5	0.8	15.1	12.0	18.0
81	169.0	74.7	39.7	0.8	19.5	14.2	18.4
82	185.6	80.6	42.7	0.7	25.4	20.3	13.0
83	160.1	30.6	56.5	1.9	21.2	17.1	26.5

Source: CBJ, vol. 20, <u>Yearly Statistical Series</u>, 1964-1983, special issue.

Table 1.B: Geographical Distribution of Imports, 1973-83 (million Jordanian dinars)

Year	Total imports	Arab Common Market	Other Arab countries	EEC	Other European countries	US	Socialist countries	Asian countries	Others
1973	108.2	11.9	2.5	30.5	4.1	11.2	7.7	6.8	26.1
74	156.5	14.4	4.0	45.6	6.9	17.6	14.7	10.3	34.9
75	234.0	14.1	3.5	77.0	16.7	24.2	18.7	21.4	29.7
76	339.5	18.8	8.8	126.0	20.6	31.0	25.1	34.7	41.1
77	454.4	23.1	8.1	158.0	26.0	67.4	41.8	32.8	56.0
78	458.8	23.6	7.8	165.0	31.2	33.6	50.2	33.6	58.7
79	589.5	23.8	16.0	211.2	50.7	44.3	51.4	40.6	80.8
80	716.0	18.9	14.0	259.7	49.5	61.6	49.8	53.3	92.8
81	1,048.0	18.7	17.6	339.5^a	58.8^b	166.7	81.2	73.6	114.7
82	1,142.5	16.0	18.0	329.6^a	69.1^b	144.3	94.8	89.7	145.1
83	1,103.3	24.5	19.2	330.1^a	52.7^b	131.0	77.8	104.3	156.6

Notes: a. Includes Greece.
b. Excludes Greece. Numbers do not add up due to rounding off errors.
Source: CBJ, vol. 20, Yearly Statistical Series, 1964-1983, special issue.

Table 1C: External Trade Balances by Some[a] Geographical Distributions, 1969-83 (thousand Jordanian dinars)

Year	Arab Common Market					EEC			
	Exports	Imports	Trade Balance	Export as % of imports	Exports	Imports	Trade balance	Exports as % of imports
1969	1584	7198	- 5614	22.006	2	22,333	- 22,331	0.0089
70	1434	5961	- 4527	24.056	3	22,153	- 22,150	0.0135
71	964	7055	- 6091	13.664	4	18,980	- 18,976	0.021
72	1530	7897	- 6367	19.374	51	26,985	- 26,934	0.188
73	1391	11,883	- 10,492	11.805	20	30,525	- 30,505	0.065
74	4001	14,409	- 10,408	27.767	63	45,629	- 45,566	0.138
75	2018	14,115	- 12,097	14.296	1,978	76,970	- 74,992	2.569
76	1660	18,825	- 17,165	8.818	2,520	125,968	- 123,448	2.000
77	2921	23,072	- 20,151	12.660	872	157,983	- 157,111	0.551
78	1824	23,648	- 21,824	7.713	1,337	164,933	- 163,596	0.810
79	2457	23,848	- 21,391	10.302	1,138	211,149	- 210,011	0.538
80	2183	18,914	- 16,731	11.541	2,096	259,731	- 257,635	0.806
81	3167	18,688	- 15,521	16.946	2,463	339,531	- 337,068	0.725
82	1922	15,998	- 14,076	12.014	3,567	329,587	- 326,020	1.082
83	1807	24,513	- 22,706	7.371	8,134	330,087	- 321,953	2.464

Note: a. Only those geographical groupings are considered which include the same group of countries in the composition of imports and exports.
Source: CBJ, vol. 20, Yearly Statistical Series, 1964-1983, special issue.